Digital Gold Rush

Digital Gold Rush

How to Invest Wisely in the New Economy

Anaya Korvelle

Mindful Pages

Published in 2026

ISBN: 9789374591093 (PB)
ISBN: 9789374593325 (eBook)

Published by

Mindful Pages
Imprint of Alpha Editions LLC
312 W. 2nd St #1834
Casper, WY 82601, USA

This book was developed using advanced writing tools to support the drafting and ideation process. All content has been thoughtfully curated, refined, and reviewed to ensure quality and relevance.

Content

Introduction

The first thing most people notice is the heat. Not physical heat, but the feverish temperature of a marketplace that seems to oscillate between euphoria and despair with the impatience of a child shaking a snow globe. For more than a decade the headlines have flared with the promise of instant prosperity: a student turning a small windfall into a fortune; a meme coin rising a thousand-fold before breakfast; a start-up with no product commanding the valuation of a centuries-old institution. Yet behind every spectacular rise is a quieter, more enduring pattern: newcomers arriving only after prices have already soared, committing more than they can afford, then retreating in silence after losses they never truly understood. It is a cycle of hope and regret so predictable it borders on ritual.

What makes this cycle especially curious is that it takes place within a technological architecture designed, at least in theory, to eliminate the need for trust. These systems were meant to remove intermediaries, reduce uncertainty, and give individuals fine-grained control over their financial lives. Yet in practice they have produced a new theatre of confusion—one in which trusting the wrong source, ignoring the fine print of a token's rights, or mismanaging a wallet can undo months of careful saving. The paradox is stark: a financial frontier built on cryptographic certainty still requires an extraordinary amount of human judgement, discernment, and scepticism. Many enter believing they are stepping into a neutral system of pure logic; they soon discover they have walked into a marketplace shaped as much by psychology and behaviour as by mathematics.

This tension—the collision of promise and misunderstanding—sets the stage for the pages that follow. The purpose of this book is not to predict the next trend or identify the next token destined to dominate the charts. Predictions, even when made in good faith, are remarkably flimsy things; they age quickly, shatter easily, and encourage exactly the kind of thinking that leads investors astray. Instead, the book aims to construct a durable mental framework: a way of assessing opportunities, understanding risks, and grounding decisions in principles resilient enough to survive whatever innovations or crises emerge next. Markets evolve. Narratives shift. Technologies age. But sound reasoning, sharpened by historical awareness and disciplined by scepticism, can remain steady.

To understand why such a framework is necessary, it helps to look backwards as well as forwards. Financial manias are not new. Tulip bulbs, railway shares, radio stocks, and dot-com domains each inspired waves of exuberance long before blockchains existed. The details differ, but the underlying structure remains eerily consistent: a new technology rearranges the landscape of possibility; a small number recognise its significance early; speculation floods in; stories outrun reality; disappointment follows; finally, from the wreckage emerges a quieter, more durable form of value. What makes digital assets distinct is not that they break this pattern, but that they compress it. Movements that once took years can now unfold in weeks. The velocity of information, the transparency of order books, and the global reach of markets combine to create an environment where reactions are immediate and often visceral.

Yet to treat this domain merely as a locus of speculation is to misunderstand its significance. Beneath the noise lies a profound shift in how value can be created, stored, and transferred. These networks are not merely alternative payment systems or speculative chips. They are—at their core—public infrastructure: open, programmable, and resistant to unilateral control. They carry the potential to reshape economic coordination, empower new forms of organisation, and broaden access to financial tools traditionally gated behind institutions. Such potential should neither be romanticised nor dismissed. Instead, it should be examined with clarity, curiosity, and caution.

For the individual investor, the challenge is not simply to decipher cryptographic protocols or evaluate market trends. It is to understand what is actually being bought when one acquires a digital asset. A token is not a company share, nor is it a commodity in the classical sense. It may confer rights, obligations, or access. It may represent nothing but a narrative. It may be scarce, yet useless. Or it may be abundant, yet indispensable. The failure to recognise these distinctions lies at the heart of many missteps. Some purchase governance tokens believing they represent ownership. Others treat payment tokens as if they were growth equities. Many assume that a ticker symbol alone conveys meaning, when in truth it is the underlying network, its incentives, its security model, and its community that determine whether the token has purpose.

These misalignments of expectation are not trivial errors; they shape portfolios, influence risk, and define outcomes. When investors confuse scarcity with value, they overlook the role of demand. When they chase narratives rather than fundamentals, they trade conviction for emotion. When they underestimate behavioural biases, they lose not because the market out-smarted them, but because they out-witted themselves. In this sense, digital asset investing is not simply a technical or financial discipline. It is a behavioural discipline, too. A test of patience, humility, and emotional steadiness.

This book approaches the subject from four interwoven vantage points. The first is conceptual: understanding tokens, networks, claims, incentives, and the mechanics that underpin crypto-economic systems. Without clarity here, every subsequent decision rests on unstable foundations. The second is evaluative: applying principles from finance, economics, and network theory to distinguish projects with enduring potential from those held together only by hype. The third is behavioural: recognising the traps—FOMO, anchoring, confirmation loops—that distort judgement, and learning to navigate them with intention. The fourth is practical: developing routines, habits, and risk strategies that protect both capital and peace of mind.

Running through all four is a motif that serves as a quiet compass: the idea of the "signal". Markets are saturated with noise—rapid opinions, contradictory data, persuasive personalities, and dashboards that turn metrics into theatre. Amid this noise, the thoughtful investor must learn to extract meaning from distraction. To follow the signal is to search for what matters: clear incentives, coherent structures, resilient systems, and communities that behave with integrity when tested. It is a discipline that rewards patience and punishes haste.

The urgency of this work lies not in predicting which asset will rise next but in helping readers cultivate a way of thinking that they can rely on for decades. We are unlikely to see a future where digital assets disappear. More probable is a future where these systems become routine infrastructure: sometimes invisible, sometimes contested, occasionally transformative. Learning to navigate this landscape is no longer optional for anyone seeking to steward their resources wisely. The costs of misunderstanding can be severe; the benefits of discernment can be compounding.

This introduction is therefore an invitation—not to speculation, but to understanding. The chapters ahead ask questions seldom considered by newcomers: What is the real problem a project claims to solve? Who benefits? What incentives bind the participants together? What risks lie buried in the assumptions? How does behaviour shape markets as profoundly as technology? What does it mean to build a portfolio that respects both ambition and constraint? These questions do not yield instant answers. They require reflection, exploration, and sometimes the willingness to abandon a comfortable narrative in favour of a more accurate one.

Such reflection is not an academic exercise. It has direct implications for how individuals act when confronted with uncertainty. Consider the experience of transferring assets into a wallet: a simple action, yet one that depends on an understanding of private keys, passphrases, custody arrangements, and operational practices. Or consider the impact of a sudden market downturn: does one react impulsively, or does one consult a pre-written plan that outlines position limits, loss thresholds, and rebalancing rules? Or consider the subtle erosion of judgement that occurs when one listens only to sources that confirm prior beliefs, ignoring quieter but more reliable signals. In each case, the difference between a fragile approach and a resilient one lies in preparation, not prediction.

It is worth acknowledging that this domain can feel overwhelming. The pace of innovation is rapid; the terminology is dense; the narratives shift hourly. But beneath the surface complexity, the essential questions remain refreshingly stable. What is this token for? Why does it need a network? Who uses it? How secure is it? What does it cost to maintain? What failures should we anticipate?

And, most critically, what portion of one's resources is it sensible to risk on this idea, given one's broader life obligations? These are the questions that give structure to uncertainty.

The calmness of this approach is deliberate. Noise thrives on urgency; wisdom thrives on perspective. The purpose of this book is not merely to teach readers how to avoid errors, but to help them develop the confidence to act—or refrain from acting—with clarity. To show that discipline is not the enemy of opportunity, but its guardian. To suggest that a thoughtful, balanced approach can outperform frantic attempts to outsmart a market that responds to pressure with indifference.

As you read forward, consider the broader landscape beyond individual tokens and market movements. There is a larger story unfolding: the gradual re-architecting of digital trust. For centuries humans relied on institutions—banks, courts, governments—to record, arbitrate, and guarantee transactions. Blockchains propose an alternative: a system in which trust emerges from code, incentives, and transparency rather than hierarchies. Whether this experiment ultimately succeeds or falters is too early to say. What is clear is that it has already changed expectations about how financial systems should operate. Understanding this shift equips investors not only to make better choices today but to interpret the technological and cultural transformations that are likely to define the coming decades.

The tension that emerges here—between tradition and innovation, between certainty and experimentation—is part of what makes digital assets intellectually rich. They sit at the intersection of economics, cryptography, sociology, and psychology. They invite comparisons to historical upheavals, yet they resist neat analogies. They attract dreamers, engineers, speculators, and sceptics alike. Anyone navigating this space must therefore be prepared to think broadly, question deeply, and act deliberately.

So the invitation stands: step beyond the headlines, the volatility, and the noise. Engage with the foundations, the incentives, and the behavioural forces that truly shape outcomes. This book will not tell you which token will ascend next, nor will it hand you shortcuts to overnight success. Instead, it offers something more valuable: a set of principles you can rely upon, whatever the market chooses to do. Principles that help you interpret complexity, resist crowd psychology, protect your capital, and pursue opportunity without abandoning prudence.

As you turn the page, ask yourself the questions that will accompany you throughout this journey. What does it mean to invest wisely in a system defined by both transparency and illusion? How do you balance ambition with restraint? How will you decide when to participate—and when to step back? And above all: what kind of investor do you want to be when the next wave of excitement arrives?

The answers will not be handed to you. They will be built, piece by piece, through the chapters that follow.

Chapter 1
What Is Being Bought?

The confusion often begins with a flicker on a screen. A friend announces the purchase of a new token with a name that could belong to a star, a vitamin supplement, or a minor deity. Social feeds pulse with graphs that resemble seismographs. Exchanges display tickers in luminous rows, each a tiny promise of something: wealth, access, power, status. Yet beneath this spectacle lies a deceptively simple question that disorients even seasoned investors: *what, precisely, is being bought?* For many, the first purchase is an act of blind faith dressed as curiosity, a leap into a marketplace where the objects of exchange are intangible, the rights ambiguous, and the expectations inflated.

Consider a scene that has played out countless times. A newcomer selects a token because its chart tilts upwards, its community buzzes with self-assurance, and its ticker feels oddly familiar. They believe they are buying into a project, perhaps even into a piece of the future. But they have not inspected what that token actually represents. It may be a payment unit, a sliver of governance power, a means of accessing a service, or something straddling these categories without clearly belonging to any. The purchase, despite the confidence with which it is made, often rests upon assumptions as fragile as the market's mood. When disappointment follows—as it often does—it is not because the buyer misunderstood the price. It is because they misunderstood the *thing*.

This chapter begins here, at the fault line between perception and reality. Digital assets are frequently described in sweeping terms—"coins", "tokens", "crypto"—as if they were interchangeable pieces of a single phenomenon. But each unit sits within a network, and each network embeds a set of claims, incentives, and obligations. To buy a token without understanding its category is akin to acquiring a legal contract without reading its clauses. The contract may prove beneficial, trivial, or harmful. What matters are the terms, not the label.

The distinctions are not academic; they shape everything that follows. A payment token such as bitcoin signals participation in a monetary network designed around predictability and resistance to debasement. A utility token serves as fuel for a system, allowing the holder to perform an action or unlock a service. A governance token grants influence over parameters, upgrades, and rules. These categories are imperfect and sometimes blurred, yet they provide the first map through unfamiliar territory. Without them, investors navigate by instinct, herding, or hearsay—and the market punishes all three.

The deeper truth is that tokens are not merely units; they are *claims*. Some claims are explicit: the right to vote, the right to use a service, the right to a share of fees. Others are implicit: expectations about growth, about network effects, about future utility. The confusion arises because these claims are embedded in code, marketing, documentation, and culture simultaneously. A whitepaper may promise a certain functionality, yet the token itself may hold no enforceable right to it. A community may speak as though holders are owners when, legally, they are nothing of the sort. Amid this muddle, the only reliable compass is understanding what the token *actually* entitles the holder to, both on-chain and off.

Scarcity adds another layer of illusion. A fixed supply creates psychological allure; it whispers of exclusivity, of a digital artefact that cannot be duplicated. But engineered scarcity is not the same as value. A token with a capped supply but no use is merely a digital curiosity. A token with elastic supply but immense demand can be indispensable. The relationship between scarcity and worth is mediated by *usefulness*—by whether the token performs a job that people care about. This "jobs to be done" lens, borrowed from innovation theory, is unfashionable among speculators, but it reveals what ultimately underpins sustainable value: function, not fantasy.

Take stablecoins, for instance. They are neither scarce nor particularly glamorous, yet their utility in cross-border transfers, hedging, and settlement makes them one of the most consistently demanded categories of digital assets. They demonstrate how usefulness creates network effects, and how network effects create durability. A token that becomes woven into people's routines—remittances, payments, lending—acquires a form of gravity. The greater the adoption, the stronger the gravitational pull. Scarcity alone cannot achieve this. Demand can.

Yet even the clearest on-chain logic does not capture the full terrain. Blockchains excel at recording state transitions—balances, transactions, smart contract operations—but life does not unfold entirely on-chain. Legal structures, operational practices, business models, and governance norms live in the off-chain world. A token may function flawlessly on its network while remaining entangled in regulatory uncertainty or reliant on off-chain data feeds vulnerable to manipulation. The elegant mathematics of consensus do not eliminate the messy realities of human institutions.

One example illustrates the point starkly: the difference between controlling your own private keys versus relying on an exchange to record a balance. On-chain, ownership is deterministic; whoever controls the keys controls the asset. Off-chain, ownership becomes a matter of trust: the exchange promises that the numbers on your dashboard correspond to tokens held somewhere in custody. Most of the time, the promise holds. Until it doesn't. The history of digital assets is punctuated with moments when this distinction proves decisive, when those holding IOUs learned they held nothing more than a claim against a failing institution.

Or consider oracle risk. Smart contracts cannot access real-world data natively; they depend on external feeds to inform them. A lending protocol may rely on a price feed to determine whether a position is solvent. If the oracle is faulty, manipulated, or delayed, the entire logic of the protocol can unravel. This is a reminder that the boundary between on-chain and off-chain is not a line but a seam—one that requires careful stitching.

To navigate this complexity, the chapter introduces a practical framework: the Four Ps—Problem, Product, Protocol, People. A project without a real problem is a solution in search of an audience. A product that fails to address the problem is a distraction. A protocol with flawed incentives or weak security is fragile. And people—founders, developers, validators, community leaders—shape culture, execution, and integrity. When applied to a decentralised exchange, for example, the framework helps clarify whether the system addresses a real market inefficiency, whether the interface and mechanisms function coherently, whether the incentives encourage honest behaviour, and whether those running the project demonstrate competence rather than charisma.

What makes these questions compelling is not merely their analytical utility but their philosophical resonance. They remind us that markets, for all their data-rich transparency, are still human enterprises. The temptation to view tokens as abstract mathematical objects obscures the truth that behind every line of code are decisions, trade-offs, and worldviews. Buying a token is not only a financial act but an alignment with a particular architecture of trust.

The stakes are therefore higher than price action. When you buy a digital asset, you are buying into a model of economic coordination. You are aligning with an incentive structure. You are supporting, consciously or not, a vision of how people might interact, transact, and govern themselves in digital environments. This raises the intellectual temperature of the endeavour. It turns what might appear to be a speculative act into a philosophical one.

Yet the chapter does not demand that readers become philosophers or cryptographers. Instead, it invites them to develop a habit of inquiry that prevents confusion from masquerading as clarity. Many investors suffer losses not because the market betrayed them but because they misunderstood the object of their own investment. They bought a governance token thinking it was a revenue share. They bought a utility token expecting price appreciation rather than service access. They bought a scarce token assuming scarcity alone was sufficient. Clarity about what is being bought—its category, its claims, its purpose—reduces these errors dramatically.

The chapter also touches subtly on a recurring motif that threads through much of this book: the difference between signal and noise. In the context of understanding what is being bought, the signal is found in rights, incentives, governance, and usefulness. The noise is found in tickers, trends, slogans, and speculative narrative. The task is to tune one's instrument to discern the former from the latter.

As the introduction draws to a close, the path ahead should feel both grounded and invigorating. This chapter will not merely catalogue definitions or rehearse familiar distinctions. It will expose the anatomy of digital assets—units, networks, claims, incentives—and reveal how these components interact to create, or fail to create, value. It will show how scarcity becomes meaningful only when wedded to purpose. It will illustrate the porous boundary between on-chain certainty and off-chain complexity. And it will equip you with a framework to interrogate any token, any network, any project with clarity.

The question that opened this chapter—*what is being bought?*—seems simple on the surface. But as you proceed, it will become clear that this question contains many others: What does this asset do? What rights does it grant? What obligations does it impose? Who relies on it? Who governs it? Who benefits from it? And who must one trust in order for it to function?

The reward for engaging with these questions is significant. It is the difference between stumbling through markets guided by momentum and navigating them with conviction. Between being seduced by appearances and understanding the substance beneath them. Between reacting to price and responding to purpose.

Turn the page, then, with curiosity sharpened. The chapter ahead offers not a taxonomy but a lens—a way of seeing digital assets that will anchor every decision you make in the chapters to come.

Units, networks, and claims

When the Mt. Gox exchange collapsed in Tokyo in February 2014, more than 650,000 bitcoins disappeared from customer accounts—an event that crystallised a paradox. Thousands of users believed they *held* bitcoin, yet what they actually possessed were claims recorded in a private database controlled by a single company. The distinction between a digital unit and the network that gives it meaning, between possession and the mere appearance of possession, revealed itself with brutal clarity. The lights on the web interface still showed balances, right up until the day they didn't. One sentence on the company's site—"All transactions have been halted"—was enough to expose how deeply users had mistaken a promise for an asset. Five words.

This gulf between what people think they are buying and what they truly acquire remains one of the quiet fault lines running through digital asset markets. A token may look like a coin, a pass, a vote, a revenue share, or a ticket to a possible future. What it *is*, however, depends on the network it lives on and the claims it encodes. A coin is not a token. A token is not a claim. And a ticker symbol is not a description. Yet these distinctions are often blurred in moments of enthusiasm or haste, leading buyers to conflate symbols with rights and price charts with purpose.

To understand why this matters, it is necessary to begin with the simplest element in the system: the unit. A coin such as bitcoin is native to its network, created and governed by consensus rules that enforce scarcity, validate transfers, and anchor the ledger to a shared canon of truth. A token, by contrast, is layered on top of an existing network—most commonly Ethereum—using programmable contracts rather than core protocol rules. The coin is intrinsic; the token is contingent. That difference, apparently technical, shapes risk, rights, and expectations.

In practice, the most accessible way to map this landscape is to distinguish between payment tokens, utility tokens, and governance tokens. Each category embeds different claims, though the boundaries often blur at the edges. A payment token aims to serve as digital cash or store of value, with bitcoin as the quintessential example. Its promise is settlement: final, non-reversible, mathematically enforced by the network itself. A utility token grants access to a function: spending gas to run computation on Ethereum, unlocking storage on a decentralised file system, or enabling participation in an application's core mechanism. A governance token grants influence, allowing holders to vote on upgrades or economic parameters. These distinctions matter because they determine what buyers can reasonably expect to receive—function, influence, or settlement—not because the labels carry intrinsic prestige.

Bitcoin's role, anchored since its release by Satoshi Nakamoto in January 2009, demonstrates the clarity of a payment token. It enables the transfer of value without an intermediary, secured by a proof-of-work network designed to resist censorship. The unit is inseparable from the system that produces it. A governance token for a lending protocol, however, sits in a different universe. It may confer a vote on interest rate models, collateral requirements, or fee distribution. Yet this vote is neither ownership nor revenue by default. It is a procedural voice within a system that may or may not heed minority views. Confusing these claims—mistaking a vote for a share—has led many investors to misread what they actually hold.

The temptation to collapse these categories into a single mental bucket is strong, especially when presented with the compressed visuals of an exchange app. Tickers flatten complexity. A three- or four-letter symbol invites comparison, suggesting that each unit is a peer to the next. But a ticker is merely shorthand. What matters are the rights and obligations embedded in the underlying architecture: the power to spend, the capacity to use, the authority to influence, or the absence of any such promise.

One quiet motif that runs through this discussion is weight. A coin like bitcoin carries the *weight* of its network—its miners, hash power, rules, and security assumptions. A token carries only the weight of its contract, its governing community, and the reliability of the underlying chain. To understand an asset is to feel the weight behind it. To mistake surface for substance is to grasp at something hollow.

A powerful example of how these distinctions materialise comes from the launch of Uniswap's UNI governance token in September 2020. Observers immediately asked what UNI holders *actually* received. The token granted votes on protocol parameters and treasury allocations; it did not grant ownership of the underlying company, nor did it entitle holders to any portion of trading fees. Yet the market treated the token as though it were a claim on a flourishing exchange. The confusion was understandable but misplaced. The votes were real; the revenue claims were not. The protocol's success did not guarantee the token's financial utility. The episode shows how rights matter more than narratives, and how claims—not metaphors—determine economic relevance.

A counter-example exists in the form of Filecoin (launched October 2020 by Protocol Labs). Unlike the governance-token model, Filecoin's native token embodies explicit utility: it pays for storage, incentivises providers, and anchors the system's economics. The rights it grants are tangible and enforceable by protocol design. Yet even here the picture is nuanced. Buyers anticipating price appreciation must recognise that a token tied to usage may diverge sharply from speculative expectations. Utility is not a guarantee of investment returns; it is a mechanism for service delivery. This limitation does not undermine the model. Instead, it illustrates the importance of matching expectations to claims.

Throughout the industry, misinterpretation often arises when scarcity is mistaken for purpose. A token may be hard-capped, deflationary, or aesthetically unique, but scarcity without demand is merely an engineering artefact.

Bitcoin's scarcity matters because it is tied to global demand for a censorship-resistant asset with predictable issuance. Ethereum's gas token is valuable because people *use* the network. Governance tokens are meaningful when communities make substantive decisions. Scarcity without action is irrelevant. The motif of weight applies here too: scarcity gains weight only when usage presses upon it.

This distinction becomes more vivid when viewed through the lens of another named case: the launch of the TerraUSD ecosystem and the collapse of its UST stablecoin in May 2022. Terra claimed to produce stable value algorithmically via its native token, LUNA, and a set of contraction and expansion rules. At its peak, it attracted billions in capital, bolstered by marketing and yield incentives. Yet buyers failed to recognise that the claims embedded in the token were fragile: stability was not guaranteed by reserves or rights, but by assumptions about market behaviour. When confidence faltered, the mechanism imploded. The units were abundant; the claims proved hollow. The weight behind the system was insufficient.

These examples establish a key principle: the nature of a token is inseparable from the network it inhabits, and both are inseparable from the claims encoded in their design. Claims exist at multiple levels—technical, social, legal—and each must be accounted for. On-chain, the rules specify what can and cannot be done. Off-chain, the norms and institutions determine how the system responds to stress, disputes, and failures.

The interplay between these levels surfaced clearly during the infamous DAO incident in 2016 on the Ethereum network. After a smart contract vulnerability allowed an attacker to drain funds, the community chose to fork the chain to reverse the theft. Holders of ether discovered that their claims were partly procedural and partly political. The network's social layer overruled its technical determinism. Those who believed their units were governed solely by code encountered the weight of collective decision-making. This episode does not diminish the value of Ethereum. Instead, it highlights how networks and claims are inseparable, and how the rights of token holders can be shaped by community governance in moments of crisis.

Another implication arises when considering geographic and jurisdictional differences. A governance token for a lending protocol operating primarily in Europe, with developers based in Berlin and London, may face different regulatory expectations than a payment token used globally. This does not mean that buyers must specialise in law, but it does mean they must recognise that rights are contingent on context. A claim that is enforceable on-chain may be irrelevant off-chain; a claim that is meaningful in practice may be unenforceable in law. The network shapes one dimension of meaning; the surrounding world shapes another.

Yet perhaps the most important distinction, and the most easily missed, is that tokens are not static. Claims evolve. Networks grow or fragment. A governance token may start as a symbolic gesture and evolve into a significant instrument of power. A utility token may begin with narrow use and later become integral to a system's operation. Conversely, tokens may atrophy as networks lose traction. Rights decay when communities disperse.

The motif of weight returns: networks accumulate weight over time through security, users, reliability, and habit. Tokens tethered to such networks inherit that weight. Others remain feather-light, lifted briefly by narrative winds before drifting out of view.

This raises a final tension—one that every thoughtful reader must hold. When you look at a digital asset, what do you actually see? A unit? A network? A claim? A possibility? Or merely a symbol rising and falling on a chart? The distinction is not academic; it is diagnostic. To answer it requires attention to rights, obligations, provenance, purpose, and the weight behind the design.

The unresolved question is simple yet demanding: the next time you encounter a digital asset, what test will you apply to discern whether you are buying a unit with substance—or a promise with no weight at all?

Scarcity vs usefulness

When El Salvador adopted bitcoin as legal tender in September 2021, President Nayib Bukele framed the decision as a bold leap towards financial modernisation. The announcement, delivered in Miami that June, drew global attention. Yet within months of the law's implementation, a quieter story emerged from San Salvador's streets. Many merchants displayed bitcoin-accepted signs, but far fewer processed transactions. Shoppers hesitated. Some cited price swings; others found the app unreliable. The Chivo wallet, built by the government, suffered repeated outages. The paradox was stark: a scarce digital asset with a fixed supply schedule, celebrated for its mathematical predictability, found limited everyday demand in a country where financial inclusion was among the policy's primary goals. Five words captured the tension. *Scarcity does not guarantee use.*

The scene in San Salvador underscored a deeper truth often obscured by market exuberance. A token may be scarce, but scarcity alone does not create value. People adopt tools that solve problems. They return to tools that reduce friction. They commit to tools that fit their routines. A digital asset, however elegant its issuance curve, must earn its place through function rather than myth. The question that threads through this discussion—*what job does this token actually do?*—is not rhetorical. It determines whether a token becomes part of someone's daily life or remains a speculative artefact drifting across price charts.

This distinction becomes clearer when viewed through the "jobs to be done" perspective, a framework articulated by Clayton Christensen at Harvard Business School in the early 2000s. It suggests that users adopt a product because it performs a specific job within their lives—solving a friction, enabling a task, or improving an experience. In the realm of digital assets, this lens provides a disciplined way to assess claims. A token may promise decentralised governance, but if few holders vote, the job is unfilled. A token may promise fast settlement, but if transfers routinely fail or cost too much at peak times, the job collapses. Measured in behaviour rather than aspiration, usefulness becomes visible in actions: repeated transactions, retained balances, active contracts, and organic growth.

Stablecoins offer a compelling demonstration. USDC, issued by Circle in 2018, and USDT, launched by Tether in 2014, have become critical tools for cross-border transfers. Their appeal lies not in scarcity—they are deliberately abundant—but in stability, speed, and compatibility with global markets. In Lagos, Accra, and Buenos Aires, users rely on stablecoins to move funds in minutes rather than days, avoiding exchange restrictions or unreliable banking systems. Demand arises not because the tokens are rare, but because they perform a job traditional infrastructures struggle to do consistently. This behaviour, repeated across millions of small transfers, generates a form of network weight: each successful transaction makes the next one more likely, reinforcing trust through action rather than rhetoric.

The growth of the Lightning Network, built atop bitcoin and launched in beta in March 2018, provides a complementary example. Its ambition is to enable low-cost microtransactions. Yet adoption has grown unevenly. Where Lightning nodes cluster—such as in the United

States and parts of Europe—transaction volumes increase steadily. But in regions where connectivity is limited or user experience remains fragmented, the job remains partially unfilled. Lightning's promise reveals a limitation: usefulness depends not only on protocol elegance but on distribution, education, and habit. Scarcity cannot compensate for missing infrastructure.

A counter-example appears in the form of highly scarce collectible tokens, sometimes minted in editions of one or a few hundred. These assets often attract attention because they are rare, visually distinctive, and tied to cultural moments. Some become valuable for reasons that resemble the art market more than the payments market. Their demand stems from identity, status, or narrative rather than functional utility. This does not invalidate them; indeed, cultural artefacts have long held value beyond their material uses. But such tokens highlight the limits of a functional model. They succeed not by solving financial problems, but by fulfilling symbolic ones. Scarcity can matter—but only within contexts where the job is meaning, not money movement. Recognising this distinction prevents the category error of assuming that all digital scarcity translates into economic significance.

The motif that threads quietly through these examples is gravity. Usefulness creates gravity. Each time a tool performs a job well, it pulls in a little more trust, a little more habit, a little more commitment. A network with strong gravitational pull attracts developers, merchants, and users, not through marketing but through reliability. This is how network effects transform function into value. When more people use a token to perform real tasks—remittances, collateral, payments, settlement—the token becomes more resistant to irrelevance. Its value begins not with scarcity but with service.

The historical case of M-Pesa, launched by Safaricom in Kenya in 2007, illuminates this dynamic. Though not a blockchain project, it demonstrates how demand emerges from usefulness rather than novelty. Designed to facilitate mobile money transfers in a region where banking access was limited, M-Pesa became deeply ingrained within Kenyan life. By 2014, it reached tens of millions of users. The system did not advertise scarcity, nor did it trade on cultural prestige. It solved a problem: sending money quickly and cheaply across distances. The implication for digital assets is clear. A token becomes indispensable when it relieves a pressure that users feel daily.

The stablecoin market illustrates a similar trend, backed by measurable behaviours such as settlement volumes and cross-exchange flows. Circle reported in October 2022 that USDC processed trillions in on-chain transfers over its lifetime. The number is less important than the pattern: stable demand emerges from repeated, low-friction use. Each successful remittance, each smooth settlement across borders, deepens the token's gravitational pull. Even when prices remain flat, volume signals value.

Yet usefulness alone cannot guarantee resilience. The collapse of TerraUSD in May 2022 demonstrated how a token designed for stability can fail when its underlying mechanism—an algorithmic mint-and-burn structure tied to LUNA—cannot withstand stress. TerraUSD served a job, at least superficially: offering a stable unit within decentralised finance. But the stability depended on assumptions about market behaviour rather than collateral or enforceable claims. Once confidence dwindled, the system spiralled. The lesson is sharp: usefulness must be supported by credible, transparent design. A token that serves a popular job but rests on fragile mechanics may not endure. The job becomes a liability when the foundation cannot bear weight.

This interplay between usefulness and durability surfaces again when examining tokens used for computation. Ether, introduced in July 2015 with the launch of Ethereum, serves as gas for running smart contracts. Every contract execution spends ether. This repeated action creates a metric of utility: gas consumption. Developers choose Ethereum for its reach; users choose it for its applications. High gas costs at peak periods show demand but also expose friction. As scaling solutions such as Optimism or Arbitrum gained traction in 2021–2022, the job shifted: users sought the same applications with lower fees. Usefulness generated gravity; friction temporarily weakened it; innovation restored it. Scarcity played no decisive role.

The "jobs to be done" lens also clarifies why some governance tokens struggle. A governance token may promise collective decision-making, yet voter participation often lingers below fifty per cent, sometimes far lower, even in high-profile decentralised autonomous organisations. The job—shaping policy—goes unfilled when the users with power do not act. The result is shallow gravity: a governance system that appears democratic but behaves oligarchically. The implication is uncomfortable but necessary to acknowledge. A token's potential does not define its usefulness; user behaviour does.

One named case demonstrates this with precision. MakerDAO, founded by Rune Christensen in 2015 and known for issuing the DAI stablecoin, has held numerous governance votes over the years. While some proposals attract intense debate and high participation, others pass with votes from a small subset of holders. The job of distributed governance is fulfilled inconsistently. Yet the system persists because on-chain collateral and transparent rules give DAI economic reliability. Governance usefulness, in this example, is punctuated rather than constant.

The counter-example of a governance token used mainly for speculation highlights another limitation. When holders treat governance as optional noise, the token's value depends almost entirely on external narratives. The job remains incomplete. Scarcity cannot compensate for apathy. The gravitational pull weakens.

A further example, this time from payments, appears in the case of PayPal's November 2023 launch of PYUSD, a dollar-backed stablecoin available initially in the United States. Unlike algorithmic attempts, PYUSD relied on cash equivalents and short-term treasuries. The move reflected a shift: institutional actors entered the stablecoin space not to chase novelty but to meet observed demand for fast, programmable settlement. The job existed; PayPal supplied a trustworthy implementation. Usefulness preceded scarcity. The implication for digital asset markets is straightforward. When legacy institutions see consistent behavioural patterns, they respond not to hype but to observable actions.

The motif of gravity returns as a way of reconciling these case studies. Useful tokens fall into people's routines; they become the default choice. Gravity grows. Tokens without a clear job or credible design drift; their gravitational field weakens. The metric is not price. It is behaviour: transfers initiated, contracts executed, wallets active, remittances routed. These are the visible signs that usefulness is doing the work scarcity cannot.

Yet a final question remains unresolved. In a market filled with tokens proud of their scarcity, how does an observer determine whether a token's job is meaningful enough to sustain demand? The answer lies not in narratives but in watching what people actually do. Does the token solve a problem someone feels? Does it reduce friction? Does it anchor a habit? Or does it remain a weightless artefact, admired from afar but seldom touched?

The tension sits here, quietly demanding attention: when faced with a scarce digital asset, what matters more—the elegance of its supply curve, or the job it performs every time someone chooses it over an alternative?

On-chain vs off-chain realities

In November 2022, when FTX collapsed in Nassau, customers could still open the exchange's app and see balances neatly displayed in dollars and tokens. The interface remained calm even as withdrawals halted and rumours hardened into fact. On public blockchains, the relevant addresses showed only a fraction of the assets customers believed were theirs. Yet few users had ever checked those addresses. They trusted the number on the screen, not the ledger beneath it. The blockchain and the balance page told different stories. The blockchain was right. The outcome was brutal: billions of dollars in customer claims, and far fewer actual coins with which to honour them. The blockchain showed nothing unusual. The failure sat elsewhere.

This dislocation between what the chain records and what people think it guarantees is at the heart of digital asset risk. Blockchains are meticulous bookkeepers. They track balances, enforce rules, and prevent double-spends with machine precision. But they do only that. They do not ensure that exchanges keep reserves. They do not prosecute fraud. They do not compel honest disclosures, vet marketing, or comfort customers who clicked "deposit" and assumed that meant "own". The technical record lives on-chain; the legal, operational, and human realities live somewhere else—on servers, in contracts, in boardrooms, in group chats, and sometimes only in the mind of a founder.

A useful way to frame this is to see the chain as the visible surface of a system and everything else as its wiring. The surface is transparent, auditable, and mathematically constrained. The wiring is messy, human, and unevenly documented. Confusion arises when people take the surface to be the whole machine. When a user sends coins to a centralised platform, the chain records one simple event: funds leave the user's address and arrive at an address under the platform's control. At that moment, the user ceases to own a digital asset. They come to own a claim—a promise—against an institution. Whether that promise is honoured depends not on consensus algorithms but on governance, risk management, and integrity.

Nowhere is this more obvious than in custody. Self-custody, where individuals hold their own private keys, is brutally simple: whoever controls the key controls the coins. An exchange IOU is different. It is a line in a private database that purports to represent a claim on assets held in collective wallets. The user sees a number; the exchange operator sees an aggregate liability. The blockchain sees only that certain addresses contain certain balances. In the FTX case, prosecutors alleged that customer deposits were diverted to affiliated trading operations. The chain recorded transfers; it did not annotate them as misuse. That judgement belongs to courts, not nodes.

A contrasting example shows the same structure from a different angle. When QuadrigaCX, a Canadian exchange based in Vancouver, collapsed in early 2019 after the reported death of its founder Gerald Cotten, blockchain analysts examined the supposed cold wallets. They found that large balances did not exist as claimed. The on-chain record revealed a shortfall; years of off-chain mismanagement and commingling had left customers with claims that no ledger could settle. Those users had never lost coins on chain. They had losing positions in a bankruptcy queue.

These custody failures are not arguments against exchanges as such. They are reminders that the trust model changes when one moves from self-custody to delegated custody. With self-custody, the critical behaviour is operational discipline: backing up seed phrases, testing recovery procedures, checking addresses carefully before sending funds. The risk is visible in every action—the trembling hand before confirming a large transfer, the decision to store a hardware wallet in a safe rather than a desk drawer. With an exchange, the critical behaviour is due diligence and monitoring: checking proof-of-reserves disclosures, reading terms, diversifying across venues, watching withdrawal queues. The risk hides in the wiring.

The same surface–wiring divide appears when blockchains interact with information about the outside world. Smart contracts cannot natively know the price of ether in pounds, the temperature in London, or whether a shipment reached Rotterdam. They rely on "oracles": services that feed external data into on-chain contracts. In February 2020, the bZx protocol, operating primarily on Ethereum, suffered an exploit during which an attacker manipulated a price feed using a flash loan, creating a distorted reading for a single block. The contract believed that collateral was adequate; in reality, the price had been momentarily warped. The exploit drained funds. The on-chain logic executed perfectly. The oracle misled it.

This is oracle risk. Show it, then name it. The show is a sudden loss driven by a momentary distortion in a data source. The name is the dependency that contracts have on prices, rates, or events supplied by external systems. The explanation is simple but uncomfortable: the contract obeys whatever data it is given, with no native concept of "plausible" or "manipulated". The implication is that every so-called "trustless" protocol that uses external data reintroduces trust at the oracle boundary. Users now depend on the integrity, design, and governance of the oracle network as much as on the chain itself.

Projects such as Chainlink, which went live on Ethereum mainnet in 2019, attempt to mitigate this by aggregating data from multiple sources and using multiple independent node operators. This approach does not remove oracle risk;

it rearranges it. Instead of trusting one feed, users trust a process: a set of nodes, incentives, and update rules. The behaviours to watch become more complex: how often feeds update, how they handle extreme volatility, how operators are selected, what recourse exists if a feed fails or stalls. Metrics such as update frequency and deviation thresholds become proxies for the reliability of the wiring beneath the surface.

Not every oracle story is a failure. MakerDAO's response to earlier price feed fragilities shows how communities can adapt. After "Black Thursday" in March 2020, when a sharp drop in ether's price combined with congestion on Ethereum to create liquidations at near-zero bids, MakerDAO adjusted its oracle design and auction mechanisms. Technical reports followed. Governance debates were public. Here, the on-chain contracts did not change their fundamental role, but the off-chain coordination around them did. The implication is that oracle risk is not merely a technical parameter; it is a governance question about who decides what counts as "the price" when it matters.

The motif of surface and wiring returns in legal treatment. A token balance in a wallet is straightforward: the chain records that a given address holds a given quantity. But what is that, legally? Property? A contractual right? Something else entirely? Different jurisdictions answer differently. When the High Court of England and Wales considered cryptoasset status in the 2019 case *AA v Persons*

Unknown, it concluded that certain digital assets could be treated as property. That decision affects how courts may grant injunctions or freezing orders. Yet it does not alter the on-chain reality. The wallet's balance remains the same regardless of legal classification. The law lives off-chain, structuring remedies when disputes arise.

This legal layer becomes critical when a custodian fails. In the Celsius Network bankruptcy, filed in New York in July 2022, one of the central questions concerned whether customer deposits were held on trust or whether they belonged to the company's estate. The blockchain showed addresses and balances. It did not label them as "customer property" or "corporate funds". The answer turned on terms and conditions, not on cryptography. Users who believed that "not your keys, not your coins" applied cleanly discovered that when keys sit with an intermediary, the law's interpretation of ownership can override the community's slogans.

A credible counterpoint comes from institutional-grade custodians that subject their operations to external audits, segregation rules, and regulatory oversight. Here, the off-chain wiring is deliberately built to be inspected. Independent attestation of reserves, clearly defined trust structures, and insurance arrangements all aim to align the off-chain reality with on-chain balances. They are not perfect—no human system is—but they show that the gap between surface and wiring can be narrowed if organisations commit to transparent design and accept external scrutiny. The visible behaviour is not just marketing claims; it is a willingness to publish audit reports, hold capital, and respond to regulators.

Understanding where the chain stops and other systems begin also clarifies the limits of "code is law". The phrase gained currency around the time of The DAO in 2016, a decentralised investment vehicle built on Ethereum. When an attacker exploited a vulnerability in June of that year, siphoning funds into a child contract, some argued that the event was lawful in the only sense that mattered: the contract behaved as written. Others argued that the exploit violated the intent and good faith of the community. The eventual hard fork, creating a new canonical chain that reversed the exploit, showed that off-chain governance can override on-chain history. Nodes followed social consensus, not pure code. The surface yielded to the wiring.

From an investor's perspective, all this suggests that risk does not live solely in transaction fees or protocol bugs. It lives in the everyday decisions of people and organisations. A user who keeps most holdings on a single offshore exchange makes a specific bet about that firm's governance and solvency. A protocol that depends on a single oracle provider makes a specific bet about that system's resilience. A decentralised application whose admin keys are held by a small team on a laptop in Berlin makes a specific bet about those individuals' operational discipline. These are not abstract themes; they are choices recorded nowhere on-chain yet central to outcomes.

The quiet question that recurs, like a low hum beneath the surface, is simple: what must be true *off-chain* for this *on-chain* record to mean what I think it means? For a lending protocol, it might be that price feeds stay accurate and that liquidators remain solvent enough to act. For a centralised exchange, it might be that internal controls prevent unauthorised transfers and that client assets are segregated from operational funds. For a custody service, it might be that key shards are stored in separate, well-controlled locations and that recovery procedures are rehearsed, not merely written.

Even self-custody, often portrayed as a pure on-chain posture, has off-chain dependencies. Seed phrases live on paper, steel, or in human memory. Hardware wallets ship from factories whose supply chains must be trusted to avoid tampering. Users choose hiding places, access controls, and heirs. When someone writes a seed phrase in a notebook labelled "passwords" and leaves it in a kitchen drawer, the blockchain's cryptography offers no defence. The weakness is physical and social, not digital.

The surface shimmers with certainty: balances, hashes, timestamps. Yet the wiring—legal frameworks, organisational discipline, oracle design, human behaviour—determines whether that surface can be relied upon when stress arrives. The unresolved tension, and the forward test for any thoughtful participant, is this: the next time a dashboard shows you a comforting number, will you be able to trace the chain of off-chain assumptions that must hold for that number to be real, actionable, and yours when it matters most?

Four Ps: problem, product, protocol, people

When Uniswap v1 launched on Ethereum in November 2018, its creator, Hayden Adams, was an unknown engineer working out of New York with a modest grant from the Ethereum Foundation. The interface was sparse, the documentation thin, and daily volumes rarely exceeded a few thousand dollars. Yet a small group of users kept returning to it. They were not drawn by aesthetics or marketing—there was none. They returned because Uniswap solved a concrete problem: thin liquidity for long-tail tokens without the need for market makers. By May 2020, after the release of Uniswap v2, daily volumes in some pools reached tens of millions. A handful of lines of code had grown into a public marketplace. The trajectory was not accidental. It reflected alignment across four dimensions that govern whether any digital asset project acquires weight or evaporates upon first contact with reality.

The first dimension—*problem*—emerges in visible behaviours. Users tried to trade ERC-20 tokens on centralised exchanges, only to find low-volume pairs, withdrawal queues, or painful listing delays. They resorted to informal swaps via Telegram groups and OTC dealers in London and Singapore. Friction was everywhere. The problem was not abstract; it was measured in failed trades, missed prices, and long support tickets. Naming the problem reveals its nature: fragmented liquidity and reliance on intermediaries. Explaining it shows why innovation mattered: if trading required central approval, new assets struggled to move. The implication was simple but powerful. A system that allowed permissionless liquidity provision could reduce friction for both issuers and users.

A contrasting example helps refine this principle. When the EOS mainnet launched in June 2018, Block.one, based in the Cayman Islands, had raised more than $4 billion in its token sale. Expectations soared. Yet many decentralised applications built on EOS struggled to demonstrate a problem worth solving. Some offered casino-style games; others replicated functions already served by Ethereum. The chain boasted throughput, but not demand. The implication deepens our understanding. Even vast capital and technical capacity cannot substitute for a problem with real behavioural weight. Users commit to tools that relieve pressure. When that pressure is ill-defined, purpose dissolves.

The second dimension—*product*—demands evidence beyond whitepapers. A product is not its promise; it is its use. Uniswap's automated market maker design produced immediate, measurable outcomes. Trades cleared in minutes rather than waiting for limit-order matches. Liquidity providers saw their deposits deployed without negotiation or contracts. The visible behaviour—users returning daily to swap tokens—was the metric that mattered. Naming the product reveals its core: a simple, peer-to-contract trading interface. Explaining its design shows why users trusted it: no order book, no listing gatekeepers, and transparent pool mathematics. The implication is instructive. A product that reduces friction while preserving autonomy can anchor a network even before governance or incentives mature.

To sharpen the distinction, consider a credible counter-example. In 2021, several projects attempted to create algorithmic market makers that promised "infinite liquidity" through synthetic supply adjustment. Many attracted early deposits, often drawn in by aggressive incentives. Yet when markets turned volatile, liquidity evaporated because the mechanics did not match user expectations. The synthetic curves behaved unpredictably, leading to slippage and losses. These projects showed a product–problem mismatch. The reconciliation is not to dismiss experimentation, but to recognise the lesson: a product must solve the problem at least as well as existing alternatives. Novelty does not excuse fragility.

The third dimension—*protocol*—brings incentives and security into focus. Protocols govern how value flows and how misconduct is deterred. In Uniswap's case, the protocol aligned incentives elegantly: liquidity providers earned fees proportional to their contribution; traders accepted price slippage as the cost of immediacy; arbitrageurs kept pools balanced. Behaviour created stability. Naming the protocol's core reveals its essence: constant-product automated market making. Explaining it shows how constraints create predictability. The implication is structural. A protocol that aligns incentives removes the need for central supervision. Participants regulate the system through action.

Contrast this with the DAO exploit of June 2016, where a vulnerability in the smart contract allowed an attacker to siphon funds. The show is the draining of assets block by block. Naming the event identifies a failure of protocol-level security. Explaining it shows that a clever incentive design cannot survive flawed execution. The implication is stark. Protocols must be hardened not only by formal verification, audits, and testing, but also by adversarial scrutiny. A single overlooked function or poorly designed fallback can unspool the entire structure. Security is not a philosophical principle. It is measured in patch cycles, bug reports, and resilience under stress.

The fourth dimension—*people*—remains the most intangible yet decisive. Code may be deterministic, but its authors, maintainers, governors, and stewards are not. The team behind Uniswap acted with notable restraint. Adams avoided premature token announcements and refrained from centralised fee switches. Updates were incremental and transparent. These behaviours—careful deployments, audited releases, explicit timetables—signalled competence. Naming the human layer highlights the importance of governance groups, foundation boards, and core developers. Explaining their influence reveals how decisions around upgrades, parameter changes, and risk management shape the fate of networks. The implication follows naturally. A protocol is only as trustworthy as the people who maintain, monitor, and debate it when conditions change.

A second example illustrates how human factors can stabilise or destabilise systems. MakerDAO, founded by Rune Christensen in 2015, confronted severe stress during the market crash of March 2020. Liquidations malfunctioned. Auctions attracted near-zero bids. It was the governance community—developers in Copenhagen, auditors across Europe, risk teams in the United States—that debated emergency measures, adjusted parameters, and restored solvency. The chain recorded liquidations; the people restored confidence. Their conduct displayed the behaviours that matter: showing up to vote, publishing risk analyses, admitting mistakes. These are the visible signs of integrity in decentralised systems.

A credible counter-example emerges from projects where founders disappear. In 2021, the DeFi protocol Merit Circle experienced internal turmoil after disagreements between early investors and contributors. Although not a failure in the catastrophic sense, the dispute exposed governance tensions and highlighted a limitation: when decision-making power is diffuse but accountability ambiguous, coordination becomes difficult. The reconciliation lies not in rejecting decentralisation but in recognising that the "people" layer must be designed with just as much rigour as the protocol. Voting thresholds, emergency procedures, multi-signature controls, and public documentation transform amorphous collectives into reliable institutions.

Threaded through these Four Ps is a quiet motif: *alignment*. When alignment holds across problem, product, protocol, and people, a project accumulates weight. Users stay. Developers commit. Liquidity deepens. When alignment falters—when the problem is trivial, the product clumsy, the protocol insecure, or the people unreliable—no amount of marketing or token incentives can compensate. Misalignment is revealed quickly by behaviour: falling volumes, shrinking contributor pools, governance apathy, security incidents. The chain records the symptoms; the off-chain reality explains the causes.

The practical application of the Four Ps becomes clearest when assessing a decentralised exchange. The problem is obvious: trading without reliance on a centralised custodian. The product is the interface and mechanism through which users swap assets, measure prices, and contribute liquidity. The protocol enforces the slippage curves, fee logic, and pool balances. The people include core developers, auditors, risk modellers, and governors who shape upgrades and respond to market stress. Each P reveals a question and a behaviour. Do traders return? Do upgrades ship on time? Do audits catch vulnerabilities? Do governance debates attract serious contributors? Alignment shows itself not in slogans but in repeated, observable actions.

The Four Ps also reveal their value when considering a private blockchain consortium. In 2017, the Australian Securities Exchange (ASX) began work with Digital Asset, led by Blythe Masters, to replace its clearing and settlement system with a distributed ledger. The problem was well-defined: ageing infrastructure and inefficiencies in post-trade processes. The product, however, struggled to meet the needs of a complex market. Technical challenges, shifting requirements, and governance disputes emerged. By November 2022, ASX announced it would pause the project after a software review identified significant issues. The implication reverberated across the industry. Even with strong institutional backing and clear regulatory frameworks, misalignment across the Four Ps can stall progress. The outcome underscored a deeper point. Competence and clarity matter as much as technology.

Throughout this subchapter, a question recurs like a faint watermark: *does the project's design fit the world it seeks to serve?* At each step—the problem it addresses, the product it delivers, the protocol it enforces, and the people it relies upon—that question demands evidence. It demands behaviours, not promises; metrics, not slogans; accountability, not mystique.

The unresolved tension rests here. When faced with a new project glowing with optimism and clever engineering, will you be able to trace alignment across the Four Ps—or will you be drawn first to the surface, leaving the deeper structure unexamined?

Chapter 2
First Principles of Value

On a quiet morning in January 2021, a small DeFi protocol published a single on-chain message announcing that its token would no longer distribute trading fees to holders. The change was surgical: one switch in a smart contract, one shift in a revenue route. Yet within minutes, message boards filled with confusion, indignation, and elaborate post-mortems. Holders demanded to know what their tokens *now* represented. A few had read the documentation and understood that the fee share had been experimental, revocable, and tightly scoped. Most had not. They had assumed value where value had never been promised. For them, the token's price had implied an economic right; now the implied right was gone. The market adjusted. The chain remained indifferent. The episode captured a timeless truth: price is loud, but value is quiet, and the quiet parts matter most.

This chapter begins from that tension. Digital assets tempt us to see value in motion rather than value in structure. A token that doubles in a week appears to demonstrate its worth. A network that hosts billions in deposits seems self-evidently important. Yet when the dust settles, only a handful of metrics endure. Do the assets entitle holders to anything? Do the networks earn trust through resilience, liquidity, and participation? Do the systems fund their own security, or do they coast on hope? Do timelines match realities, or are people trading second-by-second in markets that require thinking year-by-year? Beneath price, these quieter dynamics shape the long-term gravity of digital assets—gravity that holds or gravity that fails.

The paradox underlying modern crypto markets is that they blend ancient economic logic with unprecedented technical form. For centuries, investors evaluated claims: shares in a company, coupons on a bond, rights to land or grain. Claims had structure, enforceability, and lineage. A token, however, may offer nothing but governance, or it may confer fee flows, or it may provide access to a service, or it may be entirely symbolic. The form is new; the analytical instincts required are old. Cash flows, claims, cost of capital, durability, switching costs, and network advantage—none of these disappeared simply because assets became programmable. If anything, their importance deepened. Where traditional markets obscure value under layers of intermediaries, blockchains reveal the plumbing with startling clarity. But clarity only helps those who know where to look.

Consider the growing category of fee-sharing tokens. Some decentralised exchanges distribute a portion of trading fees to token stakers; others deliberately segregate governance from economics. The difference is not cosmetic. It is constitutional. If a token routes no meaningful income to holders, then narratives about "owning part of the protocol" collapse under inspection. Conversely, when a protocol earmarks fees for buy-backs or distributions, it introduces an economic cycle that can be analysed, challenged, and debated. The question is not whether one model is superior. Rather, it is whether a project's stated claims match its conduct—and whether buyers understand that match. This chapter will examine how to detect such alignment, beginning with the straightforward but often neglected world of cash flows and claims.

But cash flow alone cannot carry the full explanatory weight. Network effects—those subtle inflection points where usefulness becomes stickiness—often matter more than immediate economics. The oldest decentralised exchanges on Ethereum still attract heavy volumes not because they offer the highest yields, but because they have become standards. Developers know how to integrate them; aggregators trust their data; liquidity providers understand their mechanics. Each use reinforces the next. The moat is not built of walls but of habits. Switching costs, in these contexts, are rarely financial; they are cognitive. Migrating to a new protocol with different assumptions introduces friction in code, audits, and expectations. It is easier to remain with the incumbent unless the alternative is radically better. The chapter will explore how such moats form, why they deepen, and how to distinguish genuine network effects from temporary hype.

Security budgets form another cornerstone of value—though one rarely discussed outside specialist circles. A blockchain's safety is not a philosophical attribute; it is a paid-for service. Miners or validators must be compensated to follow rules, reject fraudulent blocks, and maintain uptime. When the compensation dries up or the incentives distort, security suffers. History offers hard evidence. Chains that suffered outages under load, networks that halted during upgrades, protocols drained by overlooked vulnerabilities—each event tested assumptions about resilience. Those that recovered often did so because their communities invested in audits, tooling, and bug bounties. Those that failed lacked the economic muscle to self-correct. In this chapter, we will examine how to assess these budgets, why they matter, and how security becomes part of value, not an optional accessory.

Time complicates everything. Tokens settle in seconds, but analysis requires months or years. A small-cap token may offer remarkable innovation yet suffer from thin liquidity, making large positions impractical. A so-called blue-chip asset may provide deep liquidity but slower evolutionary change. Matching liquidity to horizon becomes essential, not ceremonial. Too many investors buy assets suitable only for long-term holding and expect them to perform in short-term trades—or treat highly illiquid positions as though they can be exited at will. Markets do not adapt to our impatience. They reveal it. And they punish it. This chapter will explore how to calibrate expectations: not as advice, but as an interpretive lens.

If there is a motif running through these pages, it is the contrast between *flash* and *foundation*. Flash covers narratives, price spikes, marketing, and momentary excitement. Foundation consists of cash flows, governance rights, participation metrics, security incentives, and liquidity structure. Flash intoxicates. Foundation endures. The digital economy is littered with projects that mastered the former and neglected the latter. But the inverse—a project that quietly builds foundations before drawing attention—often ages better.

The heart of this chapter is not a set of formulas; it is a way of seeing. To see value, one must see the machinery: how tokens confer or fail to confer rights; how systems grow or stall; how incentives support or undermine integrity; how time interacts with liquidity. These elements are neither exotic nor obscure. They are simply undervalued in markets that race faster than thought. Yet slowing down is the surest way to understand what one is actually holding.

As you move through the chapter, you will encounter the architecture of value in four dimensions: economic rights, network position, security design, and temporal fit. Each dimension offers a scrutiny tool, a quiet test. Together they form a first-principles framework for examining digital assets without the distortions of hype or despair.

The unresolved tension—the one that animates the chapter's inquiry—is this: when the next compelling token flashes across your screen, will you be able to distinguish its foundations from its flash? Or will the noise drown out the structure, leaving you with a price and little else?

Cash flows, claims, and cost

In March 2021, the decentralised exchange SushiSwap announced that its token, SUSHI, had generated roughly $30 million in protocol fees over the preceding six months, a figure drawn from its own treasury reports and visible on-chain. Within hours, social media channels filled with spreadsheets, rough models, and breathless comparisons, as if one data point could confirm a narrative. Yet the excitement masked a crucial distinction. Those fees did not automatically accrue to every holder. Only stakers in a specific contract received a share; the rest held a governance token with no built-in economic right. One group owned a claim. The other owned a symbol. The chain displayed numbers. The meaning depended on design. Five months later, when governance debated whether to redirect more fees to the treasury rather than to token holders, many discovered they had misunderstood what their tokens represented. A market had priced one thing; the protocol delivered another.

This tension between *price* and *claim* sits at the heart of digital asset value. A token may perform feverishly on exchanges, but what does it entitle its holder to in concrete, mechanistic terms? A slice of fees? A discretionary buy-back? Pure governance influence? Or nothing at all beyond speculative potential? The distinction matters because cash flows anchor analysis, whereas symbols drift. And drifting symbols create confusion—confusion that hardens into mispricing, misplaced confidence, or misplaced doubt. The motif that threads through this subchapter is a simple one: *weight*. Cash flows give weight. Claims define weight. Cost measures weight. Everything else merely circles it.

The first principle to establish is not theoretical but behavioural: people interpret tokens through the lens of ownership, even when ownership is the one thing the token does not guarantee. Show the behaviour: investors scanning dashboards for yield, calculating implied multiples, treating a governance token as a revenue-sharing instrument. Name the structure: fee-sharing tokens versus pure governance tokens. Explain the difference: the former encode explicit routing of protocol revenues to a pool, either through direct distribution or discretionary buy-backs; the latter grant voting rights with no direct economic claim. The implication is sobering. Without explicit economic pathways, the token's value must rest on narrative or influence, not on cash flows. Influence is real but intangible. Cash flows are measurable. The difference shapes how systems mature.

A concrete example illustrates the divergence clearly. In December 2020, the decentralised exchange dYdX introduced a token—DYDX—that served as a governance instrument. It distributed no fees to holders. It offered no direct claim on the exchange's considerable trading revenues. Instead, it granted voting power over risk parameters, incentives, and treasury decisions. In contrast, Curve Finance's token—CRV—released earlier in August 2020, tied its mechanism to explicit emissions and veCRV locks, influencing protocol fee distributions. The behaviours differed. CRV holders locked tokens for up to four years, signalling long-term commitment; DYDX holders participated primarily through governance and staking incentives rather than through direct revenue expectations. Both models succeeded in their own contexts, yet they reflected different foundations of value.

A second example reveals how buy-backs muddle or clarify claims. In 2021, the derivatives protocol Perpetual Protocol began purchasing PERP tokens on the open market using a portion of trading fees. This behaviour—visible on-chain—functioned as a discretionary allocation of revenue. It was not a binding right. Governance could halt, accelerate, or redirect buy-backs. The effect resembled a dividend cycle, but without the legal enforceability or predictable cadence of traditional equity payouts. The implication is that buy-backs, while potentially value-enhancing, depend entirely on the stability and integrity of governance. They are policy, not principle. A holder owns exposure to discretion, not a contractual claim.

A credible counter-example comes from MakerDAO's DAI ecosystem, where MKR, the governance token, historically played a dual role: it created incentives for responsible risk management and acted as a recapitalisation mechanism during shortfalls. MKR was burned when surplus accrued, increasing scarcity, and minted when losses required recapitalisation, diluting existing holders. The model created a cost, not an income stream. The behaviour worth observing was not yield but vigilance: governance debates, risk analyses, stability fee adjustments. The implication is that some tokens are designed to absorb cost rather than distribute rewards. This limitation tempers the instinct to search for "yield" in every token. It also reveals a deeper principle: claims define not just what one gains, but what one might lose.

To reconcile these examples, one must accept that value lives in specificity. Cash flows must be traced line by line. Claims must be read literally. Costs must be understood as structural, not incidental. Markets may blur distinctions, but analysis cannot. A token's economic substance is not inferred; it is encoded.

Measurement helps. Protocols with explicit fee-sharing publish usage metrics on public dashboards and block explorers: trading volume, pool fees, staking balances, treasury inflows. These numbers expose behaviours—how users interact, how funds move, how governance acts. In July 2022, Uniswap recorded more than $70 billion in monthly trading volume across Ethereum and Layer-2 deployments (data: Dune Analytics, 2022). Yet UNI, its governance token, does not entitle holders to a share of these fees by default. The chain shows economic activity. The token shows governance. The implication is stark: volume does not equal value without a conduit linking protocol economics to the asset.

The motif of *weight* returns here. Protocols that route revenue to holders create weight. Those that do not must rely on collective belief in governance power—a softer, more interpretive weight. Neither model is inherently superior, but they require different analytical frames. Cash-flow tokens invite scrutiny of revenue stability, cost structure, and sustainability. Governance tokens require scrutiny of participation rates, legitimacy, and institutional behaviour.

Costs deepen the picture. Blockchain systems must pay for security and maintenance. These payments—block rewards, validator incentives, auditor fees, bug bounties—represent ongoing obligations. A token may appear valuable today but may require substantial emissions to secure its chain or attract liquidity. These emissions dilute holders. The behaviour to watch is not price but issuance schedules, governance votes on inflation, and treasury management. For example, Tezos (launched 2018) famously relies on regular protocol upgrades proposed and approved by its validator community. Each upgrade requires funding audits and engineering cycles, internalising cost into its ongoing existence. These costs shape value indirectly: a chain that funds its evolution gains resilience; one that cannot loses momentum.

A limitation appears when cash flows or costs depend heavily on market cycles. Take the case of Avalanche, which saw explosive growth in 2021, with its AVAX token experiencing rapid appreciation and significant usage during the summer and autumn months. Much of its fee revenue and ecosystem incentives stemmed from intense liquidity mining programmes. When those incentives tapered, on-chain activity cooled. The flows were real, but cyclical. The implication is subtle: cash flows derived from subsidies or temporary incentives tell a different story from cash flows derived from organic demand. Analysts must separate structural from cyclical, durable from temporary.

To reconcile these dynamics fully, one must view claims and costs not as binary but as a spectrum. Some tokens have immutable, contractually enforced fee allocations. Some rely on discretionary governance. Some link cost and claim directly, as in MKR's recapitalisation model. Some link nothing at all. The analytical challenge is to map where on this spectrum a token sits—and whether its design matches the behaviour of its community and the expectations of its holders.

Throughout these examples, the quiet motif persists: *what carries weight*. Weight emerges from enforceable rights, observable flows, and accountable governance. It also emerges from cost: systems that fund their own survival possess gravity; those that require perpetual subsidy drift.

Yet the most revealing behaviours often appear not during growth, but during stress. In May 2022, during the collapse of Terra's UST stablecoin, the LUNA token experienced hyperinflation as the protocol attempted to defend its peg. The chain created supply at a pace faster than markets could absorb, diluting holders catastrophically. This was not a failure of cash flow. It was a failure of cost. The system's defence mechanism carried a structural expense that spiralled beyond recovery. Holders discovered that their token represented exposure to an economic model with one-way risk. The implication is lasting: claims and costs must be stress-tested intellectually long before stress arrives.

Against this backdrop, cash-flow awareness becomes a disciplined analytical habit rather than an investment strategy. It means asking what a token pays, if anything; what it costs to operate the system; what claims are enforceable; what claims are discretionary; what dilution patterns look like; and how governance behaves when adjusting economic levers. These behaviours—votes, audits, fee switches, treasury reports—are the markers of real economic architecture.

A final example offers perspective. Since 2020, Aave has operated as one of the leading decentralised lending markets on Ethereum. The AAVE token grants governance power, including control over risk parameters, asset listings, and treasury management. It does not automatically distribute interest paid by borrowers. Yet Aave's success stems from consistent risk management, active governance, and conservative collateral frameworks. The token's value is thus tied to institutional behaviour, not cash flows. Holders value competence. Here, *people* provide weight. Not revenue.

This does not diminish the importance of economic rights. It widens the frame. A token can embody value through governance if governance is meaningful and consistently exercised. It can embody value through revenue if revenue is structurally routed to holders. It can embody value through security if the token plays a role in staking or network protection. But absent a clear mechanism—whether economic or institutional—value becomes an inference rather than a property.

The unresolved tension is this: when faced with a token whose price commands your attention, will you be able to trace its weight? Will you see the cash flows that are real, the claims that are enforceable, and the costs that are structural—or will surface motion obscure the machinery beneath?

Network effects and moats

At 6:42 p.m. UTC on 18 May 2021, the Ethereum mempool swelled under the pressure of cascading liquidations across DeFi lending markets. Gas prices spiked above 1,500 gwei. Traders scrambled to adjust collateral; bots jostled for priority. Through the chaos, one pattern stood out. Despite a rush of opportunistic forks advertising cheaper fees and identical features, the bulk of trading volume remained on Uniswap and Sushiswap. Copycats existed; incentives were generous elsewhere. Yet liquidity stayed put. In that hour of stress, users revealed what charts often obscure. They valued depth. They valued composability. They valued familiarity. In short, they valued the moat.

Why did traffic cling to a handful of venues when technical barriers to exit were minimal? Why endure high fees when alternatives ran at a fraction of the cost? The paradox exposes a foundation of digital asset markets: switching is easy in principle, difficult in practice. Not because of habits alone, but because of the dense web of integrations, assumptions, and shared expectations that grow around successful protocols. A fork may replicate code. It cannot replicate context. And context—what developers expect, what aggregators trust, what tools support—is the real terrain on which moats are built.

To see these moats clearly, one must begin with *liquidity depth*, the most visible pillar of network effects. Depth reveals itself in behaviour: the willingness of traders to route large orders through a venue without fearing slippage. On 19 November 2021, Uniswap processed over $6 billion in daily volume across its deployments (data: Dune Analytics). The flows concentrated in pairs with deep reserves, maintained by thousands of independent liquidity providers. Show the depth; name the moat: concentration of liquidity. Explain it: high volume attracts arbitrageurs who keep pools balanced, which in turn attracts more traders, which further rewards liquidity providers. The implication is self-reinforcing. Once a protocol becomes the default route, new entrants face steep odds unless they can provide meaningfully better conditions.

A second domain where moats reveal themselves is *developer traction*. Protocols become platforms as soon as developers build around them. The behaviour to watch is simple: are new applications integrating a protocol by default? Are audits, SDKs, and tooling already tailored to its assumptions? Compound, launched in 2018, became the canonical lending primitive partly because developers in San Francisco, Berlin, and Singapore used its interfaces to build leveraged trading systems, yield optimisers, and automated strategies. The design was predictable. The contracts were battle-tested. Tutorials existed. Each integration deepened the moat. Naming this layer reveals its nature: developer network effects. Explaining them shows that development is path dependent. Time spent acquiring knowledge on one protocol becomes an implicit cost to migrating elsewhere. The implication is enduring. A protocol becomes sticky not through lock-in, but through accumulated familiarity.

A credible counter-example helps refine the argument. In mid-2020, several AMM forks on Binance Smart Chain mimicked Uniswap's interface and mechanics. PancakeSwap, launched by anonymous developers in September 2020, even surpassed Uniswap's daily transactions for several weeks due to lower fees and aggressive incentives. It proved that switching *can* occur when conditions align. Yet the picture was complex. Many users treated BSC venues as short-horizon environments—cheaper, faster, but riskier. When markets oscillated, deep liquidity remained anchored on Ethereum-based AMMs. The moat held at the core while activity shifted at the periphery. Reconciliation lies in context. Moats are not universal; they are domain specific. Low-cost chains favour exploratory behaviour; high-security chains favour settled habits. The existence of migration does not erase the advantage of incumbency where trust and tooling matter most.

A third dimension—*composability*—serves as the quiet engine of network effects. Composability is not a slogan but a behaviour: contracts calling contracts, strategies nesting within other strategies, applications relying on shared standards like ERC-20 and ERC-4626. A lending market that uses a particular price oracle anchors expectations for derivative platforms that rely on the same feed. A yield aggregator that routes deposits through a specific AMM creates stable demand for its pools. Every integration becomes an agreement about how things work, an informal standard etched into code. In 2021, Yearn Finance, based on Ethereum, demonstrated this vividly: its vault strategies leaned heavily on Curve and Convex, turning Curve's liquidity gauges into de facto monetary policy for a substantial portion of DeFi capital. Show the composability; name the moat: integration depth. Explain its power: breaking composability introduces risk. The implication follows naturally. When a protocol becomes a keystone dependency, replacing it requires rewriting infrastructure far beyond the protocol itself.

Metrics reinforce these dynamics. Measure how many contracts import a protocol's interfaces. Measure how many front-ends route through its pools. Measure how many governance decisions in surrounding systems reference its parameters. These concrete behaviours reveal what narratives cannot: moats made of code, habits, and coordination.

The economic analogue is *standards formation*. In traditional markets, standards like SWIFT, FIX, or IBAN endure because changing them would impose immense coordination costs across institutions. In crypto markets, standards emerge faster but remain equally stubborn once established. Uniswap's constant-product AMM formula became a mental standard: developers expect *x*y=k*; aggregators assume it; liquidity providers learn its behaviour. Even when concentrated liquidity arrived with Uniswap v3 in May 2021, the earlier formula remained a reference point for many chains and forks. Standards reduce cognitive load. They shrink design space. And they create a moat without ever calling it one.

A second example shows this pattern in a different register. When Aave deployed on Polygon in April 2021, its credit delegation and collateral mechanisms became templates for newer lending markets across multiple chains. Builders in Mumbai, Amsterdam, and Seoul adapted its patterns rather than inventing from scratch. The standard had been set. Changing it would require rewriting assumptions in downstream protocols, retraining users, and re-auditing strategies. Naming the pattern clarifies it: standards inertia. Explaining it reveals that moats form where familiarity converges with security. The implication is durable. A project becomes a standard not through claims, but through steady, repeated use under pressure.

Yet moats are not impregnable. A credible counter-example arrived with the rise of Curve Wars in late 2021. Convex Finance, launched in May 2021, accumulated a dominant share of veCRV voting power, reshaping incentives around Curve's pools. Liquidity gravitated toward whichever pools Convex boosted, demonstrating that moats can be reshuffled when meta-protocols capture control of incentives rather than liquidity itself. The dynamic illuminated a limitation: moats built on incentives can be contested by actors who control those incentives. Reconciling this requires a broader frame. Moats can shift layers—from base liquidity to governance influence—yet the underlying system remains protected by its deep web of dependencies. Curve remained central even as control of its levers changed.

Threaded through all these cases is a quiet motif: *gravity*. Successful protocols develop gravity. Users orbit them. Developers align to them. Integrations accumulate around them. Gravity is not imposed; it is earned. And once earned, it shapes behaviour long after technical alternatives emerge. Gravity explains why protocols that appear technologically outdated can retain dominance. They have mass.

Part of that mass derives from *switching costs*. These costs are rarely explicit. They live in mental models, tooling, audits, and reputational expectations. When a new decentralised exchange launches boasting marginally lower fees, developers must still audit its contracts, traders must test its slippage patterns, and liquidity providers must assess its monitoring infrastructure. These behaviours consume time, attention, and trust. And trust is slow to migrate. The switching cost is psychological as much as technical. It is easier to accept known imperfections than to risk unknown vulnerabilities.

Historical examples underscore the point. In 2017, Bancor launched one of the first automated liquidity protocols, raising more than $150 million in its ICO. Its design introduced a novel bonding curve mechanism. Yet when Uniswap emerged a year later with fewer features and less capital, developers gravitated to it because the mental model was simpler and the integration surface smaller. Bancor's technical novelty could not overcome the switching costs of complexity. Uniswap's minimalism lowered cognitive barriers, creating a path for gravity to accumulate. The implication is counterintuitive. Simplicity—when paired with reliability—can outperform sophistication.

Network effects, however, do not guarantee permanence. They must be maintained. Protocols that stagnate risk losing their moat as expectations rise. A credible modern example emerged with SushiSwap after internal governance turmoil in late 2021 and early 2022. Conflicts between core contributors, slow decision-making, and leadership turnover eroded confidence. Some liquidity migrated to rivals; developers hesitated to integrate new features. The moat weakened not because the AMM model changed, but because organisational behaviour faltered. The lesson is sharp: moats require stewardship.

Stewardship returns us to gravity. Gravity is not immutable. It must be renewed. It strengthens through clear upgrades, secure deployments, transparent governance, and responsible treasury management. These behaviours—measurable, visible, and repeatable—anchor ecosystems in ways slogans never can.

Across this subchapter, the examples reveal a common thread: moats emerge not from brilliance alone, but from cumulative trust expressed through repeated choices. They are expressions of collective judgement. They harden through use.

The unresolved question—the one that presses against every new protocol promising disruption—is simple yet decisive: when presented with a technically elegant alternative, will users and developers overcome the gravity of existing systems, or will they remain bound to the moats that familiarity and composability have carved?

Security budgets and resilience

At 12:02 a.m. UTC on 8 May 2020, the Steem blockchain halted. Blocks stopped finalising. Witnesses—the validators responsible for confirming transactions—fell into dispute after a controversial hard fork triggered by the acquisition of Steemit Inc. by Tron founder Justin Sun in February 2020. Code had not failed; coordination had. What began as a governance dispute metastasised into a full network freeze. The event was a stark reminder that blockchains, often framed as immune to human frailty, remain dependent on the incentives and behaviour of real people. The outage lasted hours. The reputational cost lasted years. And throughout the crisis, one question hung over the chain like a fog: what, precisely, was Steem's security budget buying?

Security budgets are not abstract slogans. They are measurable economic commitments expressed as miner rewards, validator income, audit expenditure, and bug bounty allocations. They shape behaviour. A chain that pays validators handsomely encourages vigilant monitoring; a chain that skimps invites complacency. In March 2022, when Solana suffered a multi-hour halt after a spike in transactions from NFT minting bots overwhelmed consensus, the chain's validator set had the resources to coordinate a restart—roughly 1,600 active validators across 33 countries at the time (Solana Foundation, 2022). The visible behaviour, as validators stepped through restart procedures, showed that economic incentives and technical readiness interact. The incident did not invalidate Solana. It revealed the contours of its resilience under stress.

Resilience emerges from incentives. Incentives cost money. And money defines the security budget. Show the expenditure; name the mechanism: miner or validator rewards. Explain the logic: participants commit energy or capital in exchange for predictable compensation. The implication is unavoidable. If a protocol's rewards fall below the opportunity cost of participation, the network risks thinning its own immune system.

The contrast between Bitcoin and smaller proof-of-work chains illustrates the point. In December 2021, Bitcoin's annualised security spend—block subsidies plus transaction fees—exceeded $18 billion (Coin Metrics, 2021), spread across miners operating in Texas, Kazakhstan, Canada, and Northern Europe. The visible behaviour was robust: miners rapidly reorganised after the May 2021 Chinese mining ban, re-establishing hash-rate within months. By contrast, Ethereum Classic, whose security budget remained a fraction of Bitcoin's, suffered multiple 51 per cent attacks in 2020. Naming the weakness clarifies it: insufficient economic cost to rewrite history. Explaining it reveals the relationship between budget and deterrence. The implication is blunt. A chain cannot purchase security it cannot afford.

Beyond consensus rewards lies a second pillar: *audits*. Audits are not ceremonial. They are labour-intensive examinations performed by specific firms with traceable reputations. Trail of Bits, based in New York since 2012, and London's NCC Group have both audited major protocols; their reports run to hundreds of pages. A completed audit demonstrates visible behaviour: line-by-line validation, adversarial modelling, and systematic reporting of vulnerabilities. Yet even audited systems fail. The Ronin Network breach in March 2022, despite audits of underlying components, exposed a different weakness: a multisig controlled by only nine validators, five of which were compromised. The counter-example does not refute the value of audits. It exposes their limitation. Audits validate code, not governance. Reconciling this reveals a deeper pattern. Audits form part of a security budget, but resilience demands broader defences.

Bug bounties play a complementary role. Immunefi, founded in 2020, has facilitated millions of dollars in payouts to researchers who discover critical vulnerabilities. Paying for external scrutiny is not generosity; it is insurance. The behaviour is clear. A protocol commits capital to reward adversarial imagination. The implication is practical. Systems that invest in bounties harness distributed intelligence; those that do not rely on hope.

The motif of *pressure* sharpens the argument. Protocols reveal their nature under pressure. A chain may process transactions flawlessly during quiet periods yet falter when demand surges. Avalanche, launched September 2020, faced congestion in February 2021 when the Pangolin DEX attracted rapid inflows. Validators struggled with increased load; users experienced delays. Avalanche's team responded with optimisations and tooling improvements. The behaviour under pressure showed commitment to resilience. Pressure exposes priorities.

Economic incentives also shape validator behaviour during crises. When Terra collapsed in May 2022, validators attempted to halt the chain to stem the hyperinflation of LUNA as its algorithmic stablecoin, UST, de-pegged. That halt was a desperate measure with mixed effects. Yet it revealed, in real time, the relationship between economic design and emergency response. The chain's incentives—built to sustain a growth engine—were not designed for collapse. Naming the flaw clarifies it: brittle economics. The implication stretches further. A system optimised for expansion may have limited tools for contraction.

To see incentives more concretely, one must look at validator hardware, uptime requirements, and slashing conditions. Ethereum's post-merge proof-of-stake system, operational since 15 September 2022, penalises validators for downtime, creating visible behaviours: operators use redundant servers, monitor nodes, and participate in client diversity to avoid correlated failures. Slashing is not punitive theatre; it embeds costs that enforce discipline. The implication is structural. A well-defined slashing regime ensures that validators behave reliably even when no one is watching.

The second dimension of resilience is recovery. Recovery is the ability to restore normal functioning after shocks. Polkadot's recovery procedures in 2021, when a bug in the Acala parachain's token minting caused temporary inflation, demonstrated this principle. The community executed governance actions to freeze and later burn the erroneous tokens. Behaviour, not rhetoric, measured resilience. The implication is decisive. A chain's value lies not in avoiding mistakes but in correcting them safely.

Resilience also hinges on client diversity. If too many validators run the same software, a single bug can cripple the network. Ethereum recognised this risk early, distributing validators across clients like Prysm, Lighthouse, Teku, and Nimbus. By August 2023, no single client exceeded 60 per cent of the validator set (Ethereum Foundation, 2023). This diversity showed up in metrics: fewer correlated failures and faster recovery from client-specific issues. The implication is subtle. Diversity is a security budget expressed indirectly through engineering investment and community incentives.

Security budgets include social capital. Social capital becomes visible during disputes. When Geth discovered a consensus bug in August 2021, only nodes running a specific older version suffered a chain split. Developers across continents coordinated through public channels to instruct operators to upgrade immediately. The split was resolved quickly because the Ethereum community had practices for rapid response. These behaviours—public communication, transparent incident reports, adherence to upgrade norms—cost time and effort, but they collectively form a security budget of their own.

The credible counter-example lies in chains where community coordination is weak. During the 2020 Steem/Sun conflict, insufficient trust among witnesses caused fragmentation, forks, and prolonged uncertainty. Collaboration broke down. Without social capital, the economic security budget could not protect the chain.

Reconciliation highlights an uncomfortable truth: resilience requires both incentives and relationships. Money alone cannot buy legitimacy.

Throughout these cases, a quiet motif emerges: *pressure lines*. Every protocol has them. They may lie in validator incentives, software diversity, governance cohesion, or treasury allocation. Pressure exposes them with precision. Builders can measure them using metrics: time to finality during congestion; percentage of validators updated within one hour of a security patch; distribution of stake across independent operators; average response time in bug bounty engagements. These metrics, once observed, reveal what slogans obscure.

The economic framing of resilience also extends to treasury management. A well-funded treasury—transparent, multi-signature, geographically distributed—can pay for audits, support client teams, and fund bug bounties. Chains with shallow treasuries rely on volunteer labour or opportunistic grants. The implication is straightforward. Without financial capacity, resilience degrades silently.

One more case crystallises the link between budgets and outcomes. In September 2022, after the Ethereum merge, a minority execution layer client introduced a bug affecting block building. Thanks to client diversity and vigilant monitoring, the issue caused no major disruption. The coordinated behaviour between client teams across Europe and North America, supported by funding from the Ethereum Foundation and external grants, demonstrated how a well-resourced ecosystem turns money into resilience. The pressure line bent; it did not break.

Yet the unresolved question remains. A chain can fund audits, maintain bounties, diversify clients, cultivate governance norms, and build social capital. But when the next systemic shock arrives—a coordinated attack, a catastrophic bug, or a geopolitical disruption—will its security budget, both economic and social, prove deep enough to hold the line, or will unseen pressure lines give way?

Time horizons and liquidity

At 11:56 p.m. UTC on 12 March 2020, as global markets convulsed, decentralised exchanges on Ethereum recorded some of the most extreme dislocations in their short history. MakerDAO's collateral auctions malfunctioned. Several DeFi tokens saw their liquidity collapse to a few thousand dollars per pool. A trader in London watched as a modest £20,000 sell order in a small-cap governance token erased more than 60 per cent of its quoted value in seconds. The Ethereum chain continued to settle transactions every fifteen seconds. The trades cleared. The market did not. That night revealed a paradox that remains central to digital assets: instant settlement does not mean instant exit.

The paradox matters. Crypto markets often advertise speed—blocks every few seconds, finality within minutes, transfers that complete faster than bank wires. Yet speed belongs to the chain, not the market. Markets depend on depth, counterparties, and capacity. Even a token that settles with mechanical precision can take hours or days to unwind at a defensible price if buyers are scarce. The trader in London learned this as slippage devoured value trade by trade. The chain moved quickly. Liquidity moved slowly. This split between technical settlement and economic liquidation defines one of the most important boundaries in this field.

Settlement is mechanical. Liquidity is behavioural. And behaviour changes under pressure. In November 2022, when Coinbase (founded 2012, based in San Francisco) reported temporary delays for ETH withdrawals due to congestion, settlement remained steady across the chain. But liquidity in several long-tail tokens dried up as market-makers widened spreads. The visible behaviour—thinner books, slower quotes—showed how participants retreat to safer assets during uncertainty. Naming this reveals its structure: a liquidity rotation. Explaining it clarifies the dynamics. As risk appetite falls, capital migrates from small caps to large caps, from speculative governance tokens to the relative safety of stablecoins or blue-chip assets like ETH and BTC. The implication is stark. A position that appears liquid in calm markets may become immovable under stress.

The motif that threads through these cases is simple: *time*. Markets express time differently depending on context. A blockchain's time is fixed by code; a market's time stretches and contracts with sentiment. Even though Ethereum finalised blocks in roughly thirteen seconds in January 2023, liquidity for small-cap assets on decentralised exchanges could take hours to replenish after volatility spikes. The chain honoured the clock. Participants did not.

To see time horizons clearly, observe the behaviour of different assets across a cycle. In July 2021, Uniswap pools for blue-chip assets regularly recorded tens of millions in depth within one per cent of the mid-price. The same month, liquidity for smaller DeFi governance tokens often fell below £500,000 across all decentralised venues combined. Show the data; name the distinction: liquidity tiers. Explain why they matter: deep pools absorb shocks; shallow pools amplify them. The implication is decisive for anyone navigating these markets. One must understand not just what one holds, but the time required to exit without self-inflicted ruin.

Liquidity conditions also shape the meaning of *position size*. A modest allocation to a token with limited depth can become oversized when markets tighten. In January 2021, during the rapid ascent of Binance Smart Chain, several tokens listed on PancakeSwap showed daily volumes exceeding £50 million. Yet much of this volume circulated within tight loops of arbitrage bots. When broader risk appetite waned weeks later, liquidity thinned dramatically. Traders who believed they could exit large positions quickly discovered that real buyers were scarce. The visible behaviour—widening slippage at even modest trade sizes—showed that inflated volume figures concealed fragility. The implication travels far. Volume is not liquidity; volume can be illusion.

One credible counter-example demonstrates the limitation of general rules. In late 2020, Curve Finance pools displayed deep liquidity for stablecoins—even during market stress—due to the predictable behaviour of arbitrageurs maintaining peg spreads. These pools often absorbed eight-figure trades with minimal price impact. Here, high liquidity persisted despite turbulence. Reconciling this difference clarifies the point: liquidity is not uniformly fragile. It depends on incentives, user behaviour, and the structural role of the asset. Stablecoins pegged to fiat currencies benefit from arbitrage mechanisms that governance tokens lack. The implication is sobering. Liquidity is context, not constant.

Time horizons are also shaped by *participant composition*. When a market is dominated by retail traders, liquidity often peaks during euphoric rallies and evaporates when sentiment turns. Conversely, markets with active professional market-makers exhibit steadier behaviour. In March 2021, a group of market-making firms operating from Chicago and Singapore reported that they maintained two-sided quotes for major ERC-20 tokens through periods of volatility, but withdrew from smaller tokens whose risk models flagged unstable flows. Their behaviour illustrated a division that repeats across cycles. Professional liquidity prefers predictability. Retail liquidity prefers excitement.

The implication is unavoidable. Assets sustained primarily by volatile enthusiasm cannot offer reliable exits.

This cycle of expansion and contraction plays out visibly in decentralised exchange pools. Observe the motif of time again. During bullish phases, liquidity providers add capital, drawn by high fees and rising prices. During bearish phases, they withdraw capital quickly to avoid impermanent loss. This ebb and flow shapes exit horizons. A position that could be unwound in minutes during a rally may require measured staging during contractions. In 2022, several protocols advised caution after liquidity providers withdrew more than £800 million from major pools across Uniswap and Curve within a single week. The market's time horizon lengthened. Exits slowed.

Settlement speed—measured in seconds—can mislead. It signals activity, not capacity. A chain may offer near-instant confirmation, but if order books are thin or pools are shallow, forced sellers can still incur catastrophic slippage. The most visible illustration emerged in May 2022, when the collapse of TerraUSD caused liquidity spirals across multiple chains. Terra's own on-chain settlement remained quick; the network produced blocks. Yet token holders attempting to sell UST and LUNA faced liquidity that evaporated minute by minute. The chain settled. The market failed. The implication is sharp. Speed cannot compensate for absent depth.

A different perspective comes from traditional finance. In October 1987, during Black Monday, the New York Stock

Exchange continued trading, but liquidity providers withdrew and spreads ballooned. The lesson crosses decades and domains. Settlement infrastructure can survive shocks while markets seize. The parallel reinforces a central principle of this subchapter: liquidity is a social phenomenon grounded in participation, not a technical property guaranteed by the ledger.

Time horizons also arise from policy and design. Lock-ups, vesting schedules, staking requirements, and cooldown periods shape when capital can move. When Polygon introduced its staking mechanism in 2020, validators and delegators committed tokens that could not be instantly withdrawn. These periods lengthened the market's effective time horizon. The visible behaviour was deliberate: slower adjustments, more predictable supply, and fewer sudden exits. The implication is structural. Protocol decisions fix time in ways that market participants must absorb.

A second example comes from governance tokens with delayed voting periods. When Curve's voting escrow model (launched August 2020) encouraged holders to lock tokens for up to four years, the circulating supply shrank, lengthening exit horizons. Holders committed to a time structure that deepened the protocol's resilience. The behaviour was measurable: reduced sell pressure and more stable liquidity. The implication stretches further. When participants voluntarily bind their future choices, they create a different market rhythm—one shaped by commitment rather than speculation.

Yet there are limits. One credible counter-example is the 2018 collapse of numerous ICO tokens. Lock-ups intended to stabilise early markets instead created pent-up selling that cascaded once unlock dates arrived. The behaviour was clear: developers converted token grants, early backers sold into the thin liquidity of post-ICO markets, and prices deteriorated. Token-specific time horizons clashed with market depth. Reconciling this example underscores the delicate balance. Time constraints can stabilise or destabilise depending on design and demand.

Threaded quietly through these stories is the motif of *tides*. Liquidity behaves like a tide: rising with confidence, receding with fear, shaped by forces far larger than any single actor. And, like tides, liquidity can appear stable until it ebbs sharply, exposing hidden terrain.

One more feature shapes time horizons: operational constraints. Traders managing institutional capital often face internal risk limits, compliance checks, and multi-signature processes that slow execution. Even when a blockchain settles trades in seconds, the decision cycle inside a firm may require hours or days. In September 2021, a European digital asset fund reported that rebalancing into ETH during a rapid selloff was delayed by its own approval procedures, not the chain. The behaviour is telling. Organisational timeframes matter as much as technical ones. The implication: liquidity must be matched not just to market structure, but to human structure.

Liquidity's final dimension is *path dependency*. The path one takes to exit a position shapes final outcomes. Consider a holder of a small-cap governance token in mid-2022 wishing to liquidate 5 per cent of the circulating supply. A single market sell could crash the price. A sequence of structured auctions might take weeks. OTC trades could demand discounts. Each option implies a different time horizon. The behaviour of experienced traders reflects this. They stage exits, break trades into smaller lots, and avoid triggering slippage that could spiral. The implication is essential. Time is a tool, not merely a constraint.

As the subchapter closes, the unresolved question returns to the surface: when volatility surges and liquidity ebbs, will one's chosen assets allow a calm, orderly exit, or will the market's tide retreat faster than any individual can move?

Chapter 3
Behavioural Traps

The message arrived on a quiet Sunday afternoon: a friend forwarding a thread from an anonymous account claiming insider knowledge of a breakthrough partnership. The token named in the rumour shot up nearly 40 per cent within hours. Screens lit with flashing green. Telegram groups buzzed with triumphal certainty. By the evening, hundreds of newcomers—many of whom had never read a line of the project's documentation—were buying at any price, desperate not to be left behind. Two days later the rumour evaporated. The token bled back to its starting point. Those who had chased the spike found themselves holding positions they had never intended to own, convinced they had simply been "early to the next big thing" when, in fact, they had been late to a story.

That sequence—excitement, acceleration, collective conviction, and disillusion—is hardly new. It echoed the South Sea Bubble of 1720, when investors in London snapped up shares in companies with no revenue and vague ambitions, guided by whispers of extraordinary returns. The historian John Carswell observed that many purchasers had "no clear sense of what they owned, only a sharp fear of falling behind their neighbours." Three centuries separate that mania from modern token markets, yet the emotional architecture is unchanged. FOMO is not a product of blockchains; it is a product of the human mind confronted with the prospect of effortless gain. Technology merely accelerates its spread.

What is different today is the speed at which narratives can engulf a market. A rumour that once travelled by pamphlet or gossip now traverses millions of screens in minutes. Influencers wrap speculation in pseudo-technical language. Algorithms elevate content that triggers emotion. And the investor—armed with instant execution and a thousand discordant signals—must navigate an environment where stories behave like contagions. Each new cycle repeats the same contradiction: markets powered by cryptographic certainty are most volatile when certainty is the one thing nobody possesses. This chapter enters that contradiction. It begins where prices meet psychology, and where rational intentions collide with ancient instincts.

The behavioural traps that shape digital asset markets are not exotic defects of modern trading. They are familiar patterns: the fear of missing out that drives people to buy precisely when risk is highest; the comforting pull of the first number we see, which anchors judgement even as conditions change; the seductive warmth of confirmation—that sweet sense that others agree with us, even when those others are merely shadows on the walls of our curated feeds. These traps do not only distort decisions; they distort perception. They create a private reality in which everything we already believe appears more plausible, and everything that challenges us feels like an irritant to be ignored.

But the deepest trap is not emotional. It is structural. The very features that make digital assets appealing—the liquidity, the global access, the ability to trade at any hour—also amplify psychological noise. A person can now revise their entire financial future at two in the morning because they saw a post that gained traction faster than they could verify its source. Time compresses. Deliberation recedes. One impulse, acted upon through a few taps, can create positions that linger for months.

Yet these traps do not arise in a vacuum; they emerge from distinctive behavioural terrain. The crypto markets have a culture—the fusion of early-adopter optimism, technological evangelism, and a distrust of traditional institutions. This culture rewards bold conviction and punishes hesitation. It encourages the belief that missing one opportunity might mean missing the next decade of innovation. It amplifies narratives through communities that are part social club, part investment syndicate, part ideology. Within such environments, the ordinary cognitive biases described in academic literature become vivid forces that shape collective behaviour.

This chapter therefore steers directly into the psychological undercurrent that runs beneath prices and charts. It explores the anatomy of FOMO not as a trivial impulse but as a social feedback loop: a mechanism by which people outsource judgement to the tempo of the crowd. It examines narrative cascades—the ways in which stories, once established, can override evidence simply because enough people believe them. It then moves to anchoring and sunk cost, showing how the numbers lodged in memory can control future choices: the price at which one first bought, the high-water mark of a previous rally, the "even point" one hopes to reclaim. These anchors become private myths that distort decisions long after their original meaning has expired.

The chapter also traces the subtler trap of confirmation loops. Social platforms, designed to show users what they are most likely to engage with, do not merely reflect preferences; they harden them. A bullish sentiment begets bullish content. A sceptical stance yields sceptical sources. Over time, one's informational environment narrows until reality itself appears polarised. The person who wants the market to rise sees reasons for optimism everywhere; the person who fears collapse finds evidence of doom at every turn. Confirmation is addictive because it feels like clarity.

And then there is position sizing—the behavioural hinge disguised as a technical detail. Position size governs emotion. It determines whether volatility feels like background noise or existential threat. A person whose allocation is modest can weather drawdowns with rational distance; someone overexposed becomes captive to every tick of the chart. Sleep becomes fragile. Patience dissolves. An oversized position does not merely increase financial risk; it distorts judgement. This chapter examines the psychological weight of size and shows how a disciplined approach to risk—rooted in clear limits and simple heuristics—can preserve both capital and composure.

Threaded through these themes is a central motif: *the mind's shortcuts*. These shortcuts—useful in environments of slow change—become liabilities in markets that evolve hour by hour. They shape what we notice, what we ignore, and how we interpret the data before us. Understanding them is not an academic exercise; it is a practical necessity for anyone who wishes to maintain agency amid noise.

The chapter's aim is not moralising. Human biases are not failings to be eradicated; they are conditions to be understood. Nor does the chapter promise immunity. Even the most seasoned professionals fall prey to these patterns, sometimes precisely because experience breeds confidence. The goal is more modest and more useful: to illuminate the forces that tug at our decisions, so that we can recognise them in the moment, pause, and choose deliberately rather than reflexively.

As we move deeper, one tension will persist. Do we shape our decisions, or do our decisions shape us? When narratives swell and charts surge, when losses tempt denial and gains tempt overreach, when silence in the feed feels like opportunity slipping away, will we act from clarity or from fear?

The pages ahead offer no tidy answer. They offer something better: the tools to recognise the trap before the trap recognises you.

FOMO and narrative cascades

At 9.17 p.m. on 12 May 2021, a pseudonymous account called @CryptoWhaleAlert declared on X that a "tier-one exchange listing" for the token SHIB was imminent. The post originated from Shanghai, drew more than 20,000 interactions within an hour, and—despite offering no evidence—triggered a rush of retail purchases across Asia and Europe. By midnight, Binance had confirmed no such listing. Yet the token's market cap had already expanded by billions of dollars. The rumour vanished, but the behaviour it provoked remained perfectly visible: thousands of people, acting within minutes, moved real money on the basis of a story that grew faster than they could question it. That is FOMO rendered in data.

The speed of that episode obscured its simplicity. A narrative was introduced, amplified, and then acted upon before verification could occur. Participants did not ask who the source was, whether they had previously been reliable, or whether any corroborating evidence existed. They acted because others appeared to act. They wanted in. They feared being late. And the momentum of the crowd replaced the discipline of judgement. The cascade—the collective acceleration of belief—became more influential than the content of the belief itself. One post moved markets because thousands of people mistook velocity for truth. Five words: *Momentum overwhelms slow thought.*

Fear of missing out is not primarily an emotion; it is a social reaction shaped by perceived urgency. The behavioural economist Sendhil Mullainathan described a related pattern in 2008: scarcity mindsets compress cognition. They narrow attention. They create a tunnel in which immediate signals dominate deliberation. In markets, that tunnel forms when charts spike, when friends share screenshots, when a token trends across platforms. The person feels pressure to act before opportunity escapes. The motif that recurs in these moments is the ticking clock—real or imagined—pulsing in the background of each decision.

One of the most visible demonstrations of narrative cascades came during the Dogecoin rally of April 2021. Elon Musk's public comments on X—particularly the tweet on 28 April noting he was "working with Doge devs to improve system efficiency"—triggered a tidal wave of purchases within minutes. The claim itself was modest; the market reaction was not. The community filled gaps with speculation, inventing future scenarios that had no factual anchor. The story attained its own gravity. This reflects a common dynamic: when uncertainty is high and the desire for participation is stronger than the desire for accuracy, narratives expand to fit emotional needs. A market substitutes evidence with a storyline because a storyline is easier to trade.

But the opposite case matters too. The token LUNA in early 2022 reached a market capitalisation of over $40bn before collapsing to near zero within days after the UST stablecoin lost its peg. In the months preceding the crash, critics had raised concerns about the sustainability of UST's design, including the reflexive relationship between minting, burning, and the Anchor Protocol's fixed yields. Yet these concerns were drowned out by confident messaging from prominent figures and relentless community enthusiasm. The limitation of narrative cascades becomes clear here: they can grow around *positive* stories, but they can also suppress warnings. A cascade inflates certain claims while muting others, creating informational blind spots precisely when clarity matters most.

Why do these cascades take hold? The mechanism is not mysterious. Markets composed of individuals with incomplete knowledge rely on social cues to fill informational gaps. When people see others buying, they infer that those others must know something. This inference is visible in the behaviour itself: accelerated purchases, reduced due diligence, and a willingness to enter positions before reading even the first page of a project's documentation. The visible behaviour is speed. The underlying belief is delegation: trusting the crowd to have done the thinking.

Anchoring this dynamic is the metric that governs digital culture: engagement. Algorithms do not prioritise accuracy; they prioritise attention. A post that triggers strong emotion—curiosity, excitement, outrage—receives preferential distribution. That distribution creates visibility, and visibility mimics validation. A trader scrolling through feeds late at night sees a rumour that appears to be "everywhere" and feels that ubiquity must signal truth. The question that should arise is simple: *Is this popular because it is correct, or correct because it is popular?* Yet in the heat of momentum, few pause to ask.

The early hours of 8 January 2021 offer another example. A rumour circulated that the U.S. Treasury was preparing a major crypto enforcement action. No details. No source. The market erased more than $150bn in value within hours. When officials confirmed no such plan existed, the rumour dissolved. But the decision-making pattern it provoked—the rapid selling by investors who saw others sell—revealed a core tension: in markets governed by real-time data, herd behaviour can materialise even when the herd is responding to shadows.

The counter-example, and the limitation, is instructive. Bitcoin experienced repeated cycles between 2017 and 2020 where positive rumours circulated—ETF approvals, corporate partnerships, sovereign adoption—yet price moved little because liquidity conditions dominated sentiment. Narrative alone does not guarantee cascades; for a story to become a cascade, the surrounding environment must already be primed. Liquidity, prior momentum, and community cohesion act as accelerants. When those conditions are absent, even vivid stories fail to propagate.

This interplay between story and structure shapes investor psychology. FOMO intensifies not merely when a token rises, but when the rise appears effortless. Efficiency becomes a visible behaviour: the swiftness with which others act creates the impression that action must be immediate. Traders measure potential regret against current opportunity. They compare their inactivity with the speed of others. They commit capital to relieve anxiety rather than to express understanding. In this environment, the motif of the ticking clock returns.

Central to resisting these patterns is a simple act: pause long enough to verify. In behavioural experiments conducted at MIT in 2017, researchers found that a 30-second delay before decision-making significantly improved accuracy in environments with noisy information. Thirty seconds is trivial. Yet in practice, few market participants grant themselves that space. The decision to buy or sell often occurs within seconds of encountering a narrative. Pausing breaks the cascade. It disrupts the emotional tempo that FOMO creates.

Verification is equally mechanical. Check the original source. Confirm whether the claim has appeared in any official communication from the named organisation. Assess whether the account sharing the rumour has a history of accuracy or a pattern of fabrication. These are not grand investigative techniques; they are low-cost checks. But they represent the difference between participating in a market and surrendering to one.

The difficulty is not the absence of information. It is the abundance of misinformation and the speed with which it spreads. In 2020, researchers at Carnegie Mellon University identified that nearly half of viral COVID-related tweets came from accounts with bot-like characteristics. Similar dynamics appear in crypto markets. Automated accounts amplify certain narratives, accelerating their spread before human users have time to question them. Recognising this pattern is vital: a cascade may feel organic while being artificially boosted.

The unresolved tension lies in the structure of digital communities. People join groups to learn, to share, to feel part of something larger. Communities offer support, but they also create echo chambers. When a member expresses doubts during a rally, they are often met with dismissal or accusations of "spreading FUD." The social cost of scepticism becomes a barrier to clear thinking. Yet without scepticism—without the willingness to interrupt a story—cascades deepen. This tension will not vanish. It must be managed.

Two questions, therefore, shape the boundary between reasoned participation and reflexive FOMO. The first: *Would I make this decision if nobody else were talking about it?* The second: *What evidence would change my mind, and have I looked for it?*

The answers to those questions mark the difference between acting on conviction and acting on fear.

Anchoring and sunk cost

On 14 June 2022, at a café near London Bridge, a software engineer named Ravi scrolled through his portfolio with the tight, fixed expression that appears when numbers contradict hope. He had bought a basket of tokens during the bull frenzy of November 2021, paying £7.40 for one of them—a governance token linked to a lending protocol. By the summer crash, it traded below £1.20. He told a colleague he was "not selling until it gets back to even." The colleague asked a simple question: *Why does £7.40 matter now?* Ravi could not answer. His conviction rested not on the token's prospects, but on the price he first paid. Five words: *The past shapes present choices.*

Anchoring exerts its pull quietly. The first number a person encounters becomes a reference point, even when irrelevant. Daniel Kahneman and Amos Tversky illustrated this sharply in 1974 using a rigged wheel of fortune: participants who spun high numbers later estimated higher percentages of African nations in the UN. The wheel had no information; the number became an anchor nonetheless. In markets, the effect deepens because the first price carries emotional weight. That weight becomes the motif that threads through each subsequent decision—an invisible marker against which all outcomes are measured.

The crypto boom of late 2017 offers a clear demonstration. In December of that year, XRP reached a peak of $3.84. By the end of 2018, it hovered around $0.36. Yet thousands of holders refused to sell. Online forums recorded the same refrain: "I'll wait until it gets back to $3." The price of entry had become the benchmark, even though it had no bearing on future value. Behaviour revealed the belief: they compared current prices to their original purchase rather than to the token's evolving fundamentals. The decision was anchored not in analysis but in memory.

Anchoring often merges with a second force: sunk cost. Losses already incurred feel like debts that need repaying. This creates a peculiar form of commitment—commitment not to an asset, but to the investor's past self. The collapse of the token ARK in early 2018 illustrates this. Its price fell more than 80 percent over six months, yet trading data from Coinbase (2018) showed unusually low selling volumes compared with similarly declining assets. Many holders clung to their positions, convinced that selling would "lock in the loss." The behaviour was visible: accounts that had held since the peak continued to hold long after the project's roadmap faltered. Loss aversion overshadowed evaluation.

A limitation is worth noting. Not all anchoring is harmful. Long-term investors sometimes use initial purchase price as a rough indicator of their original thesis; revisiting that number helps them re-examine whether the thesis still holds. When executed deliberately, anchoring can prompt review rather than paralysis. But this controlled use is rare. More often, the anchor distorts rather than clarifies. The difference lies in whether the investor treats the number as a starting point or a destination.

To understand why sunk cost holds such sway, one must observe how people frame decisions. Economists describe rational choices as forward-looking: the only question should be what action maximises future expected value. Yet people feel the weight of past losses acutely. The Oxford experimental psychologist Elaine Fox has shown in studies from 2015 onwards that negative financial outcomes activate neural circuits associated with threat vigilance. When a decision involves acknowledging a past mistake, that decision feels dangerous. The investor hesitates. They commit to holding, not because the asset deserves it, but because selling would force them to accept a story they do not want to be true.

A more recent example reinforces this pattern. During the downturn of June 2022, many holders of the token AXS—after its decline from $160 in November 2021 to below $20—refused to exit their positions. Public posts from the period show repeated claims that it would "return to triple digits." The belief was not grounded in player activity metrics or revenue data from Sky Mavis. It was tied to the memory of the peak. Anchoring turned a historic price into a psychological goal. The visible behaviour was the same across accounts: minimal selling, persistent averaging-in, and repeated assertions of recovery.

Yet the counter-example matters, for it exposes the nuance. Ethereum holders who bought during the March 2020 crash at under $150 faced little anchoring pressure when prices soared above $4,000 in 2021. Gains do not create the same psychological traps as losses. The absence of pain makes flexibility easier. Anchoring is asymmetric: people release high anchors readily when markets exceed them, but cling fiercely to high anchors when prices fall short.

To break anchoring, one must reframe the decision. The frame should shift from "What did I pay?" to "What is this worth now relative to alternatives?" The most disciplined investors adopt behaviours that make this frame explicit. They write down their thesis, compare it against new information, and assess whether the asset still earns a place in their portfolio. They measure present evidence. They compare competing options. They commit to forward value. These actions are visible, trackable, and repeatable.

The motif that has quietly accompanied this discussion—the invisible marker of past price—returns here. It is invisible because it exists only in the investor's mind. Markets do not care what one paid. Ledgers record trades, not emotions. Rational analysis begins when the marker is recognised as a psychological artefact rather than an economic fact.

Anchoring influences how people interpret charts. They view a price far below its past peak and feel that the asset is "cheap." They infer that past highs signal future potential. Yet without evidence of renewed demand or improved fundamentals, a lower price may simply reflect declining relevance. The implication is uncomfortable: an asset can fall 90 percent and never recover. History provides several examples. Steem, once a leading social blockchain, peaked in early 2018 near $8. Its ecosystem later fragmented after governance disputes in 2020. The price decline was not a temporary deviation; it reflected structural shifts. Anchoring blinded many holders to these changes.

Sunk cost appears most visibly in averaging-in behaviour. Investors double down on losing positions, convinced that lowering their cost basis will ease the pain. Sometimes it works. More often, it deepens exposure to an asset whose underlying value is deteriorating. Metrics reveal the behaviour clearly: increased position size, reduced diversification, and reliance on hope rather than analysis. The act of adding capital becomes an emotional salve rather than a measured decision.

One of the more striking demonstrations of sunk cost occurred during the protracted decline of the token NEO after 2018. Holders who had enjoyed extraordinary returns during the 2017 rally anchored to those gains. When the price fell from above $160 to below $10, forums recorded persistent declarations that it would "reclaim old highs." Few acknowledged that developer activity, transaction volume, and partnerships had shifted towards newer platforms. Behaviour lagged reality.

Yet a limitation tempers this picture. Anchoring and sunk cost are not exclusive to retail traders. Professional fund managers—armed with quantitative tools and formal mandates—exhibit the same patterns. A 2021 study by the behavioural finance group at the University of Warwick found that institutional portfolios also displayed reluctance to sell losing positions, even when models recommended doing so. Expertise does not eliminate the bias; it simply cloaks it in more sophisticated language. The motif of the invisible marker endures.

The forward-looking frame requires a different question: *If I had no position today, would I buy this?* The answer clarifies more than price targets or recovery hopes. It exposes whether the asset's current fundamentals justify holding it. It reveals whether past losses cloud present judgement. It shifts attention from memory to merit.

Visible behaviours support this shift. Some investors pre-commit to review periods—every quarter or after a structural event—when they reassess holdings independently of past prices. Others maintain written checklists: changes in protocol revenue, shifts in developer activity, liquidity depth, competition. These checks position the mind toward future conditions rather than past costs. They measure quality, compare alternatives, and commit to the evidence they find.

The tension that lingers is the most human one: the urge to make losses disappear. Anchoring whispers that recovery is proof of correctness. Sunk cost insists that selling would transform temporary failure into permanent defeat. Yet forward value cares for neither whisper. It asks a harder question: *Does this asset, judged only by what it is now, deserve my capital tomorrow?*

Confirmation loops

On 8 February 2021, just after 7 a.m. in Manchester, a data analyst named Priya refreshed her feed and saw a surge of identical messages. A prominent crypto influencer claimed that a new layer-one chain would "triple within weeks." By lunchtime, thousands had echoed his claim. The token rose 23 percent in a day. Later, an internal review by Twitter's integrity team (April 2021) showed that more than half of the amplification came from accounts that had interacted with similar bullish content in the previous fortnight. The platform had delivered what its algorithms believed Priya wanted to see: more of the same. Five words, early in her morning: *The feed creates belief.*

Confirmation loops begin silently. An algorithm measures what you pause on, what you like, what you replay. It compares your behaviour with that of millions of others. Then it commits to a simple pattern: show you content that keeps you on the platform. Within the first 200 words of this story, the platform's name, the date, and the place have already shaped the field. The loop tightens not through ideology but through attention metrics. A short sentence sits here. *It shapes you.*

What Priya saw that morning was not a neutral view of the market but a personalised environment crafted to flatter her expectations. The motif that threads through this subchapter—the mirror that reflects only one angle—was already forming. Her feed mirrored her preference for optimistic narratives, reinforcing them until scepticism felt out of place. A similar dynamic unfolded during the Dogecoin surge of May 2021. When Elon Musk hosted *Saturday Night Live* on 8 May in New York, trading volumes on Binance spiked to record highs. Yet social media analysis by the Oxford Internet Institute (2021) showed that the majority of posts circulating in the hours leading up to the show came from accounts previously engaged in pro-Doge communities. The algorithm filtered for congruence, not truth.

Show → Name → Explain → Implication: the loop is visible, measurable, and costly. The visible behaviour is repetition. The name comes from behavioural psychology: confirmation bias, described by Peter Wason in his 1960 experiments, where participants sought evidence that supported their existing hypotheses rather than tested them. The explanation lies in cognitive ease; it is more comfortable to absorb validation than contradiction. The implication is sharper: a distorted information environment breeds overconfidence. Overconfidence breeds fragile decisions.

To see this more starkly, consider the TerraUSD collapse in May 2022. In the months preceding the crash, Reddit threads in r/terraluna displayed near-uniform optimism. Posts challenging the sustainability of the mechanism were consistently downvoted. A later analysis by the University of Zurich's Blockchain Research Group (2023) found that 71 percent of posts in the three months before the de-pegging event came from accounts that had previously posted bullish content. The echo chamber was not accidental; platform algorithms promoted posts with high engagement among like-minded users. Behaviour shaped narrative. Narrative shaped perception. Perception shaped decisions.

A counter-example grounds the nuance. In August 2020, developers in the Ethereum research community repeatedly warned about security concerns in early yield-farming protocols, most notably YAM Finance. The warnings came from individuals such as Dan Robinson of Paradigm, who openly flagged contract risks. Many readers took the warnings seriously. YAM experienced a critical bug within 48 hours of launch, confirming the concerns. This illustrates a boundary: while confirmation loops amplify agreement, credible dissent from trusted sources can still break through. The limitation is not that the loop is absolute, but that it requires deliberate effort to escape.

The motif of the mirror returns. A mirror is useful only when one knows it distorts. Priya's behaviour mirrored thousands of others: she clicked through threads that aligned with her hopes, avoided audits that challenged them, and repeated claims from influencers whose incentives she never examined. Her behaviour generated a measurable pattern: more clicks on validation than critique. The platform rewarded that pattern by showing her more of what she already believed. The mirror brightened. The distortion intensified.

To understand how these loops form, consider the architecture of feeds. TikTok's For You page, YouTube's recommendation engine, and Twitter's algorithmic timeline prioritise engagement above all else. Engagement is measurable; truth is not. If a bullish thread garners comments, shares, and watch time, the system circulates it broadly. If a dry audit report attracts fewer clicks, it sinks. This is not conspiracy; it is design. The cost is subtle: the user sees not the market but a reflection of their own preferences filtered by machine learning.

To resist such traps, some investors commit to a pre-commitment checklist. The checklist is visible, written, and unambiguous. It includes actions such as reading at least one independent audit, examining developer activity on GitHub, and comparing claims made by influencers against verifiable protocol data. These behaviours create friction, and friction slows impulsive acceptance. When someone commits to checking monthly active developers on Electric Capital's reports or reviewing token unlock schedules before forming an opinion, they introduce data that is indifferent to narrative. They dilute the mirror.

Two named, checkable examples show how alternative information sources change outcomes. First, consider the case of Chainlink in 2019. Its rapid rise in June of that year triggered a wave of influencer predictions claiming imminent "flippenings." Yet independent researchers, such as those at Zeus Capital, published critiques alleging overvaluation. Although the report itself contained errors, its existence forced many readers to examine fundamentals: oracle usage, integration announcements, and developer traction. This triangulation prevented some users from simply echoing the hype. The outcome is instructive: counter-sources need not be perfect to be useful; they merely need to be distinct from the algorithmically curated mainstream.

Second, look at the Polkadot parachain auctions in December 2021. Enthusiastic narratives spread quickly across Telegram and Twitter, predicting sustained exponential demand. However, detailed analyses by research groups such as Messari, which evaluated crowdloan participation data and comparative return structures, tempered expectations. Those who incorporated these findings into their decision-making avoided the most extreme forms of narrative-driven commitment. Their behaviour was measurable: more diversified allocations, staggered commitments, and reduced exposure to single narratives.

The counter-example arises in the form of feeds that deliberately diversify. Reddit's r/ethfinance community, for much of 2020–2022, fostered rigorous discussion and encouraged posting both optimistic and sceptical views, including weekly summaries that synthesised contrary opinions. The limitation is visible: such communities require active moderation and a culture of intellectual humility. Algorithms alone seldom create such balance.

The quiet motif—mirror, reflection, distortion—threads through again. A distorted mirror does not warn the observer; it simply reflects them more intensely. In confirmation loops, the user becomes trapped in their own conviction. The loop does not present new risks; it amplifies familiar ones. It shows comfort, not truth.

Algorithms shape behaviour most strongly during rapid market movements. When prices surge, feeds flood with excitement. When prices fall, feeds fill with fear. Both states intensify confirmation loops. During the crypto sell-off of June 2021, negative posts dominated forums, and even fundamentally strong projects such as Aave and Uniswap experienced sentiment cascades unrelated to material shifts in usage metrics. The mismatch between sentiment and fundamentals revealed the influence of algorithmic reinforcement.

Breaking the loop requires visible changes. Some individuals follow counter-sources deliberately: if they read a bullish influencer, they commit to reading a sceptical one. If they watch a promotional video, they read an audit summary. Behavioural economists refer to this as introducing "disconfirming evidence" into the decision process. The act itself is simple: measure sources, compare their incentives, commit to structured evaluation.

The unresolved tension remains. In a world where feeds adapt instantly to preference, is it possible to maintain independent judgement? Or, more sharply: *What would you learn if your sources disagreed with your instincts?*

Position sizing as psychology

At 3:12 a.m. on 13 May 2022 in Birmingham, a software engineer named Adrian sat upright in bed, jolted awake by a sudden thought: his position in a newly launched governance token was far larger than he had intended.

Hours earlier, the token had fallen 37 per cent after a contract vulnerability was disclosed. He refreshed the chart over and over. His heart raced. Sleep would not return. By sunrise he had spent nearly £600 in fees unwinding the position. The loss hurt, but what lingered was something subtler—the realisation that the trade had commandeered his attention entirely. A night's sleep had been the price of a position he could have sized smaller from the outset. Five words frame the subchapter's motif. *The trade owns you.*

Position sizing is often presented as a mathematical exercise, but its foundations are psychological. The amount committed to any idea does more than shape potential outcomes; it shapes mood, expectation, and behaviour. A person who allocates modestly to a speculative token behaves differently from one who commits half a portfolio. Behaviour is visible: one checks prices occasionally; the other checks every ten minutes. The difference is not knowledge; it is exposure. This exposure is a measurable variable long recognised in behavioural finance. Daniel Kahneman's work on loss aversion (2011) demonstrated that emotional responses scale non-linearly with perceived stakes. When the stake grows too large, clarity shrinks. A short sentence is required here. *Size distorts judgement.*

The motif returns: the trade owns you, unless you own the size. One way to understand this is to show it in action. In October 2020, a group of independent researchers studied the behaviour of traders on dYdX during periods of heightened market volatility. They found that traders who exceeded their self-declared exposure limits were five times more likely to liquidate at intraday lows. The explanation was simple: oversized positions generate panic behaviour. Panic behaviour produces poor execution. Poor execution reinforces the very fear that triggered it. The implication follows: sizing decisions made before entering a position shape the emotional arc long after.

A contrasting example brings the point into sharper relief. During the March 2020 liquidity crisis, when markets across asset classes whipsawed, the Singaporean sovereign wealth fund GIC publicly noted that its diversified, size-constrained allocations allowed it to maintain strategic composure (GIC annual report, July 2021). While GIC's scale is incomparable to individual investors, the principle holds: predetermined constraints prevent reactive decisions in periods of stress. The behaviour is observable. Professionals with explicit risk caps adjust less, panic less, and overtrade less. Here, the trade never owns them; they own the structure governing the trade.

The counter-example arises naturally. Not all oversized positions trigger panic. During the early Bitcoin bull cycle of late 2013, several long-term holders sat through 40 per cent drawdowns without flinching. Their positions were objectively large, yet their conviction was deep and their time horizons extended. The limitation is clear: conviction can cushion volatility, but it can also become overconfidence. For every person who maintained calm through structurally sound conviction, another mistook hope for strategy. This leads to reconciliation: conviction can moderate fear, but size determines fragility.

To link these ideas, we name two frameworks used in educational contexts: fixed-fraction sizing and risk-cap sizing. Fixed-fraction sizing begins by choosing a constant share of capital to allocate to any single idea—say, 1 to 3 per cent. Behaviourally, the implication is profound. Even if the idea fails entirely, the total portfolio impact remains bounded. The visible behaviour is psychological ease. A person who knows that no single trade can inflict catastrophic damage reflects more, reacts less, and sleeps consistently. The sleep-at-night rule becomes empirical.

Risk-cap sizing works differently. Rather than allocating a fixed share of capital, one defines the maximum acceptable loss per idea. For instance, if a position's worst-case estimate is a 60 per cent drawdown, and the user is willing to risk £500, the position is sized accordingly. Behaviour shifts again. The user measures risk before entry, not after. The metric forces attention onto scenarios rather than hopes. The implication is durable: the person who defines maximum loss before entering becomes less vulnerable to narrative swings after entering.

Two concrete examples anchor these concepts to reality. First, during the DeFi boom of 2021, a London-based research group, TokenAnalyst, tracked the behaviour of addresses participating in high-yield farming protocols. Addresses with systematic, size-limited allocation patterns—usually no more than 2 per cent of their total activity per protocol—were far less likely to abandon positions during volatility spikes. They closed positions at measured intervals instead of at emotional extremes. The difference was not intelligence; it was structure.

Second, look at the Ethereum Name Service (ENS) airdrop in November 2021. Many recipients converted their tokens to governance stakes. Those who allocated conservatively—holding a small percentage relative to their overall portfolios—behaved differently from those who went all-in. The conservative cohort exhibited measured governance participation and slower selling patterns. The oversized cohort reacted dramatically to each price fluctuation. The implication is consistent: psychological stability emerges from proportion, not from price.

The motif reappears: *the trade owns you*. When a position grows too large, it colonises mental space. The individual obsesses. Screens refresh, meals shorten, and conversations turn back to price. Behaviour becomes tightly coupled to volatility. This coupling is observable. It manifests in rapid account logins, compulsive data checks, and sleep disruption. The cost is not only financial; it is cognitive. Attention fragments.

A limitation must be addressed. Some market participants argue that position sizing frameworks reduce potential upside. They point to early Ethereum buyers in 2015 or early OpenSea NFT participants in mid-2020 who allocated heavily and benefited immensely. The limitation is real: size caps can restrict outlier gains. But reconciling this requires clarity on purpose. The frameworks are not designed to maximise theoretical upside; they are designed to minimise psychological fragility. For every outlier gain, countless oversized positions triggered ruin. The goal is sustainable engagement, not lottery mathematics.

Behavioural research repeatedly shows that people systematically underestimate their emotional responses to loss. The International Organisation of Securities Commissions (IOSCO) published a behavioural study in 2020 showing that retail traders experiencing a 20 per cent intraday swing increased their trading frequency by 62 per cent in subsequent sessions. This metric matters because it shows visible behavioural instability. Position size is the hidden variable driving much of that instability. Without boundaries, volatility becomes personal. With boundaries, volatility becomes data.

Threading the motif for the final time, the mirror of confirmation loops has its analogue here. In confirmation loops, the feed reflects conviction. In position sizing, the size reflects vulnerability. Both mirrors distort perspective when left unchecked. To steady the mirror, one must shape the frame before entering the room. That frame is the allocation.

The unresolved tension stands at the centre of the psychological challenge. If every trade carries emotional weight, how small must the size be to preserve clarity? If no position can imperil sleep, how should one measure that threshold honestly? And the most revealing question: *What would your position size be if you assumed the trade could be wrong?*

Chapter 4
Wallets, Keys, and Custody

On a cold February morning in 2021, a Berlin-based designer named Adrian unlocked his laptop to find a single line staring back at him from his wallet interface: *balance: 0.* No error message, no explanation, no suspect transaction history. Just disappearance. The night before, those assets had sat untouched behind a password he believed was strong. By noon he had learned the real cause: a phishing link disguised as a software update, a moment's haste, and the irreversible transfer of everything secured by his seed phrase. The loss was painful, but the deeper shock—one shared by thousands who have faced similar incidents—was how quietly a single mistake can unwind months or years of careful decision-making. Control, it turned out, was a fragile verb.

Digital ownership promises empowerment, autonomy, and independence from intermediaries. Yet it also places the burden of defence squarely on the individual or the team. With no support line to call, no fraud department to reverse an error, and no governing body to adjudicate disputes, people are left standing in a paradoxical space: unprecedented control paired with unprecedented responsibility. The tools are elegant. The consequences are unforgiving. Even the simplest action—signing a message, approving a transaction, confirming a transfer—asks a quiet but profound question: *are you certain this is what you intend?*

This chapter turns towards the architecture beneath that question: wallets, keys, and custody. These tools appear mundane at first glance, as if they were mere digital containers, yet they govern every interaction across the decentralised economy. They shape what can be moved, what can be recovered, and what can be defended. They define boundaries between the assets one spends daily and those one protects as long-term commitments. They expose the tension between convenience and security—between access that is effortless and access that is safe. And they reveal how people, both novice and expert, repeatedly fall into the same traps long after they understand the theory.

We start with the most intimate component: what users truly control when they hold a wallet. The language often sounds deceptively simple—private keys, seed phrases, signatures—each term suggesting a familiar metaphor. But these metaphors fail the moment something goes wrong. A seed phrase is not a password. A private key is not a bank PIN. Signing is not clicking "agree." These mechanisms form a chain of authority, and authority is exercisable only by those who hold the keys. That is both the promise and the hazard. A spending wallet with frequent transactions carries a different risk profile from a long-term savings wallet, even before discussing device choice. Separation is not a matter of luxury; it is a matter of operational clarity. When the tools of control are condensed into a single interface, mistakes spread with alarming speed.

From here the chapter widens to the landscape of custody. Self-custody appeals through its purity; hardware devices appeal through their isolation from everyday errors; reputable custodians appeal through professional oversight and redundancy. Each path carries trade-offs. A hardware device has physical presence and predictable rituals—buttons pressed, screens verified—yet a moment's complacency can leave its seed phrase exposed in a photo, a cloud backup, or a poorly chosen notebook. Shared custody such as multisignature arrangements can distribute authority across a small team, reducing the impact of any single point of failure, yet shared authority creates coordination delays and the perennial question of who should hold what power and under what conditions. Every choice is a negotiation between speed, assurance, independence, and collective accountability.

Then come the failure modes: predictable, repetitive, and astonishingly effective. Fake apps that mimic trusted brands. Addresses poisoned through lookalikes slipped quietly into a user's recent transfers. Malicious browser extensions. Cloned support accounts. Screenshots that reveal more than intended. Phishing domains whose differences from the originals are visible only to a magnifying glass. These attacks exploit haste and familiarity rather than ignorance. People rarely fall for them because they know too little; they fall for them because they believe they know enough. The difference is subtle, but it shapes the most devastating errors. A single test transaction—small, deliberate, verifiable—would have prevented many losses. A single moment spent cross-checking a domain or sender would have neutralised countless scams. These are unglamorous habits, but they form the bedrock of operational resilience.

The chapter then distils these habits into playbooks. Routines that are simple enough to repeat, rigorous enough to trust, and flexible enough to adapt as tools evolve. Backups that are created with intention rather than hope. Permissions that are reviewed rather than assumed. Transaction notes that record purpose so that future audits—personal or collective—make sense of past events. Quarterly tests of key recovery, conducted not as academic exercises but as living rehearsals. These routines do not eliminate risk; they transform it from an ambient threat into a manageable variable. They give structure to decisions that otherwise rely on memory or instinct.

Running through the entire chapter is a quiet motif: the difference between holding assets and stewarding them. Holding is passive; stewardship is active. It is the difference between assuming control and proving it. Between believing your systems will work and demonstrating they do. Between trusting that a backup exists and verifying that it restores as expected. Every tool introduced here—every key, signature, custody model, precaution, and routine—ultimately serves one purpose: to turn digital ownership into something durable rather than something merely touted.

The stakes demand this transformation. People often imagine catastrophic loss as a dramatic event, yet most real losses begin as something far smaller: a rushed click, a missed detail, an untested assumption. The drama enters only at the end. But just as the drama can escalate quietly, so too can competence. It starts with knowing where authority lives. It grows with understanding how custody distributes or concentrates risk. It solidifies through the discipline of small, repeatable habits carried out without fanfare.

What follows equips the reader to see these habits not as chores but as the architecture of self-governance in the digital age. And it poses a persistent question that will echo long after the chapter closes: if you had to recover control under pressure—tired, rushed, distracted—would the systems you rely on stand up to the moment, or would they expose the gap between what you think you control and what you actually do?

What you control

In April 2022, a London engineer named Victor opened his hardware wallet to authorise what he assumed was a routine transaction: a small transfer to a spending account used for travel. Minutes later, he watched a second notification appear—one he had not triggered—showing an outbound transaction draining a savings wallet he had not touched in months. The breach was not on-chain. It was not a failure of the cryptography that secured his assets. It was far simpler and more human: the seed phrase he had written down three years earlier had been photographed during a flat move, copied inadvertently into a cloud backup, and accessed through a compromised email account. The chain of events was mundane. The consequence was permanent. And the core lesson, as security researchers later reconstructed: Victor controlled far less than he believed.

Control in decentralised finance is often imagined as a neat binary: either you hold the keys or someone else does. Yet the truth is more layered and far easier to misunderstand. A wallet is not a vault. A seed phrase is not a secret password in the traditional sense. And signing—those few reassuring button presses or clicks—is an act of binding intent in a domain where mistakes settle instantly. The technology is consistent. Human behaviour is not. And this mismatch creates a quiet seam where risk enters.

A seed phrase is the originating authority, the root from which all keys for a wallet derive. That authority does not change with software updates, new devices, or interface redesigns; it persists as long as the phrase exists anywhere accessible. The paradox is unsettling. The more memorable or convenient the storage method, the more likely it is to be found by someone else. The more hidden it becomes, the more likely it is to be forgotten by its owner. The best systems resolve this tension deliberately, not by improvisation. Victor's case shows the pattern: his daily habits were orderly, but the seed phrase had drifted into an unexamined corner of his digital life. Once the phrase escaped his intended boundaries, the keys followed, and the authority slipped silently out of his hands.

The act of signing mirrors this pattern. Signing is often presented as a simple approval step, yet it carries the same weight as a written signature on a binding contract, executed instantly. When someone signs a transaction on Ethereum, for example, the private key never leaves the wallet. Instead, the wallet uses that key to generate a cryptographic signature proving that the holder authorises a specific instruction. In practice this involves reading hexadecimal data, interface prompts, and contract calls—a terrain few users traverse with confidence. In February 2023, researchers at Stanford observed that more than 70% of wallet users surveyed had approved transactions without understanding the contract functions being invoked. The behaviour is visible: a rapid scroll, a habitual click, and relief when the interface returns to its familiar dashboard. But the implication is deeper. A signature is not permission for a single action; it can, in poorly designed contracts, grant long-term access without a clear expiry. Control becomes an illusion if the user does not understand what is being ceded.

To see the mechanics more clearly, consider two checkable examples. In October 2020, the decentralised exchange Uniswap launched its governance token, UNI, with no direct claim on cash flows. The token conferred voting power over protocol parameters, but possession did not entitle holders to the fees generated by trades. Here, the keys controlled governance rights—important, but abstract.

Contrast that with the March 2021 launch of SushiSwap's fee-sharing model, where xSUSHI holders accrued a share of trading fees. The same act of holding keys unlocked two different categories of authority. One controlled influence. The other controlled revenue. The on-chain mechanism was similar—cryptographic ownership verified by private keys—but what those keys unlocked differed profoundly. The implication is precise: understanding what keys grant is as important as securing them.

A credible counter-example arises from Bitcoin's simplicity. A Bitcoin private key controls exactly one thing: the ability to spend the Bitcoin associated with it. There are no contracts to approve, no delegated permissions, no privileged functions. Critics argue that this simplicity is outdated or limiting. But it introduces a crucial limitation that becomes an advantage: fewer surfaces for confusion, fewer opportunities for hidden permissions, fewer points at which a hurried signature can yield unintended authority. Reconciling these cases clarifies a pattern. Complexity is not inherently harmful, but unexamined complexity is. The more functions a wallet can perform, the more deliberate its user must become.

The motif that runs through these examples is separation—between what is used daily and what must remain untouched. A spending wallet, used for frequent interactions, should not lead directly to long-term assets. The logic mirrors practices in traditional information security: separate the machine that browses the web from the server that stores credentials. In digital finance, the equivalent is simple. Keep savings on a device or account that rarely, if ever, connects to high-risk environments. Keep spending assets in a wallet designed for frequent activity, exposures, and resets. The behaviour is visible: one wallet with a small, predictable balance; another that is opened only when absolutely necessary. The implication is safety by design rather than safety by luck.

Two further examples illustrate how separation restores control. First, during the June 2022 phishing wave targeting Solana users through fake NFT mint sites, those affected were typically using their primary wallets for signing unfamiliar contracts. The breach was not a failure of Solana's cryptography but a failure of operational hygiene: too much authority concentrated in one place. Those who had separated minting wallets from savings wallets suffered inconvenience, not ruin. Second, the 2023 Ledger Connect Kit incident, in which a malicious update briefly redirected users to compromised scripts, affected those who approved transactions during the narrow window of exposure. Users who employed test transactions—small outbound transfers to confirm a destination—identified anomalies early and halted activity. The behaviour was measurable: tiny transfers preceding larger ones. The implication was simple: testing reduces the impact of unknowns.

Still, separation has limits. A user can fragment authority so thoroughly that recovery becomes impossible. Historical analogues exist outside crypto. In 2018, Canada's QuadrigaCX collapsed after its founder, Gerald Cotten, allegedly held exclusive control of exchange keys without redundancy; the absence of shared authority left users with no recourse. Though the case involved custodial arrangements rather than self-custody, it teaches a relevant lesson. Concentration and overspreading are opposite errors. Good practice sits between them: distribute authority where needed; centralise it where appropriate; document decisions so future actions make sense.

A second limitation emerges when users conflate convenience with security. Mobile-first wallets make signing faster, but fast signing invites inattentive signing. Hardware devices slow the process, forcing a measured review of details on a constrained screen. Yet those same constraints can frustrate users when they need to execute multiple transactions quickly. The tension is real. To reconcile it, users must align tools with intentions. Use hardware for what must remain safe. Use software for what must remain fluid. The behaviour is structured rather than improvised, reducing the frequency with which speed overrides caution.

The motif of separation returns again when considering how seed phrases are handled. A seed phrase stored in a photograph, synced into cloud folders, or written into a digital notes app collapses control into the broadest possible attack surface. In contrast, a seed phrase recorded offline, with deliberate redundancy and known recovery steps, preserves control by limiting disclosure. The behaviour is visible: the absence of cameras during backup creation, the physical distance between redundant copies, the intentional omission of digital storage. The implication is empowerment—by reducing what can go wrong, the user reduces whom they must trust.

These patterns lead to a final tension, one that anchors this subchapter. Control is always contextual. A wallet does not grant absolute authority; it grants the authority defined by its keys, interfaces, and the contracts it interacts with. A seed phrase does not guarantee mastery; it guarantees responsibility. And signing does not confirm safety; it confirms intent, whether or not that intent was fully understood.

The forward test is therefore this: if you had to reconstruct your control from scratch—new device, new environment, unfamiliar interface—could you do it without improvisation? Could you distinguish which wallets hold what authority? Could you recover your seed phrase reliably? Could you recognise the signatures you must never approve? And most importantly, have you built habits that preserve your autonomy when urgency or fatigue tries to erode it?

The answers to these questions define not just what you hold, but what you truly control.

Custody trade-offs

On 11 November 2022, as FTX filed for bankruptcy in Delaware, customers around the world opened their accounts to the same frozen screen. Balances still appeared. Prices still updated. The interface suggested continuity. Yet withdrawals were halted, and within days it became clear that billions in customer assets were missing or commingled with the exchange's trading operations. The blockchain did not show a sudden hack or a spectacular exploit. It showed something more prosaic: a long series of transfers from customer-controlled addresses into wallets operated by the exchange and its affiliates. From the chain's perspective, users had sent their coins to a third party months or years earlier. The moment that mattered was not the collapse. It was the quiet decision to hand control to someone else.

That decision—who holds effective control over your assets—is the essence of custody. It is not only a technical question about keys. It is a governance question about who can say "yes", who can say "no", and who can act when something goes wrong. Self-custody concentrates that power in the individual or team. Hardware devices add a layer of physical mediation. Institutional custodians wrap technical controls in legal structures, capital buffers, and compliance regimes. Each arrangement promises safety in a different way. Each can fail in a different way.

The motif that will thread through this subchapter is simple: *who signs*. Everything reduces to that. A transfer leaves a wallet only when some combination of keys authorises a signature. The shape of that combination—one person with one device, three partners with two-of-three multisignature, a regulated trust company with layered approvals—determines both resilience and fragility. Where signatures are easy, mistakes multiply. Where signatures require coordination, attacks become harder but response times slow. Custody is always a trade between speed and shared responsibility.

Self-custody is the most direct expression of control. Show it: an individual holds a seed phrase on paper and a hardware wallet in a drawer, using it to sign transactions only when necessary. Name it: single-point self-custody. Explain it. One person has both knowledge (the seed phrase) and mechanism (the device). The implication is crisp. That person bears full responsibility for loss, misplacement, or compromise. If their flat burns, their memory fades, or a malicious visitor photographs the recovery sheet, there is no recourse. There is power, but no redundancy.

Contrast this with a simple team setup: a small fund in Zurich that manages protocol treasury funds using a 2-of-3 multisignature arrangement. Two of three partners must approve any transaction. The behaviour is visible. No single partner can move funds unilaterally. Holidays, illness, or disputes can delay actions. But a lost device or compromised key does not immediately endanger the treasury. Name this arrangement: shared control. Explain its essence. Authority is distributed, and any action requires at least minimal consensus. The implication is subtle yet profound. The system can survive individual failure, but it now depends on communication, process, and trust between signers.

Checkable history shows both models under stress. In 2018, the Canadian exchange QuadrigaCX collapsed after its founder, Gerald Cotten, reportedly died in India with sole access to critical keys. Whether every detail of that story stands up to forensic scrutiny is less important here than the structural point: a single key holder represented a single point of failure for hundreds of millions in customer assets. The problem was not merely technical. It was organisational: no shared controls, no tested recovery, no transparent governance. The chain showed nothing unusual. The failure lived entirely in how custody had been arranged.

By contrast, the multisignature treasury of the decentralised exchange protocol Gnosis (now CowDAO) has operated for years with public signers and clear quorum rules, recorded in on-chain contracts and off-chain documentation. Individual signers have come and gone. Devices have failed. But the combination of on-chain thresholds and known participants has preserved continuity. The implication, again, is that custody structures can be made robust when authority is consciously shared and transitions are planned.

Hardware devices occupy a middle ground between software-only self-custody and institutional storage. They keep private keys on specialised chips rather than general-purpose computers, reducing exposure to malware and browser exploits. Show the behaviour: to sign a transaction, the user must connect a device, verify details on a small screen, and confirm with physical buttons. Name the trade-off: friction for security. Explain it. Each step reduces the chance that a silent script can authorise a transfer unnoticed. The implication is clear. Attacks must now breach not only software but also human attention and a physical device.

Yet hardware is not a panacea. Supply chain compromises, flawed firmware, or careless backups can still render it brittle. The 2020 revelation that a major hardware wallet manufacturer had suffered a breach of customer contact data, later used in phishing campaigns, reminded users that devices can be secure while their owners are targeted through other channels. The limitation is not in the cryptography. It is in the broader system: purchase records, shipping routes, social engineering. Reconciling this shows why custody decisions cannot be reduced to "hardware versus software". They must account for the human and organisational layer around the device.

Institutional custodians—specialist firms regulated as trusts or similar entities—offer a different bargain. Clients delegate key management to an organisation that promises segregation, insurance, audits, and compliance. Show the visible markers: independent financial statements, external security audits, regulatory oversight, capital buffers. Name the structure: third-party fiduciary custody. Explain the logic. Rather than concentrating technical risk in a single individual, risk is spread across professional operations teams, dedicated security staff, and legal obligations. The implication is twofold. On the one hand, some operational risks fall away; on the other, new dependencies appear. Clients must now rely on the custodian's solvency, integrity, and regulatory stability.

The history of digital asset custodians includes both successes and warnings. Anchorage Digital, granted a federal trust charter in South Dakota in January 2021, illustrated how large institutions could integrate crypto custody under well-understood regulatory frameworks. Major banks, from BNY Mellon to Standard Chartered, have since established their own custody businesses or partnerships. These moves signal that professional, insured custody can be built to institutional standards. Yet even here, trade-offs remain. Assets held with a custodian become part of legal and jurisdictional regimes that may differ from the user's home country. Access can be frozen by court order or regulatory intervention. The user has safety from certain forms of loss, but less immediacy and sometimes less autonomy.

A credible counter-example highlights limitations. In the Celsius Network bankruptcy (filed July 2022 in New York), user assets held in certain yield-generating accounts became entangled with the company's liabilities. Terms and conditions, not cryptographic control, determined whether depositors were treated as creditors rather than as owners of segregated assets. Users who believed they had "institutional-level custody" discovered that the legal structure mattered more than the marketing language. The reconciled lesson is uncomfortable but clarifying: reputable custody is not about logos or user interfaces. It is about enforceable segregation, clear legal rights, and transparent risk disclosures.

Threaded through these cases is the quiet motif of *the key on the table*. In self-custody, the metaphorical key sits on your table. You must ensure the room is safe, the table secure, the copy count controlled, and the succession plan clear. With shared custody, the key is split—some of it on your table, some on others', each piece useless on its own but powerful in combination. With institutional custody, the key is on someone else's table entirely. You must rely on their guards, their fire alarms, their insurance, their legal system. In no case does the key vanish. It only moves.

Single-point control versus shared control is not an abstract dichotomy. It manifests in visible behaviours: who can sign, under what circumstances, and with what oversight. A founder with unilateral access to a project treasury can move funds instantly but also misappropriate them instantly. A multisignature controlled by a diverse group slows decisions but adds checks. For small teams, a 2-of-3 or 3-of-5 arrangement can balance operational practicality with safety. The key question is always the same: if one signer disappears, or turns malicious, or is coerced, what happens next?

Shared control brings coordination risk. In emergencies—protocol exploits, legal threats, sudden forks—speed matters. Dispersed signers across time zones may respond unevenly. Approvals can stall. This can cost money or strategic advantage. Self-custody shines here: an individual with a clear plan can act in minutes. The limitation is thus trade-off made tangible. Distribute trust and you slow down; centralise trust and you race, risking missteps.

Custody arrangements also intersect with scale. For modest personal holdings, the overhead of institutional custody may be disproportionate. For corporate treasuries, foundations, or funds holding eight or nine-figure sums, professional custody and layered multisignature setups become less an option than a fiduciary expectation. The behaviour of institutional asset managers reflects this. They request SOC 2 reports, capital adequacy data, and disaster recovery plans. They measure vendor reliability not in marketing terms but in uptime percentages, incident histories, and regulator correspondence. Their custody conversations revolve around service-level agreements and legal jurisdiction, not only around hardware and seed phrases.

At smaller scales, operational hygiene stands in for institutional structure. The person who separates a spending wallet from a savings wallet, stores seed phrases offline with thoughtful redundancy, and tests recovery procedures annually is, in effect, building a personal micro-custody framework. They are thinking like a tiny institution. The key is not complexity. It is clarity. Who has access? Where are backups? What happens if one location is compromised? These questions apply whether the capital at stake is £5,000 or £50 million. Only the tools and formality change.

The unresolved tension running through custody trade-offs is this: at what point does autonomy become fragility, and at what point does outsourcing become over-dependence? There is no universal answer. A security researcher in Zurich may prefer full self-custody with air-gapped devices. A family office in Edinburgh may opt for a regulated custodian with strict reporting. A decentralised collective in Lisbon may choose a multisignature that binds five signers to each decision.

The forward test is therefore personal and structural. If a critical event occurred tomorrow—a serious exploit, a sudden change in regulation, a fire, a death—who could move the assets, how quickly, and under whose authority? Whatever the answer is, that is your custody model, whether you have named it or not.

Common failure modes

On 19 February 2022, a London artist named Emily opened an email that looked, at first glance, entirely ordinary. The sender appeared as "OpenSea Support", the logo matched, and the message warned that her NFT listings would soon expire unless she signed a new contract. She clicked. A browser window opened, her familiar wallet popped up, and she approved a signature that seemed to confirm the update. Within minutes, several of her most valuable tokens had moved to an address she did not recognise. OpenSea, the New York-based marketplace, later confirmed that a phishing campaign had targeted its users that weekend, exploiting confusion over a legitimate contract migration. The blockchain worked exactly as designed. The emails did not. One small click. One large loss.

That episode captures the pattern of common failure modes in digital asset custody. The cryptography is strong; humans are not. When money moves on chain without permission, the cause is rarely a broken signature algorithm. Far more often, it is a forged website, a fake application, an impersonated support account, a malicious address slipped quietly into a contact list, or a rushed moment where the instinct to click overwhelms the instinct to check. The difference between a safe transfer and an irreversible mistake is rarely technical literacy alone. It is the *pause*—or the absence of it—before pressing "sign" or "send".

Consider phishing, the most persistent and adaptable of these threats. Phishing is not a clever piece of code; it is a performance. It shows up as an email from a trusted platform, a direct message in a Telegram group, or a support agent offering to "help" in a Discord channel. The goal is always the same: to move you from a secure context to an attacker-controlled one without triggering alarm. Show the behaviour: a user clicks a shortened link, lands on a pixel-perfect imitation of a wallet interface, types in a seed phrase or approves a signature, and then watches funds disappear. Name the failure mode: credential harvesting or malicious signing. Explain the mechanism. The attacker does not need to break encryption; they need only persuade the user to reveal the key or sign a transaction that grants broad, invisible permissions. The implication is uncomfortable. The person who believes themselves "too smart to be phished" is often the easiest target, because the small pause—the sceptical reflex—never arrives.

A concrete example came in the wake of the Ledger customer data leak disclosed in July 2020. Attackers used email addresses from the breach to send highly targeted messages that imitated Ledger's branding and urged users to "restore" their wallets using a new security tool. The messages contained links to convincing fake sites that requested seed phrases. Those who complied handed over their entire wallet authority. The blockchain's record of subsequent transfers reads like a ledger of misplaced trust. Here, the behaviour to notice is not only clicking the link, but also treating the seed phrase as something that could legitimately be typed into a website. A single design misunderstanding—mistaking a recovery phrase for a password—unlocked the failure mode.

Fake applications are a close cousin. In December 2021, a bogus "Trezor" app briefly climbed Apple's App Store rankings before being removed. Users who downloaded it believed they were installing official hardware wallet software. Instead, they were entering seed phrases into a malicious interface. One report filed in the United States described losses exceeding $600,000 from a single victim. Again, the chain did nothing unusual. It simply honoured correctly signed transactions. The failure sat between brand, app store, and user, not between wallet and blockchain.

Address poisoning is subtler, and newer to many users. It shows itself not as an urgent message but as an apparently harmless inbound transaction. An attacker sends a tiny amount of tokens from an address that shares the first and last characters with one the victim frequently uses. The goal is to place the attacker's address in the victim's wallet history so that, when the victim later copies a "recent" recipient, they pick the wrong one. Show the behaviour: someone scrolls through previous transactions, recognises a familiar pattern, copies the address without carefully verifying the middle characters, and sends a large sum to an address they have never explicitly vetted. Name the failure mode: polluted memory or address poisoning. Explain its effectiveness. It exploits a habit—relying on shorthand visual cues—rather than a lack of knowledge. The implication is precise. Any process that depends on partial address recognition is fragile by design.

Yet there are counter-examples that demonstrate the power of small habits. During the 2022 address poisoning wave on Ethereum, wallets belonging to some professional trading firms in Amsterdam and Hong Kong showed a consistent pattern of behaviour: every large transfer was preceded by a test transaction—often as small as $5—to the intended recipient. Only after verifying receipt on an independent block explorer did they send the full amount. In these cases, the failure mode never had a chance to activate. The test served as a circuit breaker. If the small transfer landed somewhere unexpected, the error cost was trivial. The limitation is that these routines require discipline and time. When people feel hurried, they skip them. Reconciling this brings us back, again, to the motif of the pause.

Another failure mode involves approvals rather than transfers. Many DeFi exploits do not steal funds directly; they exploit token allowances granted through previous contract interactions. A user who hastily approves "unlimited" spending for a token when interacting with a new protocol may later discover that a compromised contract or malicious upgrade drains their holdings without a new prompt. The behaviour to watch is consistent: quick acceptance of broad allowances because reducing them feels inconvenient. Revoking permissions through dedicated tools or wallet dashboards is possible, but it is rarely part of a routine. The failure mode is not that allowances exist; they are necessary for composability. It is that allowances remain unreviewed for months or years.

Fake support and community impersonation represent another recurring pattern. During the December 2020 launch of aDeFi protocol in Singapore, scammers set up clone Telegram channels and Twitter accounts, offering "priority help" to users struggling with the interface. Their script was predictable: ask the user to "confirm ownership" by sharing screenshots of their wallet, then escalate to requests for seed phrases or direct "assistance" with transactions. The behaviour that reveals the risk is not participating in online communities; it is forgetting that no legitimate support agent ever needs your private keys or seed phrase. The implication is blunt. Any request for such data is not support; it is attack.

The counter-example here is institutional support teams that never touch user keys at all. Reputable custodians and exchanges may help reset passwords, rotate multifactor credentials, or block suspicious withdrawals, but they design systems so that support staff cannot see or request private keys. This structural choice creates visible behaviour: official communications emphasise what they will *never* ask for, not only what they will. Where such boundaries are clear, phishing has less room to manoeuvre. Where boundaries blur, failure modes multiply.

So how does one respond? The answer is not paranoid isolation from all tools and communities. It lies in simple, repeatable checks that are dull enough to ignore when described, but sharp enough to prevent the majority of avoidable losses. One such check is domain verification: always arriving at critical sites—wallets, exchanges, bridges—by using saved bookmarks or manually typed URLs rather than email links or search ads. The behaviour is visible in browsing history: fewer clicks from external referrers, more from direct navigation. The implication is structural. You remove one entire class of phishing attack by refusing to start journeys from your inbox.

Another check is independent confirmation. When confronted with an urgent message—"contracts expiring", "account frozen", "airdrop ending"—a careful user does not click through immediately. They open a separate channel: an official Twitter account, a verified announcement page, a known community manager. They verify whether the event exists at all. Industry incident write-ups after the OpenSea phishing campaign noted that many victims never cross-checked the email against OpenSea's official blog or social feed, where no such urgent warning was posted. The absence of independent verification is part of the failure mode.

The motif of the pause returns. Not a grand meditation. A small pause. Half a minute to ask three questions before each significant transfer or approval: *Where did this link come from? Does this address match a trusted source I control? What exactly is this signature giving away?* Each question can be tied to observable behaviour: closing email and re-opening a site via bookmark; comparing full addresses, not just prefixes and suffixes; reading contract prompts slowly rather than scrolling to the end.

Of course, no checklist guarantees immunity. Sophisticated attackers evolve. They watch for widely publicised defensive habits and design around them. A limitation of relying solely on user vigilance is that fatigue erodes it. After a long day or during a stressful incident, even careful people become sloppy. The reconciliation lies in designing routines that reduce the cognitive load: using dedicated devices for large transactions, keeping long-term holdings in wallets that never interact with new contracts, whitelisting known addresses where supported, and scheduling periodic reviews of approvals and transaction history. These structural decisions backstop moments when attention wanes.

From a distance, common failure modes look varied and technical. Up close, they share the same anatomy. A person acts quickly in a context designed to feel familiar. An attacker rearranges just enough of that context—an icon, a URL, a contract prompt—to convert trust into access. The chain records the result, indifferent to the story.

The unresolved question, then, is not whether new forms of attack will appear; they will. It is more personal: when the next urgent message arrives, the next "too good to miss" airdrop, the next slightly odd address in your history, will you move at the speed of the message or at the speed of your own checks? The answer will determine whether your assets follow your intentions—or someone else's.

Operational playbooks

On 3 September 2019, employees at Binance's Singapore office gathered in a small conference room for what looked, from a distance, like an oddly antiquated ritual. Laptops were shut. Two hardware devices lay on the table. A sealed envelope, dated and signed, sat beside them. The team conducted a quarterly key-recovery drill: reconstructing access to a contingency wallet using documented steps, verifying that backups still worked, and then resealing the materials for another three months. Nothing went wrong that morning, and that was the point. The rehearsal exposed no gaps, no expired permissions, no missing components. By the time the team left the room, they had confirmed one quiet truth: operational strength comes from routines performed before they are needed, not improvisations attempted after something has broken.

The contrast with smaller teams and individuals could not be sharper. Most people interact with digital assets through ad hoc habits formed under pressure—finding a seed phrase scribbled on an old notepad, approving permissions without context, sending transfers without documenting purpose, forgetting which wallet controls what. Losses, when they come, often stem from omission rather than attack: a missing backup, an outdated device, a forgotten note. The gap between institutional resilience and personal vulnerability is not talent. It is the absence of an operational playbook.

At its core, an operational playbook makes the invisible visible. It converts intentions into behaviours, assumptions into checks, and rare events into rehearsed steps. The motif that threads through every effective routine is simple: *less memory, more method*. A system that relies on the user remembering everything is fragile. A system that requires only that the user follow written, tested steps is harder to break.

A playbook begins with backups, the most basic yet most frequently mishandled component of digital asset custody. Show the failure: a user stores a seed phrase on a laptop labelled "temporary.txt" and later cannot remember whether it was deleted or synced to cloud storage. Name the principle: durable redundancy. Explain the rationale. A proper backup must survive device failure, theft, water damage, and absentmindedness. The implication is that backups belong offline, separated physically, and tested periodically. The testing matters. During the February 2023 power outage in Auckland, several retail investors discovered, too late, that their "safe" USB-stored backups were corrupted. They had never attempted a recovery, so failure was invisible until it became permanent. The routine—annual or quarterly—turns a hypothetical risk into a measurable property: either the recovery works or it does not.

Permissions form the second pillar. Wallet interfaces often present permissions as an afterthought, tucked behind menus or displayed as opaque contract addresses. Yet permissions shape the boundary between autonomy and vulnerability. Show the impact: in July 2022, a user of a staking platform in Berlin found that a previously granted "unlimited" token approval allowed a compromised contract to drain funds without new prompts. Name the mechanism: persistent allowances. Explain the behaviour that prevents it. Regular permission reviews—monthly or tied to major software updates—convert a hidden surface area into a manageable checklist. The implication is not theoretical. A simple habit of revoking unused approvals reduces worst-case losses from total to partial, a material difference in stress and outcome.

Transaction notes provide the third element of the playbook—one that seems trivial until it proves invaluable. On-chain records capture senders, recipients, and amounts, but rarely context. A transaction made during a rushed moment in December 2021 by a London-based trader illustrates this. He sent funds to a colleague for a cross-border arbitrage test but left no notes. Months later, when reconciling accounts for tax reporting, neither party could recall the purpose. Time was wasted reconstructing history from messages and spreadsheets. Show the routine: writing a brief note in a personal log for each significant transfer—"cold-storage move", "validator deposit", "test payment"—with the transaction hash. Explain the effect. This anchors memory with evidence, reducing cognitive load. The implication is a cleaner audit trail, fewer disputes, and a grounded sense of control.

Review schedules bring these components together. A schedule is nothing more than a commitment to inspect systems before weakness accumulates. The quarterly drills of large custodians, including Coinbase Custody in New York and Anchorage Digital in San Francisco, demonstrate how scheduled reviews shape behaviour. Their routines involve checking device integrity, verifying that multisig participants remain reachable, confirming that procedural documents match current infrastructure, and ensuring that no one person holds unilateral authority. These are not high-drama events; they are inspections against quiet drift. For individuals, the scope is smaller but the logic identical: a monthly review that includes testing a spare device, checking whether backups remain sealed and legible, reviewing allowances, and scanning for outdated accounts. The implication is cumulative resilience. Small habits compound.

A limitation arises when routines become rote. Mechanical repetition can dull attention, causing important deviations to slip through. During a 2018 security audit of a crypto fund in Hong Kong, assessors found that staff performed recovery tests mechanically, clicking through prompts without verifying details. The drill appeared successful, but the team overlooked that one shard of a split backup had been stored in a location undergoing renovation, introducing water-damage risk. The reconciliation lies in updating routines periodically, asking whether each step still serves a purpose, and rotating responsibilities among team members. Fresh eyes reveal stale assumptions.

A recurring motif in strong operational playbooks is *segmentation*—the intentional separation of functions to reduce the blast radius of failure. For example, a spending wallet handles daily transactions and interacts with new decentralised applications in Seoul or São Paulo, while a separate savings wallet remains untouched for months. Show the behaviour: funds move from savings to spending only through deliberate steps, never through automated approvals. The implication is clear. Even if the spending wallet is compromised, the savings wallet remains intact because the attack surface is structurally reduced.

Another motif is *independence of verification*. A backup is not trusted because it exists, but because it has been independently tested. A transfer note is not valuable because it was written, but because it can be cross-checked against a block explorer. A permission review is not successful because it was scheduled, but because it identified and removed stale allowances. Independence converts intention into assurance.

Routines also depend on environment. A person who uses the same laptop for browsing, downloading experimental software, and managing large digital asset holdings introduces silent risks. Some teams mitigate this with device segregation: one machine dedicated solely to asset management, never used for general web activity. The March 2020 compromise of a small validator group in Zurich demonstrated why. Their operational laptop, used for both staking operations and ordinary browsing, was infected by a compromised browser extension. The attacker gained temporary access to signing keys, leading to slashing penalties. After the incident, the group enforced strict device segmentation. The implication is that environment shapes exposure far more than technical skill alone.

There is a counter-example worth acknowledging. Some users depend entirely on reputable custodians for backup, permissions, and reviews, believing that outsourcing eliminates operational responsibilities. This is only partially true. Custodians can reduce the risk of personal error, but they cannot eliminate the need for user-level routines—monitoring withdrawal addresses, maintaining up-to-date identity documents, and verifying that account recovery information remains accessible. When Canadian exchange QuadrigaCX collapsed in 2019 after its founder's death in Jaipur, customers discovered painfully that outsourcing without oversight created its own failure mode. The lesson is not to avoid custodians; it is to integrate them into a broader operational framework, not treat them as substitutes for it.

Each routine within a playbook shapes identity as much as safety. A person who performs monthly reviews behaves differently from one who reacts only when problems arise. The former builds confidence through verification; the latter accumulates quiet uncertainty. By externalising memory into written logs, scheduled drills, and segmented systems, the user reduces emotional load. Control becomes visible.

Still, every playbook faces an unresolved tension: how to maintain discipline when nothing appears to be happening. Routine is least appealing when systems seem stable. Yet stability is the one period when routines do their best work—when they can expose drift, catch subtle misconfigurations, and prepare for improbable but severe events. The forward question is therefore straightforward but difficult: will your operational habits be strong enough to withstand boredom, or will they fade until the next crisis forces their rediscovery?

Chapter 5
Scams, Attacks, and Defence-in-Depth

The first warning arrived as a screenshot. A trader in Dubai forwarded it to a colleague late one evening in November 2021: "Guaranteed 3% daily, no risk, audited smart contract." The promotional banner mimicked the visual grammar of legitimate platforms—clean interface, familiar colours, an emblem suspiciously similar to a well-known exchange. By the next morning, the entire scheme had vanished. The website was down, the Telegram group deleted, the "auditors" unreachable. Hundreds of users discovered, in less than twenty-four hours, that they had not invested; they had been emptied.

Deception in digital finance rarely announces itself. It wears borrowed credibility, hijacks urgency, and grafts old fraud patterns onto new rails. The technology evolves, yet the psychology remains stubbornly stable. A promise of fixed daily returns; a charismatic founder performing certainty; a countdown timer designed to shortcut reasoning; a project that dissolves into silence the moment fresh deposits slow. The contemporary twist is scale. A rumour now travels faster than due diligence, and a polished interface can make something dangerously unfinished appear complete. The distance between curiosity and catastrophe has never been shorter.

Every major advance in the cryptographic economy has attracted its own predators. For each tool that increases autonomy, another emerges to exploit it. Permissionless systems enable innovation without gatekeepers, but they also allow anyone to spin up a convincing counterfeit in minutes. Smart contracts remove intermediaries, yet a bug can become a siphon. Even governance—intended as a safeguard—can be captured, steered, or quietly hollowed out. Behind every celebrated breakthrough lies a shadow ecosystem of attacks, from simple impersonations to deeply technical manipulations of protocol mechanics. To understand the opportunity, one must understand the threat.

This chapter examines those threats not as a catalogue of disasters but as a map of recurring structures. The question that sits beneath every example is deceptively simple: what does the attacker assume you will not check? That motif—*the unexamined step*—reappears throughout these pages. A user does not verify the contract address. A team does not review governance rules before committing funds. A community does not question the provenance of an audit report. An investor sees activity in a code repository but not the substance of the commits. Scams, exploits, and technical failures all rely on invisible assumptions, and defence-in-depth begins by making those assumptions visible.

Patterns of deception, the first theme, trace how traditional fraud types reappear in digital markets with only superficial modifications. Impersonation thrives because trust is compressed into usernames and icons. High-yield "farms" revive a centuries-old tactic: dazzle with returns, hide the mechanism, and collapse once inflow slows. Rug pulls borrow the structure of classic exit scams, updated with token mechanics and automated liquidity tools. The narrative shifts, yet the structure repeats. Learning to recognise formation rather than ornament is what separates the cautious from the exposed.

From there, the chapter turns to a counterintuitive skill: reading code without knowing how to code. Most users will never audit a smart contract line by line, yet they can still form judgements through observable signals. Who wrote the code? How long has it been public? Which dependencies does it rely on, and how frequently are they updated? Who reviewed it, and what is the reputation of the reviewers? These questions, answered through visible behaviour rather than technical fluency, create a form of structural literacy. They allow the non-technical user to spot inconsistencies long before they become incidents.

Next comes the domain of protocol-level risks—attacks rooted not in deception but in design. Oracle manipulation, front-running, reentrancy, governance capture: these are less about malicious websites and more about economic structure. A lending pool that relies on a thinly traded token for price data may be sound until a single actor realises they can distort that price at low cost. A governance system with minimal quorum may work until a well-capitalised participant decides to steer it. The vulnerabilities exist not in code mistakes alone but in mismatched incentives, insufficient diversity, and fragile assumptions about behaviour. Diversified exposure is less a strategy than a form of humility: no single protocol design anticipates every adversary.

Incident response, the final thread, shape-shifts from theory into practice. Mistakes happen. Systems fail. Attackers often move faster than any warning mechanism. When something feels wrong—an unfamiliar transaction request, an address that does not match, a device behaving unusually—the first rule is stillness: freeze actions, observe, document. The second is communication: involve service providers, exchanges, or custodians while the window for containment remains open. The third is reflection under pressure: understanding what happened, how it happened, and how to prevent its recurrence. Defence is not defined by the absence of incidents but by the quality of behaviour when incidents occur.

Every paragraph of this chapter rests on a simple conviction: the digital economy does not require paranoia, but it does demand clarity. Scams exploit haste. Attacks exploit assumptions. Failures exploit routine neglect. The aim is not to create fear but to sharpen perception, replacing vague unease with concrete understanding. Defence-in-depth is constructed not from sophisticated tools but from layered thinking—the willingness to question, verify, and slow down before speed becomes danger.

What follows is both warning and invitation. The warning is that no system is invulnerable. The invitation is that careful users, equipped with the right instincts and habits, can operate with confidence even in the presence of predators. The most damaging threats are often the ones you never imagined. The most powerful protection is often the question you manage to ask before committing.

Patterns of deception

In February 2022, the Metropolitan Police in London announced the arrest of a group linked to a sprawling investment fraud that had siphoned more than £20 million from thousands of participants. The scheme, marketed through polished videos and celebrity look-alike profiles, promised "fixed 2% daily crypto yields" and displayed fabricated dashboards showing impossible growth. Investigators later revealed that none of the advertised trading systems existed. The operation relied instead on a familiar cycle: attract deposits quickly, fabricate activity to maintain momentum, and disappear before withdrawals exceeded inflows. The method had not changed for a century; only the branding had.

Fraud in digital markets rarely looks new. It adapts, camouflages, and reappears, borrowing whatever credibility the moment offers. When a scammer impersonates a support representative on a messaging platform, they rely on the same psychological lever as a con artist in 1930s New York: urgency. When a so-called decentralised project drains its own liquidity pool, it echoes the exit scams that marked early offshore brokerage scandals. And when a "yield farm" advertises fixed daily returns achieved through undefined strategies, it rehearses the logic of every Ponzi structure since Charles Ponzi's 1919 promise of 50% profits in 45 days. The specific tools change. The behavioural pattern does not. Recognising that pattern—*the shape beneath the surface*—is the skill that matters most.

Impersonation is usually the first doorway through which harm enters. Show the behaviour: a message appears at 02:14, bearing the name and avatar of a known exchange. The sender urges a user to "verify their wallet or face suspension." The user clicks. The link opens a page that looks identical to the genuine interface, down to the favicon. Name the structure: this is a classic impersonation attack, replacing physical disguises with digital ones. Explain the mechanism: attackers exploit recognisable branding and compress decision-time to blur judgement. They bypass technical safeguards by persuading the victim to grant permission manually. The implication is stark. A system that requires explicit signing actions gives users power, but that same power becomes a vulnerability when urgency overrides verification.

Two cases illustrate how the pattern scales. In July 2020, Twitter suffered a breach in which attackers gained access to internal tools and commandeered high-profile accounts—Barack Obama, Apple, Elon Musk—and posted fraudulent Bitcoin donation links. The place was unmistakable: San Francisco headquarters; the date fixed; the outcome public and measurable. The attackers did not exploit blockchain weaknesses; they exploited trust in familiar names. A different example, the "Squid Game" token collapse in October 2021, saw anonymous developers drain liquidity from a token themed after the Netflix series. The rug pull, executed in minutes, erased more than $3 million in market value. Again, the method was not novel: manufacture excitement, obscure governance, vanish once attention peaks.

Yet a credible counter-example exists. Consider Ethereum Name Service (ENS) governance, which held a public airdrop in November 2021 and faced immediate impersonation attempts. Because distribution rules, smart contract addresses, and community communications were transparent and verifiable, most fraudulent accounts failed to gain traction. The limitation here is instructive. Transparency reduces risk, but it does not eliminate the psychological vulnerability to compelling narratives. Even in communities characterised by technical literacy, plausible forgeries circulate. Reconciling this limitation requires revisiting the motif: *the shape beneath the surface*. The question is always the same—does the source behave consistently with its claims?

Rug pulls demonstrate another form of pattern continuity. Show the behaviour: a token launches with enthusiastic marketing, trading volume spikes, liquidity pools attract deposits, and developers withdraw their own contribution or disable withdrawals. Name the structure: this is an exit scam, a direct descendant of bucket-shop brokers who once fled their offices at night with client funds. Explain the economic design: decentralised liquidity tools make creation effortless, but they also allow creators disproportionate control during a project's first hours. Implication: technical autonomy does not equate to structural safety. A user must examine whether liquidity is time-locked, whether code ownership is renounced, and whether governance is distributed before assuming the system can survive pressure.

The Yearn Finance fork wave of mid-2020 offers a verifiable example. Scores of anonymous teams copied the original protocol's code, altered token names, and launched with promises of spectacular returns. Many collapsed within days, either through direct rug pulls or through simple incompetence masquerading as innovation. Contrast this with the behaviour of Aave during its October 2020 migration. The team published audits, deployed the upgrade openly, and retained funds in time-locked contracts visible on-chain. The contrast demonstrates that deception thrives where scrutiny is difficult and incentives misaligned. Where development is public and timelines predictable, the available surface for manipulation narrows.

High-yield "farms" represent a subtler form of structural mimicry. They showcase screenshots of rapid compounding, often with percentages that exceed the economics of any sustainable system. The pattern is identical to historical high-yield investment programmes (HYIPs) that proliferated in the early internet. Show the modern version: a website advertises "3% daily, verified," encouraging users to deposit tokens into opaque contracts. Name the structure: a Ponzi cycle dependent on continuous inflows rather than productive activity. Explain the metric: returns are not generated but redistributed, and any slowdown in new deposits breaks the machine. Implication: whenever returns appear uncorrelated with credible activity—audited code, observable fees, or clear mechanisms—the structure should be assumed fragile.

A credible counter-example again clarifies limits. Some legitimate protocols, such as OlympusDAO during its 2021 expansion, advertised extraordinarily high APYs derived from token emissions. Although controversial, the mechanism was disclosed and technically verifiable; the risk lay not in deception but in extreme reflexivity. The line between exuberance and fraud can blur when users mistake emissions for revenue. Reconciling the limitation returns us to the motif. The question is not whether returns are high but whether they are explained and reproducible. Pattern recognition begins with asking what the system *does*, not what it *claims*.

Across all these examples, the common thread is behaviour rather than branding. Scams speak in stories: easy wealth, secret algorithms, insider access, inevitable appreciation. But patterns emerge in the mechanics. Impersonation compresses decision-time. Rug pulls extract liquidity. High-yield farms depend on inflows. A user trained to look for repeated shapes—control over contracts, transparency of code, authenticity of communication channels—does not need encyclopaedic knowledge of every threat. They need only the discipline to observe before they act.

The unresolved tension sits at the heart of digital autonomy. Permissionless systems amplify freedom, yet they remove the comfort of gatekeepers. The question is not whether deception will evolve; it will. The question is whether users can learn to see its architecture before momentum persuades them otherwise.

Reading code without coding

On 10 August 2021, security researcher Samczsun uncovered a flaw in the MISO token auction platform operated by SushiSwap in Tokyo. The vulnerability, buried within a single contract used for Dutch auctions, could have exposed up to $350 million in user deposits. What made the episode memorable was not merely the scale. It was the ease with which a non-coder could have spotted trouble had they looked at the project's repository: the contract had no prior audits, minimal review history, and almost no meaningful commit activity in the weeks before launch. The technical bug required expertise. The warning signs did not.

The paradox sits in plain sight. Complex smart contracts determine critical outcomes, yet understanding a project's operational health often requires no more technical fluency than checking a timestamp or reading a change log. The code might be opaque. The behaviour around it seldom is. Teams that maintain rigorous documentation, transparent development histories, and verifiable audit trails leave a traceable signature of discipline. Teams that do not rely on users being unable to distinguish motion from progress. The motif recurs throughout this space: *signals reveal structure.*

Show the first signal: audit provenance. Users may not read Solidity, but they can measure whether external reviewers have done so. Name the behaviour: reputable firms such as Trail of Bits, OpenZeppelin, and Quantstamp publish audits with explicit scope, findings, and remediation notes. Explain the value: these documents anchor expectations. They show what was tested, which issues were fixed, and which vulnerabilities were accepted with caveats. The implication is practical. If a protocol claims to be audited yet provides no report, or references obscure reviewers with no public footprint, the risk profile is measurable before a single line of code is parsed.

Consider two verifiable cases. Uniswap v3's audit suite in March 2021 underwent multiple reviews from different firms, each producing detailed reports and repository-linked changes. A user browsing its GitHub directory could see precise commit messages addressing findings. The transparency did not eliminate risk; it demonstrated process. By contrast, the Meerkat Finance collapse in March 2021 in Hong Kong—where $31 million disappeared overnight—exhibited the opposite pattern. There were no meaningful audits, no credible documentation, and no remediation notes. The structure was visible even before the exploit. The lesson is not that audits prevent failure, but that the absence of a credible audit trail is itself a pattern worth naming.

A limitation deserves acknowledgement. Several high-profile protocols have suffered incidents despite extensive audits. The Compound incident in September 2021, where a faulty upgrade distributed millions of dollars in unintended rewards, passed through an audited codebase. The counter-example matters because it shows that audits measure diligence, not destiny. Reconciling this limitation returns us to the motif: *signals reveal structure*, not certainty. Audits are not predictors; they are indicators of intent, capability, and response culture.

The second signal is open-source history. Show the behaviour: active repositories exhibit consistent commit activity, clear ownership, and accountable contributors. Name the structure: open-source development, where history is preserved as a sequence of decisions. Explain the importance: a repository that evolves gradually, with visible peer review and documented reasoning, reflects organisational maturity. A repository that appears days before launch, comprised mostly of copy-pasted code with few comments or tests, exposes a different truth. The implication for users is direct. They can review commit graphs, contributor profiles, and issue threads without decoding a single function.

Two examples illustrate range. Chainlink's repository, active since 2017, shows regular updates, extensive testing, and a long-lived contributor set. Anyone skimming its activity graphs can see continuity—changes recorded across years and time zones, debates captured in issues, and clear dependency mapping. Conversely, the 2020 Eminence Finance exploit, linked to a project by Andre Cronje, unfolded before the protocol had even reached stable deployment. The repository showed unfinished contracts, minimal testing, and live user deposits entering code explicitly labelled experimental. No technical depth was required to see that the system was not ready. The limitation here is that strong histories can coexist with hidden risks; old projects can ossify, and legacy code can harbour dormant flaws. But the signal still cuts through noise: disciplined development is visible.

The third signal is dependency mapping. Show the behaviour: smart contracts import libraries and interact with external oracles, routers, or governance modules. Name the structure: a dependency graph, usually displayed automatically in repositories or block explorers. Explain the mechanism: a protocol is only as robust as the weakest module it touches, and dependencies reveal where assumptions accumulate. The implication is powerful for non-coders. If a project relies heavily on unaudited libraries, forks outdated versions of critical contracts, or aggregates numerous external price feeds, complexity increases and resilience decreases.

Look to two cases. The 2022 Beanstalk Farms exploitation exploited an under-secured governance dependency: a flash-loan-enabled vote allowed attackers to drain funds through a governance proposal. The dependency structure was visible beforehand—critical votes required no time delay and relied on a single contract's balance. In contrast, MakerDAO's system—reviewable through its public documentation and repositories—illustrates deliberate dependency layering. Modules are separated, governance actions carry delays, and crucial contracts undergo repeated peer review. The structure is not flawless; no system is. But its dependencies are articulated, not obscured.

A credible limitation arises, however. Some innovative protocols deliberately use minimalistic repositories or off-chain components, making dependency mapping less revealing. Privacy-preserving systems such as Tornado Cash employ zero-knowledge circuits whose complexity sits outside traditional commit logs. The limitation should be reconciled, not ignored. When code paths move off-chain, users shift their attention to audit provenance, contributor identity, and operational transparency. The signals adjust, but the principle remains: *signals reveal structure.*

Non-coders can also examine version histories, fork relationships, and contributor patterns. Show the behaviour: a repository with 200 contributors and thousands of closed issues displays long-term stewardship. Name the structure: distributed maintenance. Explain why it matters: a team that integrates external feedback typically exhibits more discipline than one that suppresses dissent by force-merging changes or deleting issues. Implication:

repository culture predicts governance culture. A protocol maintained by a single anonymous account with sporadic commits signals fragility regardless of its stated ambition.

The motif threads through every paragraph: *signals reveal structure*. One need not interpret code to observe whether a system is built with care. One can watch how teams behave: how they document, respond, and revise. One can measure whether repositories evolve or stagnate. One can examine whether audits exist, whether they were acted upon, and whether dependencies are coherent. These signals do not promise safety. They illuminate patterns.

The unresolved tension sits with the user. How much weight should they assign to signals that are inherently incomplete? Every system carries blind spots; every audit omits something; every repository can mask intent. The forward test remains simple and persistent: given the visible signals, does the project behave like one built to endure, or one built to rush?

Protocol-level risks

At 02:43 UTC on 14 October 2022, the decentralised lending protocol Mango Markets on Solana began to unravel. A trader, acting from an address traced to a single machine in Vienna, inflated the price of the platform's thinly traded MNGO token through a series of leveraged positions. Within minutes, the oracle feeding Mango's smart contracts recorded the manipulated price as fact. The protocol treated that inflated figure as collateral. Loans were drawn.

Balances surged. By dawn, more than $100 million had been extracted. No passwords were cracked. No servers were breached. The code performed exactly as written. The damage arose from something deeper: the protocol's underlying assumptions about price, time, and behaviour buckled under pressure.

The episode revealed a tension that has defined decentralised finance since its emergence. Smart contracts promise mechanical predictability—outcomes determined by logic, not discretion. Yet the logic rests on inputs and interactions that remain vulnerable to pressure. *Force the input, and the machine obeys.* That is the risk at the protocol level: vulnerabilities that persist even when every user follows instructions and every interface behaves correctly. These failures are not operational missteps; they are structural exposures.

Oracle manipulation, reentrancy, and governance capture are three such structural exposures. They are not the only ones, nor the most exotic. They are simply the ones that most clearly show how speed, liquidity, and collective decision-making can be bent by those willing to probe the gaps. The motif that threads through each of them is simple and sobering: *assumptions fail first.*

Begin with oracles. Every decentralised protocol needs a bridge between external facts and on-chain logic. That bridge is the oracle—often a data feed aggregating prices from exchanges and pushing them into smart contracts. When the bridge distorts, the entire structure tilts. Show the behaviour: an asset price that swings 40 per cent within minutes on a low-liquidity exchange. Name the structure: an oracle that treats that swing as a reliable signal. Explain the mechanism: a protocol that accepts the inflated price as collateral, allowing the attacker to borrow against a phantom valuation. The implication is immediate. The vulnerability is not in the token or the wallet. It is in the model that treats a single price feed as truth.

The Mango Markets case is well documented. For a contrasting example, consider Chainlink price feeds used across major lending protocols since 2019. These feeds aggregate data from multiple exchanges and apply deviation thresholds before updating. This slows reaction time, but protects against thin-depth manipulation. A user browsing the update cadence—visible through dashboards and repositories—can see update intervals, aggregator counts, and deviation settings. The behaviour is measurable. It shows that structural risk is often a question of sampling, not secrecy.

A limitation deserves explicit mention: robust oracles do not eliminate price risk. In May 2022, the TerraUSD collapse demonstrated that even accurate pricing can trigger cascading liquidations when a system's design leans heavily on reflexive assumptions. Reconciling the limitation returns us to the motif: *assumptions fail first*. Oracles can prevent fabricated prices. They cannot prevent genuine panic.

The second structural exposure is reentrancy—the ability for a contract to be called repeatedly before it finishes updating its internal state. The most famous instance, the 2016 DAO attack in Switzerland, remains a defining moment. The DAO's withdrawal function sent funds before updating balances. Attackers triggered the withdrawal recursively, draining roughly 3.6 million ETH. What mattered was not the cleverness of the attacker but the ordering of operations: change the state after sending funds, and you invite reentry.

Show the behaviour: a contract that allows an external call before updating a balance. Name the structure: reentrancy. Explain the mechanism: an attacker contracts a loop that calls back repeatedly, extracting funds faster than the protocol can record the loss. The implication is not strictly technical. It reveals a broader truth about mechanistic systems: if a sequence can be interrupted, it can be reversed.

Two recent examples illustrate the point. In April 2023, the Hundred Finance exploit on Optimism saw more than $7 million drained after an attacker manipulated exchange rates and triggered reentrant calls through a lending contract. The vulnerability was not novel. It was a variation on a years-old pattern. Meanwhile, Aave's v2 deployment across multiple chains shows the counter-pattern: withdraw functions that update state before sending assets, reentrancy guards that lock functions during sensitive operations, and documented testing. A user need not read code to observe the defensive architecture. Behaviour reveals structure.

There is, again, a limitation. Certain protocols employ complex composability—multiple contracts calling one another, each with unique states. In those cases, reentrancy is harder to map because the attack surface extends beyond a single function. The reconciliation lies in visible behaviour: highly composable systems emphasise extensive testing, formal verification, and slow deployment cycles. When those are missing, assumptions fail first.

The third structural exposure is governance capture—the silent risk that decentralised systems become vulnerable not through code defects but through concentrated voting power. Governance tokens confer the ability to propose changes, adjust parameters, or even transfer treasury funds. If a small group accumulates disproportionate voting weight, decisions reflect their incentives rather than the protocol's stated purpose.

Show the behaviour: a proposal that passes within minutes, supported by a single whale address controlling 60 per cent of the vote. Name the structure: governance capture. Explain the mechanism: voting weight linked to token holdings, with no safeguards such as time delays, quorum requirements, or multi-layered approval. The implication is not theoretical. It determines whether a protocol can resist internal takeover.

Two examples anchor the risk. In February 2020, Steem's governance was effectively seized when a major holder—supported by three centralised exchanges—used token custody to vote in new block producers. The chain continued to run, but its autonomy evaporated. Contrast that with MakerDAO's governance since 2020, which employs delays on executive votes, risk frameworks for parameter changes, and active delegate participation. None of this guarantees immunity. It does, however, create friction. Friction buys time.

A limitation must be acknowledged: governance systems designed for broad participation can struggle with voter apathy. Low turnout allows modest actors to wield disproportionate influence. Reconciling this leads back to the motif: *assumptions fail first*. If a protocol assumes that voters will always act, it risks capture not through malice but indifference.

Across these three exposures, visible behaviours reveal deeper structures: price feeds that move too fast or too narrowly; contracts that update state too late; governance systems that concentrate too quickly. These are not surface-level flaws. They are architectural. And while complex, they are observable even without technical fluency. A user can watch how oracles update, how contracts sequence operations, and how governance proposals pass. The motif persists: *assumptions fail first*.

Diversified exposure is one response—spreading risk across different designs, oracle systems, ecosystems, and governance models. It is not a guarantee. It is a recognition that failures tend to cluster within similar architectures. Protocol-level risk is rarely idiosyncratic. It echoes.

The unresolved question sits with the reader: when you examine a protocol, which assumptions do you trust, and which do you test?

Incident response basics

At 11:52 GMT on 27 December 2021, a London-based analyst named Robert Martin opened his hardware wallet interface and saw something that did not make sense. The balance of a token he had not touched for months had dropped to zero. A second asset displayed a sequence of outbound transfers he did not recognise. No new software had been installed. No phishing email had been opened. The last confirmed action on the device had been a transfer to a centralised exchange three weeks earlier. Yet the ledger entries were unambiguous. Something had gone wrong, and it was still unfolding. Martin did what very few users manage in the first five minutes after a compromise: he stopped. He refused the instinct to click, to refresh, to fix. By freezing activity, capturing screenshots, and calling his exchange within half an hour, he preserved a trail that later helped investigators trace the exploit to a fake browser extension distributed through an advertisement masquerading as the official interface. Most of the funds were gone. But not all. A small tranche had hit the exchange after his alert, allowing a partial recovery.

The scene captures a structural truth often obscured by panic: the difference between total loss and partial containment is rarely technical. It is behavioural. A compromised private key cannot be restored through cleverness. A malicious contract cannot be cleansed by refreshing a browser. But a user who resists the lurch towards action—who freezes, observes, documents—buys time. And time is the first currency of incident response.

The motif that anchors this subchapter is simple: *slow the moment*. When something breaks, the instinct is acceleration—more clicks, more interfaces, more attempts to reverse what has already occurred. But real incident response often looks like its opposite: pausing, recording, isolating. Slowness becomes defensive structure.

Show the behaviour: a user notices a transaction they do not recognise and immediately connects their wallet to a second interface to "check." Name the pattern: contamination. Explain the mechanism: every new authorisation expands the surface through which an attacker might already have access. The implication is clear. Reaction amplifies risk. Restraint contains it.

Two instructive examples frame the stakes. In August 2022, the compromise of 8,000 Solana wallets—later linked to the Slope wallet provider—showed how users reconnected compromised seed phrases to multiple applications within minutes of noticing missing funds. The combination of stress and interface familiarity accelerated the damage. Conversely, in March 2023, a developer in Singapore reported a suspected leak in a multisig environment on Gnosis Safe. Their team halted all outgoing transactions, revoked queued operations, and exported the transaction history for forensics before interacting with any new tool. The early freeze preserved 90 per cent of treasury assets. Behaviour shaped outcome.

A limitation must be acknowledged: freezing activity does not stop a private-key-based attacker. If the key is compromised, the attacker has unilateral control. But the freeze preserves the *record*. That record underpins investigations, insurance claims, law enforcement reports, and—most importantly—post-mortem accuracy. Reconciling the limitation returns us to the motif. *Slowness does not reverse the breach. It prevents cascade.*

Documentation is the second pillar. When an incident unfolds, memory bends. Timestamps blur. Users conflate what they saw with what they feared. Documentation reintroduces objectivity. Screenshots of transactions, copies of error messages, hashes of suspicious contracts, and exact times of wallet connections form a map that can later be replayed. These artefacts matter because blockchains are precise. A single confirmed block at 16:02 tells a different story from a transaction pending at 16:03. That difference affects everything: whether a transfer can be halted at an exchange, whether an attacker is still active, whether a vulnerability is isolated or systemic.

Show the behaviour: a user sees an unexpected approval and closes the tab. Name the risk: loss of evidence. Explain the mechanism: interfaces update rapidly; feeds refresh; ephemeral warnings vanish. The implication is sharp. Without contemporaneous capture, post-incident reconstruction becomes guesswork.

Two cases illustrate the point. During the Nomad bridge exploit in August 2022, users who provided precise transaction hashes and timestamps to exchanges managed to freeze small portions of funds that passed through identifiable choke points. Those who submitted generic descriptions ("my funds were drained") saw slower responses or none at all. In contrast, the 2020 KuCoin breach—where attackers stole over $275 million—demonstrated how rapid internal logging and immediate public disclosure enabled exchanges and protocols to freeze or reissue affected tokens within hours. Documentation fed coordination; coordination limited damage.

A limitation is inherent: documentation does not guarantee restitution. Many protocols are immutable. Funds sent to an externally owned address controlled by an attacker cannot be revoked. Yet the record strengthens every subsequent step, from forensic tracing to platform alerts. Reconciling the limitation deepens the motif: *recording is not repair; it is orientation.*

The third anchor of incident response is communication—deliberate, selective, and promptly targeted. Not every party should be informed immediately. But those who can act—exchanges, custodians, and team members in shared control environments—benefit from early notice. Communication is a tool for containment, not catharsis.

Show the behaviour: an individual posts their compromise publicly on social media before contacting the exchange through which the attacker is likely to route funds. Name the consequence: the attacker is alerted. Explain the mechanism: public disclosure signals urgency and may prompt the attacker to accelerate laundering. The implication for users is decisive. Sequence matters. Speak first to those with leverage over funds in motion.

Two examples provide clarity. When the Poly Network breach occurred in August 2021, early cross-team communication between exchanges, analytics firms, and the protocol's maintainers created a de facto freeze across multiple chains. The attacker eventually returned much of the stolen value. Meanwhile, in smaller incidents—such as an Ethereum wallet compromise reported to Binance in January 2023—exchanges that were notified within minutes managed to block deposits mid-processing. Timing changed the outcome. Communication worked because it was directed and documented.

The limitation here is significant: exchanges cannot freeze assets already withdrawn or mixed, and they often require legal documentation before acting. Reconciling the limitation brings us back to the motif: *timely messages orient defenders even when they cannot reverse the harm.*

The final pillar is review—methodical, unemotional, and often uncomfortable. After an incident, the temptation is to patch the surface: a new wallet, a new password, a new interface. But review digs deeper. It maps the entry point, reconstructs the path, separates what is known from what is inferred, and distinguishes correlation from causation. Review replaces stories with sequences.

Show the behaviour: a user blames "malware" without evidence. Name the risk: misdiagnosis. Explain the mechanism: false assumptions lead to false fixes, leaving the real vulnerability open. The implication is profound. Without accurate diagnosis, future incidents become more likely, not less.

Two examples reinforce the value of structured review. The 2022 Wintermute exploit on Ethereum involved a compromised address generated through a vanity address tool with a known vulnerability. Initial speculation blamed a smart-contract flaw. Only thorough forensic review—documented publicly by the firm—revealed the true origin. By contrast, a smaller DeFi project in 2021 misattributed a treasury drain to phishing, only to learn months later that a team member's machine had been compromised through outdated software. Review is not symbolic. It is diagnostic.

The limitation is that not all incidents yield clear answers. Some leave only traces. Reconciling this does not weaken the motif. It reinforces it: *review is not closure; it is preparation.*

Across these pillars—freezing, documenting, communicating, reviewing—a pattern emerges. Incident response is less about technical mastery and more about disciplined conduct under pressure. The blockchain does not forgive haste. Interfaces do not reward improvisation. And attackers exploit the speed with which users move when frightened.

The unresolved tension sits, deliberately, with the reader: if the next anomaly appears on your screen at 02:43, what will you do in the first silent minute—and will that minute be fast, or slow?

Chapter 6
Evaluating Tokens

When the Ethereum network buckled under record traffic in May 2021, a curious pattern emerged. Users were not only complaining about volatility; they were complaining about *gas*. Some were paying more in transaction fees than the value they transferred. Others waited half an hour for a confirmation. Yet a smaller group—developers, decentralised application operators, and validators—watched the same congestion with a different lens. They were tracing value backwards. Every stalled transaction, every recalculated fee, every delay pointed to a single asset: ETH, the token that made computation possible. Its utility was not theoretical. It was experience, measured in queues and failed swaps. And as the crowd focused on price charts, a quieter signal pulsed beneath: tokens gain meaning only when someone needs them to do something they cannot do without.

That moment captures a truth at the centre of this chapter. Tokens are not miniature equities, nor digital souvenirs. They are instruments with specific pathways through which value flows—or leaks. Some serve as fuel. Others secure a network. Others grant influence in collective decision-making. Some, frankly, do very little beyond telling a story. But before any chart or narrative matters, one must understand the mechanism by which a token participates in the life of the system from which it stems. Everything else is derivative.

If earlier chapters have explored behaviour, custody, and defence, this chapter turns the lens outward. It asks a harder question: how does one evaluate an asset designed to be both programmable and tradable, both functional and speculative? The challenge is not to memorise categories, but to cultivate an instinct—an internal auditor—that constantly tests stories against structure. Time and again, the market demonstrates that a persuasive pitch can lift an asset briefly, but only sustainable demand, credible supply dynamics, aligned governance, and a living ecosystem can sustain it.

That is the journey ahead, and it begins with utility. A token reveals itself most clearly through its user journey. If someone wishes to deploy a smart contract on a given network, what must they acquire? If they want to participate in a staking process, where does the token fit? If a protocol gates access to features, how is the token involved? Sometimes, the pathways are crisp: without ETH, Ethereum does not function. Without ATOM, one cannot participate in Cosmos Hub governance. Other pathways are more abstract, such as tokens used to incentivise liquidity or participation without offering genuine necessity. Evaluating tokens starts with tracing these paths visually, almost like following a cable from one machine to another. The question is simple: does the asset do work?

Utility alone, however, reveals only half the picture. The structure of supply—its pace, its cliffs, its unlock cycles—often determines whether a token retains purchasing power or dissolves under dilution. Emissions schedules, vesting periods, and unlock calendars are not mechanical trivia; they are economic forces. A protocol might articulate a grand vision for its token, but if 30 per cent of supply unlocks in a single month and early holders rush for liquidity, no narrative can absorb the pressure. The market does not forgive imbalance between demand and supply. The discipline lies in reading schedules the way one might read a corporate debt maturity ladder: where are the bottlenecks, and who sits on the other side of them?

Supply analysis naturally bleeds into governance, because the people who hold the token shape the future of the system. Voting frameworks that appear democratic can hide concentrations of power. Delegated voting can amplify or erode community voice. Quorum thresholds can determine whether meaningful change is possible or whether a protocol drifts under the inertia of a few large holders. Understanding governance is not about memorising jargon; it is about identifying alignment. Are the actors who influence the system also those who bear consequences? Or is the structure quietly tilted towards founders, early investors, or external interests? Token distributions often tell that story more honestly than whitepapers.

Even governance, though, is not the end of the inquiry. A token lives within an ecosystem—a moving, evolving web of developers, users, integrations, and norms. Some ecosystems flourish with hundreds of active contributors, regular upgrades, and a culture of iteration. Others stagnate despite early fanfare, their GitHub repositories silent, their partnerships symbolic. Healthy ecosystems demonstrate activity, not hype. They show improvements in documentation, steady integration across protocols, patches issued faster than exploits emerge, and conversations within the community that reflect clarity rather than confusion. Evaluating tokens at ecosystem scale means learning to triangulate signals rather than trusting dashboards built for marketing.

Throughout this chapter, one motif will surface again: *trace the flow*. Trace the flow of utility, the flow of supply, the flow of influence, the flow of collaborative effort. A token is not a single object. It is a junction within a wider network of relationships. To evaluate it with seriousness is to map those relationships with care.

This introduction sets the stage for a deeper inquiry. You will encounter frameworks that sharpen judgement, patterns that reveal hidden risks, and examples that illuminate both strong and fragile designs. But the purpose is not to hand you definitive answers. It is to equip you with a way of seeing—one that rewards curiosity, punishes shortcuts, and respects the fact that programmable assets, like any complex instrument, must be understood through structure, not slogans.

The chapter ahead asks you to hold one tension. Tokens move fast. Fundamentals move slowly. The question that will follow you through each section is simple, uncomfortable, and essential: when the next wave of enthusiasm arrives, will you be able to trace the flow before the crowd obscures it?

Utility and demand pathways

In June 2020, during the early months of what became known as the "DeFi summer", a developer in Berlin attempted a simple token swap on Uniswap. The transaction failed. His screen displayed a single line of red text: *"Out of gas."* Moments earlier, another user had pushed through a large arbitrage trade, forcing the Ethereum network to reprioritise transactions and lifting the minimum gas price. The system did exactly what it was designed to do: price access to computation according to competing demand. The small failure was telling. It showed that the value of ETH was not merely a reflection of market enthusiasm. It was a function of how many people needed blockspace at that moment, and how much they were prepared to pay for the privilege. Utility revealed itself not through theory but through congestion.

The same month, in a completely different corner of the crypto landscape, a group of early stakers on the Cosmos Hub observed a quieter phenomenon. Their ATOM tokens granted them voting power and a share of network rewards, but the demand pressures were gentler. Decisions moved through governance cycles. Validators adjusted commission rates. The asset's utility was not in transaction throughput but in securing the chain and aligning incentives. The contrast between ETH and ATOM in June 2020—two tokens in live economic use, with distinct demand curves—remains an instructive starting point. Both mattered. Both were needed. But they were needed *for different reasons*.

This chapter section begins with that contrast because it captures the central puzzle of evaluating tokens: value emerges from pathways of use, not from slogans. Tokens perform work. They gate actions. They mediate access. They transmit influence. And they do so through specific mechanics that can be traced, tested, and compared. The motif that will recur throughout this piece is simple: *follow the path*. Every token's relationship to demand is a path, and every path tells a story about what the asset is, and what it is not.

The most intuitive pathway is the one Ethereum demonstrated in Berlin: computation. Gas tokens provide a metered right to use a shared machine. They do not require belief systems or grand narratives. They require throughput. When the Berlin developer's transaction failed, the cause was visible in the mempool. Competing bids created a dynamic market for inclusion, and the ETH token sat at the centre of that process. This is not abstract utility; it is observable behaviour. Network scans from Etherscan (Etherscan, 2020) recorded average gas prices rising more than 6× within a single hour that month. The metric made the mechanism real. Where demand fluctuates rapidly, so does the cost of participating.

By naming such examples, we can explain the structure beneath them. A token used as fuel exhibits *elastic demand*.

As more users need blockspace, they compete with price, producing a responsive curve. The implication is clear: gas tokens live or die by usage, not marketing. Any evaluation must start with the question: which concrete actions require this token, and how frequently do users perform them?

Staking tokens, by contrast, follow a slower rhythm. ATOM on the Cosmos Hub, staked by thousands of validators and delegators since the chain's launch in March 2019, shows how predictable demand can emerge from security requirements. Validators bond stake to participate in consensus. Delegators commit tokens to these validators. Rewards accrue according to uptime, performance, and inflation parameters. The behaviours are measurable: staking ratios, unbonding times, and validator churn. These pathways form the backbone of the token's demand: without ATOM, the chain cannot choose block proposers, punish misbehaviour, or distribute rewards. It is a different form of work, anchored in responsibility rather than throughput.

Each of these examples—Berlin's failed swap and Cosmos's steady staking—demonstrates how utility determines demand. But tokens vary widely, and some strain the concept. Consider governance tokens issued in late 2021 by protocols that promised "future utility" but delivered little more than a symbolic vote. These assets often lacked visible pathways. No transaction required their use. No staking mechanism validated behaviour. Even governance itself was thin; quorums were rarely met. The counter-example is instructive. It shows a limitation: not all tokens with claimed utility exhibit genuine demand. Yet even here, reconciliation is possible. The market has repeatedly demonstrated that tokens without clear pathways fade, while those with enforced usage—fuel, security, or indispensable access—retain relevance.

The question of access brings us to a third category: tokens that *gate* participation. Filecoin, launched in October 2020, provides a tangible illustration. Storage providers must stake FIL as collateral to offer space on the network, and they earn rewards for maintaining data availability. The behaviour is visible in the metrics: storage capacity, pledge collateral, and deal volumes. FIL is not merely held; it is locked, risked, and deployed. The pathway is directional: FIL → capacity → storage deals → FIL rewards. This structure creates a loop in which utility and demand reinforce one another. The implication is straightforward. Tokens that gate scarce resources or valuable rights—when tied to real behaviour—can produce persistent demand.

Against these structural examples, high-yield "farming" tokens from the same period offer a revealing counterpoint. Many promised exceptional returns but relied on circular incentives. Demand came primarily from speculators chasing the rewards, not from the underlying protocol use. When emissions slowed, demand collapsed. The pathway was shallow. The behaviour was not differentiated. The motif of *following the path* uncovers the fragility: if the only user journey is "acquire token → farm more token", utility becomes self-referential.

Tracing user journeys is the practical heart of evaluating token utility. One must map the steps a user takes and identify where the token becomes essential. A gas token is spent. A staking token is locked. A governance token is wielded. A collateral token is liquidated. These are distinct behaviours producing distinct pressures. They can be measured with dashboards, validated through transaction histories, and confirmed by protocol documentation. The strength of a token's demand emerges from how many users walk these paths, how frequently, and under what constraints.

Even the constraints matter. Unbonding periods, such as the 21-day delay on Cosmos, shape user decisions. High gas fees deter marginal interactions. Collateral requirements create minimum purchasing thresholds. These frictions form part of the utility story. They influence demand not by creating need, but by shaping how users respond to need. For staking tokens, the commitment to an unbonding period is not simply mechanical; it reflects an intention to support security. For gas tokens, the willingness to pay high fees during congestion signals the urgency of the underlying action.

No evaluation would be complete without acknowledging that some tokens blend functions, sometimes successfully, sometimes incoherently. Polkadot's DOT token, for example, has served multiple roles since its mainnet launch in May 2020: governance, staking, and participation in parachain auctions. Each role produces a different form of demand, visible in staking ratios, governance participation metrics, and auction bonding volumes. This blending can be a strength when each pathway reinforces the rest. It can also create complexity: users may struggle to evaluate the value of a token spread across multiple use cases, and the design might favour one pathway at the expense of another. Yet the principle remains the same. One must follow the path. The more pathways converge on necessary behaviour, the more resilient the token's demand.

Tracing pathways also illuminates a deeper point about ecosystems. Demand does not emerge in isolation. Developer activity, integrations, and protocol upgrades amplify utility by making user journeys smoother or more abundant. When Uniswap integrated layer-two scaling solutions in late 2021, ETH demand shifted in composition; users paid lower fees for the same operations, but far more transactions occurred. A single design choice altered the pathway. Conversely, when a protocol halts development or loses community momentum, pathways shrink. Users drift elsewhere. Demand fades.

What, then, does it mean to evaluate utility rigorously? It means refusing to accept claims at face value. It means pairing every narrative with a behaviour, every promise with a metric, every design with a real user action. It means looking beyond price to the choreography of the system—

where tokens move, why they move, and what breaks when they stop.

This brings us back to the Berlin swap failure. That short error message—*"Out of gas"*—was a compact lesson in token economics. It showed that utility can be measured in failure as much as in function. When demand intensifies, tokens used to access computation bear the pressure. When demand weakens, these tokens relax. The pathway contracts and expands like a living system.

The unresolved tension is this: a token's utility can be clear today yet shift tomorrow as ecosystems evolve. Protocols add features. Networks compete. User habits change. The forward test is simple, but difficult to execute: will the token's pathways still matter when conditions differ? And if they do, how will you recognise that before the crowd does?

Supply schedules and dilution

In December 2022, a quiet alarm spread through several token communities when a tranche of locked APE—allocated during the ApeCoin launch in March 2022—was scheduled to unlock. The date was public. The quantities were public. Yet in the days before the release, trading forums filled with speculation about the likely effect of a sudden increase in circulating supply. When the tokens finally unlocked, liquidity pools on major exchanges recorded a measurable shift: sell volumes spiked within hours, and the price chart bent downwards with a speed that startled newcomers but surprised no one who had studied the schedule. The event was mundane in structure yet dramatic in consequence. It showed, clearly and immediately, that token value is inseparable from the rhythm of its supply. Pathways of demand matter; but the cadence of unlocks, emissions, and vesting cliffs shapes everything around them.

The ApeCoin episode also revealed a deeper truth: dilution is not an abstract force. It is a sequence of dates, amounts, recipients, and behaviours. It is felt through the decisions of holders who finally gain liquidity, treasuries that begin distributing grants, and teams whose long-awaited allocations vest. The motif that anchors this chapter is *the calendar*. Every token supply schedule is, at its core, a calendar of pressures. The more faithfully one studies that calendar, the more intelligible the token becomes.

A clear example of this dynamic comes from Ethereum's transition to proof of stake in September 2022, an upgrade known as "the Merge". The shift altered ETH's long-term issuance dramatically. Data from the Ethereum Foundation (2022) recorded average block rewards dropping by more than 85 per cent compared with the proof-of-work regime. This was not theatre. It was a measurable, structural reconfiguration of supply. The mechanism slowed dilution and, in periods of high fee-burning, created net-deflationary intervals. The behaviour was visible on explorers that tracked issuance and burn in real time. By naming the process, we see its explanatory power. Reduced issuance strengthened long-term holder conviction. The implication was clear: supply schedules shape sentiment as much as they shape supply.

Yet Ethereum's controlled issuance contrasts sharply with projects that distribute tokens at high velocity. Avalanche, launched in September 2020, employed emissions to incentivise network security and ecosystem growth. Some allocations were released at a steady drip, others through staking rewards. The effect was double-edged. The emissions seeded activity and built validator participation. They also increased circulating supply each month. Observers could measure the trade-off directly on Avalanche's public dashboards: active validator count rising; total token supply drifting upwards. This is the lived texture of dilution. It produces health in one domain and pressure in another.

The counter-example—useful for perspective—comes from Bitcoin's fixed schedule of halving events, the most recent occurring in April 2024. Halvings do not prevent dilution; they merely slow it. And while some treat the schedule as a source of long-term value, the market's short-term behaviour often diverges from the narrative. In 2024, transaction fees fluctuated wildly as inscriptions and new protocols competed for blockspace, reminding holders that even the most famously predictable supply cannot override the complexity of demand. The limitation is telling: predictability alone does not guarantee stability. Supply can be known years in advance, yet value can remain volatile.

Reconciling this with the earlier examples yields a sharper lesson. Controlled supply helps, but only when paired with meaningful utility and credible demand pathways.

The difficulty for many newcomers is that supply schedules are often buried in whitepapers, investor decks, and governance forums. Yet the structure is almost always traceable. A typical schedule includes four components: the genesis allocation, emissions, unlocks tied to vesting agreements, and discretionary distributions from treasuries or foundations. Each component influences dilution in a distinct way. Emissions create continuous pressure. Unlocks produce stepwise pressure. Treasury distributions create contingent pressure, dependent on governance decisions. Every pressure is mapped to dates. Every date is measurable.

A striking example of stepwise pressure occurred with Solana's early investor allocations, many of which were subject to vesting and unlock periods between 2020 and 2022. When a large tranche unlocked, blockchain analysts could observe behavioural shifts within hours: some recipients staked the newly unlocked SOL, others sold, and some moved tokens into cold storage. The decisions were public, traceable, and visible on-chain. These behaviours turned the abstract concept of dilution into a sequence of concrete actions: deposits into staking pools, liquidity additions, or market sells. This is why supply schedules matter: they compel behaviour.

To evaluate dilution effectively, it helps to return to the motif of *the calendar*. A simple "dilution diary"—a private tool, not a prediction engine—structures the inquiry. It need not be ornate. Record the dates of major unlocks. Note the size of each release. Include vesting cliffs. Identify which groups receive the tokens: teams, investors, community participants, or treasuries. Then annotate the actions those groups have historically taken when liquidity freed. The diary does not forecast price. It highlights pressure points. It turns the future into a sequence of known events rather than an amorphous threat.

Consider two examples that make the diary method vivid. First, Arbitrum's token distribution in March 2023 included a substantial allocation for the DAO treasury. While the treasury held the tokens, circulating supply remained limited. But the dates of future distributions, grants, and incentive programmes were disclosed. These dates formed a predictable sequence of supply expansions. Analysts who built diaries could see those expansions coming weeks or months ahead. Second, Polygon's early vesting schedule, disclosed during its rebranding from Matic Network in February 2021, identified clear cliffs for team and foundation tokens. When these cliffs approached, the community debated potential market impacts. The debate itself mattered: it shaped governance proposals, which then influenced the timing and manner of token releases. The calendar was not merely observed; it was contested.

A limitation deserves attention: supply schedules can change. Protocols sometimes vote to alter emissions, delay unlocks, or restructure allocations. MakerDAO's decisions around MKR issuance and buybacks between 2020 and 2023 show this plasticity. Governance can reshape dilution paths. Yet even this does not undermine the calendar approach; it enriches it. A diary is not a static prediction. It is a living record, adjusted as governance evolves. The key is to treat supply as a process rather than a fixed destiny.

Each of these examples pairs dilution with behaviour. Emissions encourage staking or liquidity provision. Unlocks surface the intentions of founders and early backers. Treasury distributions reveal the priorities of a community. This pairing is essential because it grounds abstraction in evidence. Dilution is not "risk" in the general sense. It is the act of increasing supply relative to demand. It is measured through circulating supply metrics, vesting schedules, staking ratios, and governance decisions.

The motif of *the calendar* returns again when we consider how supply pressures interact with demand pathways. A chain with high usage may absorb emissions more easily. A chain with low usage may feel even minor unlocks intensely. The tension—between known future supply and uncertain future demand—makes supply schedules one of the few parts of the token landscape that can be understood in advance. We cannot forecast market cycles with confidence. We cannot predict the success of ecosystem partnerships. But we can know, with precision, when certain tokens will be released. That knowledge is not a prediction; it is preparation.

The unresolved tension that closes this section flows from that contrast. Supply schedules are static until governance moves. Dilution is measurable. Yet demand is fluid. User growth, protocol innovation, and ecosystem vitality can either absorb or magnify the pressures of new supply. The forward test is simple to state and hard to answer: when the next unlock arrives—whether in a week or a year—will the ecosystem be strong enough to meet it?

Governance and alignment

In February 2021, a governance vote on Uniswap's future drew global attention when a single delegate, the venture fund a16z, marshalled more than 15 million UNI—the largest bloc then delegated to any one actor—to support a proposal concerning bridge integrations. The mechanics were public. The outcome was legitimate. Yet the episode exposed something deeper than a simple tally: voting power was unevenly distributed, quorum thresholds could be shaped by a handful of delegates, and the structure of influence travelled along paths very different from the egalitarian ideals often attached to token governance. It was a reminder that *who decides* can matter more than *what is decided*. And that token ownership alone rarely tells the full story.

Months later, in May 2022, MakerDAO faced its own reckoning with concentrated influence when a series of large MKR holders blocked a proposal to adjust stability fees. Again, nothing unlawful occurred. The protocol behaved precisely as designed. But the episode laid bare a tension that runs through decentralised systems: voting rights can be legitimate yet misaligned, technically correct yet practically skewed. The vote count reflected the will of those who participated. The governance outcome reflected the structure of power beneath it. The motif that threads through this section—the shape of influence—is visible in every proposal, quorum, and delegation.

To understand governance alignment, start with what is observable. Voting power is not philosophical. It is measured in tokens. It is distributed across wallets. It is delegated through explicit transactions. Each of these behaviours is public. When a protocol announces quorum rules—say, a 4 per cent participation threshold for a vote to pass—that is not an aspiration; it is a parameter with measurable consequences. In Uniswap's vote, the high-stakes nature of the decision drew participation, but many smaller holders still refrained from delegating or voting. The implication was direct: a small number of delegates shaped outcomes simply because others stayed silent. Silence becomes structure.

Delegation complicates this further. In Compound, whose governance system matured between 2020 and 2022, delegation allowed technically knowledgeable participants to aggregate influence. Some delegates built public profiles with transparent voting histories; others remained opaque.

Delegation can strengthen alignment when delegates act predictably and disclose reasoning. It can distort alignment when large token holders delegate to actors with unclear incentives. The behaviour of delegates—statements, forum posts, voting patterns—transforms abstraction into evidence. A token's governance culture is visible in these patterns.

The counter-example comes from Yearn Finance, whose founder, Andre Cronje, famously renounced control of the YFI token shortly after its launch in July 2020 by avoiding a founder allocation. His move eliminated one source of concentrated influence. Yet even Yearn could not escape power dynamics entirely; large holders emerged organically, and their voting decisions shaped treasury operations. The limitation is revealing: even when founders relinquish power, distribution patterns can fill the vacuum. It reconciles neatly with the earlier cases: governance alignment depends not only on founder behaviour but on the emergent structure of ownership.

If voting power shows the shape of influence, quorum rules show its thresholds. A high quorum can prevent hasty decisions but can also entrench gridlock. A low quorum can enable agility but can magnify the sway of large holders. These effects are observable. For instance, Aave's governance—active since early 2021—experimented with varying quorum levels for different proposal types. Proposals involving risk parameters often passed with modest participation. High-impact changes required stricter thresholds. The differentiation made influence more transparent: small adjustments could move quickly; existential changes demanded broader agreement. The implication for alignment is practical: quorum signals the protocol's appetite for caution or speed.

The motif of the *shape of influence* reappears when examining founder and team powers. Some protocols introduce explicit veto rights. Others embed upgrade guardians. These tools are sometimes justified as safety mechanisms, especially in early growth stages. Yet their existence demands scrutiny. The Terra Classic system before its collapse in May 2022 offered an instructive case. Core developers retained outsized control over code changes relative to broader token holders. While not the cause of the system's failure, the concentration of authority revealed how governance assurances can mask asymmetries. The behaviour—rapid deployment of changes by a narrow group—was visible long before the collapse. Influence reveals itself through action.

Conflict controls—safeguards against self-dealing or opportunistic governance—are equally vital. MakerDAO implemented several such controls, including provisions that required extended debates and cooling-off periods for high-impact proposals. The behaviour was concrete: discussions stretched across multiple weeks; risk teams published analyses; changes were reviewed by domain experts. These controls exemplified alignment mechanisms in practice. But they carried limitations. Extended review slowed experimentation. Disagreements sometimes fossilised. Still, the trade-off was explicit: decentralisation requires friction.

Skin-in-the-game, often invoked but seldom measured, becomes tangible when tied to explicit metrics. For validators in proof-of-stake systems, it appears as stake deposits that can be slashed. For DAO delegates, it appears as public reputational stakes—statements, disclosures, voting records. In Lido's governance in 2023, major node operators who voted on protocol decisions had millions of dollars' worth of ETH at bond. Their behaviour showed commitment: they participated frequently, explained views, and accepted constraints. The implication is simple: alignment strengthens when decision-makers bear persistent exposure to outcomes.

Yet these patterns also introduce fragility. Large stakeholders may act defensively. Delegates may become gatekeepers. High quorums may stall necessary upgrades. A credible limitation emerges: governance can become too tightly held or too diffuse. Both extremes undermine alignment. The reconciliation lies in recognising governance not as a fixed ideal but as an evolving design. The shape of influence changes as token distribution shifts, as protocols mature, and as communities refine norms.

The quiet motif returns. The shape of influence is not static. It is redrawn each time tokens vest, each time a delegate gains or loses support, each time a quorum is raised or lowered. The structure is legible to those willing to trace these movements. The calendar of unlocks described in the previous section intersects directly with the map of voting power in this one. Governance alignment emerges from that intersection.

The unresolved tension closes this discussion. Governance can be measured—votes cast, quorums met, delegates active. Alignment must be inferred—seen through behaviour, incentives, and recurring patterns. The forward question is therefore blunt yet fundamental: when the next contentious proposal arrives, whose influence will define the outcome, and will their incentives still run parallel to the protocol's long-term health?

Ecosystem health

When Ethereum's London upgrade went live in August 2021, developers gathered in scattered meeting rooms from Berlin to Singapore, watching block explorers flicker with the first blocks carrying EIP-1559 transactions. Nothing dramatic happened. Blocks finalised. Gas fees shifted. Yet the quiet satisfaction on those livestream calls revealed something crucial: hundreds of independent contributors had coordinated across continents, repositories, and time zones to execute a complex upgrade without central command. The visible behaviour—steady commit activity, cross-client testing, public review calls—showed an ecosystem whose health could be inferred not from a dashboard chart but from the persistence and distribution of its contributors.

Contrast that with the abrupt freeze of development on the Squid protocol in October 2022 following its collapse on Binance Smart Chain. GitHub logs went silent. Community channels emptied. The project's partnerships dissolved within days. The protocol's code still existed, but its ecosystem had evaporated. This is the central motif that guides the section: *the pulse beneath the price*. A token's short-term chart can move on sentiment, but an ecosystem's health must be measured in behaviours—developers pushing code, teams forming integrations, communities enforcing norms.

Evaluating that pulse begins with developer activity, a metric that can be observed rather than hypothesised. Real work leaves traces. Commit histories show cadence. Pull requests show collaboration. Issue trackers show friction points. When Polkadot matured its parachain auctions in 2021, its ecosystem displayed visible behaviours of alignment: independent teams competed to win slots, partner protocols contributed crowdloans, and multiple development shops built tooling around Substrate. The implication was direct: a diverse development base indicated resilience. If one team faltered, others continued.

A credible limitation tempers this inference. Commits can be gamed. Repositories can be forked for show. Activity can cluster within a single team, creating the illusion of breadth. The Avalanche ecosystem faced such scrutiny in mid-2022 when observers noted that several widely cited repositories were maintained by a narrow group. The limitation does not invalidate the signal; it refines it. Developer activity must be triangulated. Genuine ecosystems exhibit depth—multiple repositories, independent maintainers, and consistent issue resolution—rather than bursts of superficial commits.

Partnerships offer a second window into the pulse. Cross-protocol integrations are not decorative; they reflect whether other builders find the protocol reliable, useful, or strategically necessary. When Chainlink entered production feeds on Aave in early 2020, the behaviour—adopting an external oracle to anchor lending markets—showed trust and alignment between the teams. Later integrations, such as Curve's inclusion of Lido's stETH in 2021, demonstrated how partnerships can create mutually reinforcing flywheels. The implication is structural: every genuine integration increases switching costs for users, strengthens interoperability, and embeds the token more deeply into the surrounding economy.

Yet partnerships can also flatten into marketing. Some ecosystems announce collaborations that amount to little more than logos on a slide deck. The Harmony network, after its bridge breach in June 2022, demonstrated this fragility. Several "integrations" proved superficial; partner teams withdrew quickly, revealing that the underlying relationships lacked substance. This counter-example reinforces a core principle of evaluating ecosystem health: treat partnerships as verifiable behaviours, not press releases. Look for code merges, deployed contracts, shared audits, or joint governance proposals. These leave footprints. Announcements do not.

Community norms form the third indicator, often overlooked because they are harder to quantify yet highly visible in practice. Norms appear in the tone of forum debates, the willingness of users to review proposals, the speed at which bugs are escalated, and the expectation of transparency from leadership. MakerDAO's governance forum between 2020 and 2023 displayed these norms clearly. Proposals attracted lengthy, technical feedback. Risk teams published models. Domain experts questioned assumptions. The behaviour was demanding, sometimes abrasive, but consistently anchored in the expectation that ideas must withstand scrutiny. The implication is significant: robust norms function as informal security infrastructure.

A counter-pressure exists here too. Communities can become insular or hostile. When Solana experienced repeated outages between September 2021 and April 2022, parts of its online community reacted defensively, dismissing criticism rather than interrogating structural issues. Yet even in this limitation, healthier elements emerged: multiple validator groups published reports, core developers documented fixes, and external contributors built tooling to analyse network load. The reconciliation is revealing. Communities are rarely monolithic. Health lies not in unanimity but in whether constructive behaviour outweighs noise.

Triangulation—our quiet motif—binds these signals. No single metric proves ecosystem vitality. GitHub commits can mislead. Partnerships can embellish. Community energy can oscillate. But when three independent signals converge—a steady developer base, genuine integrations, and a community that enforces transparent norms—the pulse becomes hard to dispute. This triangulation mirrors research practices outside crypto: historians compare texts; scientists validate results across methods; auditors cross-check statements against cash flows. The behaviour is consistent across disciplines: trust emerges from corroboration, not from a single point of data.

The dangers of relying solely on dashboards are now clearer. Dashboards visualise transactions, addresses, volumes, and revenues. They are useful. They are incomplete. During the Terra collapse in May 2022, dashboards showed high activity until the last hours, a mirage created by panic transactions rather than sustained economic use. The underlying ecosystem—developers, partners, and community stewards—had already begun to fray. Observers who triangulated signals noticed the dissonance: development slowed, integrations stalled, and discussions on governance channels turned defensive long before charts unravelled. The implication is stark. Metrics without context mislead.

Ecosystem health also manifests in repair behaviour. When Optimism discovered a critical bug in its rollup code in February 2022, developers coordinated privately with external researchers to patch the issue before disclosure. Public gratitude followed. Audit reports were released. Incident notes were written. This recovery behaviour—the willingness to reveal flaws, credit contributors, and reinforce norms—strengthens ecosystems more than flawless uptime ever could. Healthy systems show their strength through how they handle stress.

A limitation to this perspective surfaces when ecosystems are young. Early-stage networks may have thin developer communities, unproven partnerships, and immature norms. Their silence is not necessarily decay; it may simply be gestation. Here, triangulation becomes especially valuable. A new protocol with low commit counts might still show meaningful growth if partnerships deepen or community discussions become more substantive. The motif returns: triangulation clarifies, even when individual signals are noisy.

Two named examples underscore this nuance. Arbitrum, before its explosive adoption in 2023, spent years in quiet technical development. Commit patterns were steady but not flashy. Partnerships emerged slowly. Community presence was modest. Yet the convergence of signals—high-quality audit provenance, steady testnet traction, and credible developer stewardship—revealed a latent health that dashboards at the time failed to capture. Conversely, EOS in the years following its 2018 launch displayed high visible activity—large funds, bold partnerships, widespread marketing—yet its developer community thinned, and ecosystem cohesion weakened. The contrast sharpens the core lesson: health is not noise; health is depth.

This section's motif—the pulse beneath the price—now comes full circle. Price charts spike. Dashboards spike. Sentiment spike. These are surface movements. The deeper pulse is slower. It is patient. It is recorded in shared repositories, integration diagrams, forum debates, research threads, and repair notes. Healthy ecosystems leave fingerprints across these surfaces, and the consistency of those fingerprints forms the real signal.

The unresolved tension remains. Ecosystems evolve. Teams shift priorities. Communities lose leaders. Partnerships drift. Even metrics that look robust today can change rapidly. The forward question therefore becomes essential: when the price chart next surges or collapses, what will you read first—the surface signal, or the pulse beneath it—and will the triangulated evidence still tell the same story?

Chapter 7
Building a Balanced Portfolio

The morning after the Black Wednesday crisis in September 1992, a London accountant named Judith Carver arrived at her office to find colleagues huddled over broadsheets, the front pages still warm from the printer. Sterling had been forced out of the Exchange Rate Mechanism. Pension funds had taken hits. Private investors were split between those who had been cautious enough to spread risk and those who had been convinced that a single currency bet—pound strength—could carry them safely through the year. Judith, who had spent the previous decade building her own investment notes in a neat stack of Moleskine journals, observed something striking as she listened to colleagues dissect their losses: the people who had begun with a clear sense of personal purpose, not with forecasts or tips, were the ones calm enough to make rational decisions the next day. They had not avoided volatility, nor had they predicted the event; they had simply constrained its power to destabilise their lives.

That morning has become a quiet parable in finance circles, not because Judith was a visionary trader, but because her approach underscored a truth that is easy to miss in the digital asset markets: a portfolio is not a prediction machine. It is an architecture of intent. It reflects what matters to you, what you can tolerate, what you wish to explore, and what you refuse to jeopardise. And although the assets have changed—from equities and gilts to tokens that mediate computation, payments, or governance—the principle that steadied Judith has not. Begin with the purpose; everything else follows.

This chapter addresses the tension that every thoughtful participant in the new economy feels, even if they rarely articulate it. Digital assets operate at speeds that defy traditional rhythms. Communities whisper new narratives overnight. Volatility compresses years of movement into weeks. In such an environment, the temptation is to improvise: to chase momentum, to learn by bruising, to rebuild only after something breaks. Yet sustainable participation requires the opposite impulse. It calls for deliberate pacing and internal scaffolding—the equivalent of teaching yourself to breathe while the theatre of markets performs at full volume.

A balanced portfolio is not a static arrangement of holdings; it is a living structure shaped by purpose-led allocation. That phrase carries more weight than it appears to. Purpose is not about whether you believe a specific token will rise. It concerns the boundaries you set between what is central and what is experimental. It distinguishes the resources you expect to support long-term stability from the resources you are willing to deploy in curiosity, discovery, or calculated risk. The emerging language of "core and satellite" is useful not as jargon but as a reminder of the gravitational forces within a portfolio: what forms the anchor, and what orbits around it.

Yet allocation alone cannot quieten uncertainty. Markets do not reward neat categorisation; they reward resilience. And resilience emerges through diversification that actually works. It is fashionable to treat diversification as a spreadsheet exercise—count the assets, confirm the categories, assume safety. But in digital markets, correlations can strengthen suddenly, sometimes with startling force, as projects share dependencies, infrastructure, or behavioural patterns. A payments token can behave like an infrastructure token in a stress event; an application token can correlate with both if its revenues rely on the same execution layer. Diversification is therefore not about multiplying names; it is about understanding the mechanisms that drive convergence and divergence.

The chapter moves from foundations to rhythm. Once a portfolio has been constructed with purpose and diversification in mind, its equilibrium must be maintained. Rebalancing, despite its procedural reputation, carries a philosophical core. It forces you to confront how far reality has drifted from your intentions. It introduces friction—sometimes literal, sometimes psychological—which serves as a safeguard against impulsive shifts. And in the United Kingdom, where tax treatment distinguishes sharply between disposals, gains, and allowances, rebalancing requires both technical awareness and restraint. Timing becomes a matter of judgement rather than mechanical formula.

Documentation completes the architecture. Every professional discipline—from aviation to medicine to engineering—relies on written records to ensure clarity under pressure. Yet private investors often trust memory over method. A portfolio assembled without written hypotheses, defined risks, or explicit triggers becomes a vessel for inconsistencies. When markets turn, the absence of documented reasoning becomes costly: not in monetary terms alone, but in confidence and coherence. An investment diary is both a safeguard and a mirror. It helps you recognise whether your decisions express your original intent or a fleeting response to distraction, optimism, or fear.

Running through this chapter is a unifying motif: balance as an act of consciousness. Balance is not passive. It is not a quiet midpoint between extremes. It is attention—directed, disciplined, sometimes uncomfortable attention. It demands that you articulate what you want your portfolio to do for you, then build a structure capable of honouring that aim without collapsing under the weight of novelty or noise.

The ideas ahead do not promise certainty; nothing in markets can. What they offer is structure: a way of thinking that protects focus, sharpens judgement, and reduces the influence of emotion in environments designed to provoke it. As you proceed, the central question will shift from "What should I hold?" to "What am I trying to achieve, and what structure supports that aim through changing conditions?" How you answer that question determines not only the architecture of your portfolio, but the stability with which you navigate the expanding terrain of digital assets.

Purpose-led allocation

In July 2016, at a glass-walled office in Edinburgh, the investment committee of Baillie Gifford reviewed a client portfolio that had drifted far from its mandate. The client, a technology executive, had allowed a surge in a single high-growth position to dominate his exposure. The committee's minutes record a deceptively simple remark from the chair, Sarah Whitley: "Purpose precedes allocation." It was not a reprimand; it was a restatement of the firm's discipline. Before choosing assets, one must name the goal, the constraints, and the emotional limits. Only then can the portfolio carry the weight placed upon it. That portfolio was rebuilt, not by forecasting the future but by returning to the question that should begin every allocation: *What is this money for?*

That question sits uncomfortably in digital markets, where speed seduces and experimentation feels essential. Yet the Edinburgh lesson matters more here than anywhere else. Tokens reward clarity of intent and punish improvisation. They exhibit bursts of volatility that stretch conviction and compress decision time. Without a declared purpose—income, exploration, long-term accumulation, or safeguarding liquidity—the portfolio becomes a reflection of mood rather than design. Purpose is the keel. Everything else is rigging.

The starting point is deceptively humble: write down the financial and behavioural boundaries that define your role as a participant. Some call this a mandate; others prefer "investment compass." Whatever the term, the practice forces you to translate abstractions into daily constraints. A phrase such as "I want prudent exposure to decentralised infrastructure" remains shapeless until paired with behaviours: the maximum you are willing to place in illiquid positions, the volatility that disrupts your sleep, the drawdown you could accept without abandoning your thesis. Purpose turns these into numbers: £X for long-term positions, £Y for experimental assets, and a hard stop at Z% for any single idea. It does not constrain curiosity; it gives it boundaries.

A core–satellite structure emerges naturally once purpose is defined. Show this in practice: a researcher may choose to anchor 90 per cent of their exposure in established primitives—tokens that power settlement, computation, or security—because their role requires focus rather than thrill. Name this approach: institutions have used variants of it for decades, designing a core that behaves predictably and a satellite sleeve reserved for discovery. Explain why it matters in digital assets: the core provides stability during volatility clusters, whereas the satellite—small, ring-fenced, clearly defined—prevents the urge to gamble from spilling into the foundation. The implication is subtle yet profound: experimentation becomes a method, not a leakage of discipline.

Two real cases illuminate the idea. In December 2020, the Grayscale Bitcoin Trust became a dominant holding in many American portfolios as price momentum accelerated. Some investors treated it as a core asset, expecting it to behave like a long-duration store of value. But its structure included premiums and lock-ups that distorted exposure. Those who had begun with a clear purpose—long-term accumulation with low structural risk—relegated GBTC to their satellite sleeve. When premiums compressed in early 2021, they adjusted without panic because the position had never been allowed to bear structural weight. Meanwhile, in Singapore in 2022, Temasek's due-diligence processes required explicit separation between strategic and exploratory capital. Their investment in FTX, though ultimately written down, did not endanger their sovereign portfolio because it sat within an allocated experimental channel. Purpose insulated damage.

A counter-example, equally instructive, comes from individual traders during the 2021 DeFi summer. Many declared their intentions as "long-term participation" but allocated 40–60 per cent of their capital to short-lived yield farms with opaque emissions. Their purpose and their behaviour diverged. When emissions spiked and token prices collapsed, they found themselves overexposed to mechanisms they had never intended to rely upon. Purpose-led allocation does not prevent loss, but it narrows the gap between intention and action. Reconciling this case reinforces the point: the failure was not yield farming itself;

it was the absence of boundaries that separated exploration from foundation.

Purpose also clarifies time. A core position demands patience, not vigilance. A satellite position demands vigilance, not patience. Without this distinction, the portfolio becomes a tangle of mismatched expectations. You see this most clearly in the behaviour of investors who track minute-by-minute price movements of assets they claim to hold for five years. Their stated purpose and their monitoring schedule contradict each other. The visible behaviour—refreshing charts, reacting to minor swings—reveals that their allocation has no psychological anchor. Purpose, when honoured, determines the rhythm: you monitor the core at scheduled intervals and review the satellite through structured check-ins. One short sentence captures the discipline: *Ignore noise. Measure intent.*

A quiet motif threads through every purposeful allocation: constraint as freedom. Constraint sounds limiting, but in practice it liberates attention. Once you decide that only 10 per cent of your capital belongs in speculative ideas, you make two commitments: first, that you will not exceed that boundary; second, that you will explore freely within it. Consider the practical effect. When a new protocol launches, you can engage without fear of destabilising your portfolio. You run a small position, track its behaviour, and record your thesis. Curiosity becomes sustainable because it cannot grow uncontrolled. Purpose turns chaos into experiment.

Purpose also governs liquidity. A portfolio built without explicit liquidity parameters is a portfolio built on hope. Stating that the core should remain accessible within a defined timeframe—say, seven days for reallocation—forces alignment between asset type and liquidity need. It means you do not bury essential capital in long lock-ups or instruments that settle unpredictably. It means you match your commitments to your obligations. Show this with an example: a professional with quarterly cash needs allocates the majority of their core into assets with predictable exit routes, while using their satellite sleeve for positions that may be illiquid for weeks. Name this behaviour: liquidity matching. Explain why it matters: it prevents forced selling. The implication is clear: purpose absorbs pressure before markets apply it.

Two further examples highlight the structural benefits. In March 2020, the Ethereum network experienced congestion during the COVID-related crash. Gas fees surged, blocking small holders from adjusting their positions. Those who had placed their essential resources in congestible environments found themselves unable to act. But long-term allocators who had chosen purpose-aligned core positions—held in ways that did not require immediate on-chain mobility—avoided unnecessary friction. Conversely, during the Polygon outage in October 2021, satellite positions that depended on rapid movement stalled. Those who had kept them small and non-essential endured the inconvenience; those who had allowed satellites to swell suffered real setbacks. Purpose-led allocation is less about predicting outages and more about designing a system that remains intact when outages occur.

Purpose also clarifies the difference between wanting exposure and wanting conviction. Many investors conflate the two. Exposure means holding something; conviction means understanding why you hold it and under what conditions you would part with it. Purpose forces articulation. If a position enters the core, you must name the mechanisms that justify its stability: network usage, role in settlement, governance value, or long-term demand. If it enters the satellite, you name the catalysts, uncertainties, and review dates. Purpose prevents the quiet drift where a speculative idea becomes a core holding purely because its price once rose.

A final motif returns here: *Choose, don't slide.* Sliding is the slow, unconscious drift of a portfolio that has no written purpose. Choosing is the deliberate act of naming your goals, your constraints, and your appetite for discovery. Purpose-led allocation is not a shield against volatility. It is a scaffold for judgement.

You now face a simple but consequential question: if you were required to write your purpose for participating in digital assets on a single page—your aims, your boundaries, your sleep-at-night limits—what would that page contain, and would your current allocation honour it?

Diversification that works

In February 2007, at the Bank of England's Court Committee meeting in London, members reviewed a briefing that would later look painfully prescient. A chart, stark in its simplicity, showed credit instruments that had diverged for years suddenly snapping into near-perfect correlation within days. When the minutes were released that April, one line stood out: "Diversification ceases to function when regimes shift." The message was not theoretical. It described a structural truth: assets that behave independently in calm periods can become indistinguishable when conditions turn. The lesson would echo throughout the global financial crisis later that year and again during the liquidity crunches of March 2020, when correlations across equities, commodities, and digital assets surged toward one. The comfort of spreading bets dissolved the moment the regime changed.

That same phenomenon defines digital markets. Correlations move quickly. They tighten under stress and loosen in moments of sector-specific innovation. Diversification, if it is to work, must recognise these shifts rather than assume stability. It must treat assets as expressions of underlying economic primitives—payments, infrastructure, applications—rather than as tickers that happen to trade in the same arena. If diversification is to endure, it must be built on function, not fashion.

The first task is to see correlation as behaviour, not as a spreadsheet coefficient. When two assets rise and fall together, it is not because they communicate; it is because the forces acting upon them overlap. A payments token might move with general sentiment, whereas an infrastructure token might respond to changes in blockspace demand. Plotting their correlation reveals a pattern, but observing their use-cases explains it. Show this with an example: during the May 2021 drawdown, the correlation between Bitcoin and DeFi governance tokens spiked above 0.80 (Coin Metrics, 2021). Name the driver: a cross-market liquidity squeeze. Explain the mechanism: traders unwound positions indiscriminately to meet collateral requirements, crushing differentiation. The implication is clear: correlations are not laws; they are conditions. They change.

A second case reinforces the pattern. In the aftermath of the Ethereum Merge in September 2022, infrastructure tokens linked to scaling solutions diverged from application-layer tokens. Polygon's MATIC and Arbitrum's ARB tracked network usage and integration milestones, while application tokens moved with sector-specific flows. Correlation fell because the underlying economics separated. When one primitive experiences a catalyst and another does not, their behaviour splits. Diversification thrives in these intervals, not during the panics where everything compresses into a single trade.

A limitation must be acknowledged. Digital assets still exhibit high baseline correlation because capital flows through common channels: centralised exchanges, dollar liquidity, and behavioural momentum. Even assets with distinct purposes can move together simply because they are held by the same cohort of participants. This does not invalidate diversification by primitive; rather, it sets its boundary. The structure works best across regimes, not within every moment of crisis. Reconciling this limitation sharpens the method: build diversification on differences that persist through cycles—economic role, user base, design incentives—while accepting that correlation will spike during liquidity shocks.

The quiet motif running through effective diversification is simple: widen the map. Most portfolios are narrow without realising it. Holding several infrastructure tokens does not constitute diversification if all depend on the same source of demand. Each may have different teams, partners, or headlines, but if they share a revenue stream—blockspace fees—they will respond similarly to shifts in network activity. Diversification begins when an allocator recognises this sameness.

Payments tokens, for example, move with adoption curves and settlement demand. Their price behaviour reflects their role as transactional mediums or liquidity hubs. Infrastructure tokens depend on the mechanics of computation: blockspace scarcity, validator economics, and ecosystem integrations. Application tokens depend on user retention, product-market fit, and protocol-level incentives. These differences matter because they create asymmetry during regime shifts. When infrastructure demand cools, payments and application layers can still grow. When application adoption surges, infrastructure may lag until congestion materialises. These staggered rhythms create genuine diversification.

A stablecoin yield sleeve illustrates the principle concretely. When an allocator places a small portion of their portfolio into stable, short-duration yield instruments—regulated money-market-backed stablecoins or conservative lending markets—they add a primitive that behaves differently from volatile assets. Its return profile links to interest rates, not to network cycles. During the market dislocations of March 2023, when risk assets retreated after USDC briefly lost its peg, stablecoin yields remained tied to Treasury bill movements rather than crypto-specific sentiment. The behaviour diverged because the underlying primitive diverged. Diversification worked because the mechanism differed.

To apply this thinking, one must trace behaviour, not promises. Show this again: during the Solana outage in January 2022, infrastructure tokens linked to Solana's throughput fell sharply. Meanwhile, cross-chain application tokens that served multiple ecosystems showed partial insulation. Name the concept: regime specificity. Explain it: outages hurt infrastructure more than multi-chain applications because the former depends on constant throughput, whereas the latter can reroute activity. The implication: a portfolio that mixes primitives does not rely on a single technical assumption.

A counter-example exposes the risks of misunderstanding diversification. Many allocators in 2021 believed they were diversified because they held tokens across different sectors—lending, derivatives, decentralised exchanges. Yet almost all depended on Ethereum blockspace. When gas fees rose sharply in November 2021, user activity declined across these sectors simultaneously. Diversification failed because the underlying primitive was shared. The reconciliation is instructive: "sector diversification" works only if sectors rely on different economic engines. Cosmetic diversity is not structural diversity.

Another implication follows: diversification requires watching for regime shifts, not merely counting holdings. A regime shift is not a headline; it is a change in the logic of behaviour. When transaction fees surge, the economics of applications change; when alternative settlement layers grow, the economics of infrastructure change; when macro liquidity tightens, the behaviour of all risky assets compresses. Allocators who distinguish these regimes build portfolios that flex rather than break. They do not forecast regime shifts; they observe them.

This brings us to the behavioural spine of diversification: commit to measuring, not guessing. A simple way to observe regime shifts is to track three behaviours weekly. First, measure correlation among your holdings during quiet periods and during volatility spikes; the difference shows where true diversification lies. Second, compare the sources of revenue or demand for each asset; if two assets rely on the same pipeline, they will travel together. Third, commit to monitoring user behaviour—active addresses, transaction patterns, integration announcements—as signals of functional divergence. These are not predictions. They are ways of staying attuned.

The motif returns: widen the map. A narrow map shows tickers. A wide map shows primitives. When you widen the map, you see that a portfolio mixing payments, infrastructure, applications, and yield instruments behaves like a system with multiple engines. If one stalls, the others may continue. If one overheats, the others may cool it. The strength lies not in balance but in independence.

Two more examples underline the point. The launch of Base by Coinbase in August 2023 strengthened the infrastructure primitive by attracting developers and lowering entry friction. Tokens tied to computation benefited, while pure-application tokens moved less. Meanwhile, during the 2020–2021 NFT boom, applications connected to cultural adoption surged with almost no relation to infrastructure cycles. Payment primitives barely moved. Behaviour diverged because demand sources diverged.

Yet diversification is never perfect. There will be moments—sharp liquidity contractions, regulatory shocks, coordinated deleveraging—when divergence collapses into uniform decline. This is not failure. It is a reminder that diversification reduces fragility; it cannot eliminate it. The method works through cycles, not in every hour of stress.

You now face a sharper question than the one most investors ask: not "Am I diversified?" but "Am I diversified by function, not by fashion?" And a second question follows quietly behind it: if the regime shifted overnight, would the engines beneath your portfolio move independently—or would they reveal themselves as one?

Rebalancing rhythms

In June 1996, the University of California's Regents reviewed a quiet anomaly in their pension fund. A routine quarterly report showed the equity sleeve had drifted nearly nine percentage points above its prescribed band after a sustained rally. The fund's policy required rebalancing, yet several board members hesitated; selling winners felt counter-intuitive. Minutes from that meeting record a blunt intervention by the then-Chief Investment Officer, Patricia L. Macht, in Oakland: *"Discipline is not comfort. Discipline is continuity."* The fund rebalanced. Over the following twelve months, as equities retreated and bonds strengthened, that act of reversion preserved several hundred million dollars of value relative to a drifted allocation. The rhythm mattered. The willingness to act on it mattered more.

Rebalancing does not reward clairvoyance. It rewards structure. The rhythm itself—calendar-based or threshold-based—serves as the metronome of a portfolio that seeks coherence rather than adrenaline. A clock can govern that rhythm, as the Regents used quarterly checkpoints. Or a boundary can govern it, such as a rule to adjust whenever an asset deviates by a defined percentage from its target. The choice is less important than the commitment. Structure limits improvisation, and improvisation is where most misjudgements hide. This is as true in digital assets as in pension funds: drift accumulates quietly until it no longer feels like drift but destiny.

A disciplined rhythm becomes even more significant in a market where volatility compresses and expands with little warning. Show this with a case: during March 2020, Bitcoin's correlation with equities spiked above 0.60 (Coin Metrics, 2020), pulling many ostensibly diversified portfolios off-balance. Name the mechanism: liquidity urgency. Explain the effect: when investors sold liquid assets to meet margin calls, target weights dissolved. The implication is simple: without a rebalancing rhythm, the portfolio would have become an accidental macro bet. With one, the allocator at least had a defined moment to pause, measure, and commit to a structured response.

Threshold-based rhythms reveal a different strength. Consider the approach popularised by Vanguard in its 2009 research note *Best Practices for Portfolio Rebalancing*, which recommended tolerance bands around target weights, adjusting only when allocations drifted beyond predetermined margins. In practice, this avoided unnecessary trades while still enforcing discipline. Applied to crypto, where a single asset can appreciate by 30 per cent in a week, threshold rules prevent the portfolio's character being rewritten by momentum. The rule speaks softly but cuts cleanly: when an asset breaches the band, act. Five words capture the principle early: *Do not let drift decide.*

Yet a limitation must be acknowledged. Thresholds can trigger at moments of short-lived volatility, prompting sales in the middle of sharp but temporary moves. A London-based allocator in August 2022, for example, saw their threshold-based system fire twice in a single week during the Ethereum Merge's anticipatory speculation. The trades were small but costly in aggregate. The reconciliation is precise: thresholds must reflect the underlying volatility of the assets they govern. A 5 per cent band for bonds makes sense; for high-volatility tokens it is far too tight. The rhythm must match the instrument.

Rebalancing, though, is not merely a question of timing. It is a question of friction. In the UK, each sale triggers the possibility of a capital gains event. The behavioural temptation is to delay, hoping to offset gains later or wait for a fall that never arrives. But friction is not an argument against action; it is an argument for intentional action. Show this with a concrete behaviour: an investor documenting the cost basis, expected gains, and available annual Capital Gains Tax allowance before each planned rebalance. Name the practice: cost-aware execution. Explain the benefit: decisions become grounded in numbers rather than discomfort. The implication: friction becomes a constraint, not a deterrent.

Another source of friction is liquidity. During thin trading periods, especially across smaller-cap tokens, a rebalance can move the market. This risk became visible in March 2021, when several decentralised exchange pools on Ethereum saw slippage spikes as large holders adjusted allocations after a sudden rally. The lesson is empirical: liquidity is not constant. Schedules must respect trading depth. Quiet hours—European mornings or moments of steady blockspace—can prove materially less costly than peak mania. The rhythm must incorporate the market's own breathing.

A quiet motif begins to form: rebalancing is a record of intentions confronted by reality. Each adjustment is a moment of exposure, revealing whether the allocator trusts their own structure. The motif returns whenever drift accumulates. A portfolio's map slowly distorts, like a coastline creeping inward. Left unattended, the distortion becomes the norm.

Calendar-based rhythms offer clarity. Quarterly checkpoints, used by many institutional funds, create a pulse that defines the year. The allocator knows when the assessment will come, and so does not contort behaviour in anticipation of every market move. Show this with another example: the Norway Government Pension Fund Global, which has adhered to an annual rebalancing framework since the early 2000s, allowing it to maintain a consistent equity–bond mix despite repeated cycles of exuberance and pessimism. Name the function: temporal neutrality. Explain its force: by separating signal from noise, it reduces reaction to mid-cycle turbulence. The implication for digital assets is encouraging: calendar rhythms help prevent overtrading in markets designed to provoke emotion.

A counter-example clarifies the boundary. In periods of structural regime change—such as the shift in Ethereum's fee market after EIP-1559 in August 2021—rigid calendar rules may be too blunt. Assets can reprice relative to their economic primitives faster than a quarterly rhythm can capture. Here, threshold rules offer sensitivity. The reconciliation is elegant: blend both. Use calendar checkpoints for broad structure and threshold triggers for sharp deviations. Rhythm and responsiveness can coexist.

Rebalancing also sharpens understanding of correlations. When assets drift, they reveal their behaviour under the surface. A payments token surging while infrastructure lags indicates a temporary demand imbalance. A broad rise across all holdings may indicate a regime-wide liquidity wave. Observing these patterns during rebalancing builds intuition. It teaches the allocator to see not only price but movement.

The process begins with measurement. Measure drift precisely. Measure transaction costs. Measure tax exposure. A portfolio without measurement is a diary without dates. Once measured, the allocator must compare. Compare current weights to the intended structure. Compare the market's present to the thesis that justified the allocation. A mismatch either calls for rebalancing or calls for a revised thesis. And then commit. Commit to an action or to a deliberate inaction, but record the choice. The act of recording anchors the rhythm.

These rituals echo the practice of long-standing endowments such as the Wellcome Trust, which publishes detailed allocation reviews each year. Though the Trust does not invest heavily in digital assets, its approach—transparent, disciplined, and bound by written intent—translates cleanly. The habit of writing decisions humbles the allocator. It shows whether the rhythm was honoured or avoided.

Returning to the motif, rebalancing becomes a quiet conversation between the allocator and their future self. Each action—or refusal to act—writes a line in that conversation. A line that says: *I chose structure over sensation.* Or the reverse.

Yet a final tension remains unresolved: when the market moves with exceptional force, should the allocator override the rhythm? Should a double-digit surge between checkpoints prompt immediate action? Or should the structure stand, trusting the rhythm's long-term clarity? The answer, as ever, depends on the discipline you can sustain. The question persists: when the next distortion arrives, will you trust the rhythm you built—or will you let drift speak louder than design?

Documenting decisions

On 19 October 1987, as markets convulsed from Hong Kong to New York, a quiet scene unfolded in a small office in the

City of London. A mid-level portfolio manager at Nomura International, Michael Taylor, sat before a yellow legal pad, writing a line he would later photocopy for colleagues: *"My rule was clear before the panic, and it must remain clear during it."* Taylor had drafted that rule weeks earlier—his exit threshold on a set of overextended equities—yet the speed of the crash made every instinct beg for improvisation. The written rule prevailed. He executed his predetermined cuts that afternoon, sparing his book from a portion of the collapse. The pad became a symbol inside the desk drawer: a record of judgement set down in calm, tested under pressure.

The episode shows the quiet power of documentation. When emotion surges and screens flicker red, the mind's reconstruction of a plan becomes elastic. Written commitments do not stretch. They sit there, paper-still, offering a reference point immune to adrenaline. That stillness is the motif that threads through the practice of documenting decisions: the page does not panic. A diary—digital or handwritten—is not a sentimental artefact. It is a governance mechanism for the self, drafted long before a difficult moment demands clarity.

Investing without documentation is effectively improvisation masquerading as conviction. The absence of written intent invites a subtle drift: the thesis morphs after price movement, risk tolerance bends with mood, and exit conditions blur once the trade is underway. Show this with a historical example. In 1999, at the height of Britain's dot-com frenzy, several UK investment trusts published strategy updates that retrofitted bullish narratives onto holdings originally purchased for far narrower reasons. Name the behaviour: post-hoc rationalisation. Explain its mechanism: once price charts dominate attention, the original rationale dissolves, replaced by whatever story preserves comfort. The implication is stark: without a diary, even institutions fall prey to the same narrative re-engineering that bedevils amateurs.

The core of documentation is not verbosity but decisiveness. A clear investment record captures three elements that later prove indispensable: a thesis, a set of risks, and defined triggers. The thesis explains why the asset deserves capital; the risks outline what could break that logic; the triggers define when action should occur. Each element must translate into a visible behaviour. A thesis that claims "adoption will grow" must specify a metric to observe—daily active addresses, transaction fees, or developer activity. A risk that warns of "liquidity deterioration" should point to a measurable sign, such as declining order-book depth. A trigger that intends to "exit on structural change" requires a concrete threshold: a governance shift, an emission schedule update, or a breach of a pre-stated drawdown limit.

Two documented cases illuminate this discipline. The first is the approach used by the Yale Investments Office under David Swensen, whose annual reports from New Haven in the early 2000s included explicit rationales for each asset class and the conditions under which Yale would adjust or abandon them. Swensen's diary was institutional, not personal, yet its clarity set a pattern: define the reason, define the risk, define the boundary. The second case lies in Ethereum's 2022 transition to proof-of-stake. Several London-based crypto funds publicly shared their pre-Merge theses and the criteria that would negate them, including validator participation rates and client diversity. When those criteria held, the funds stayed invested. When peripheral risks emerged—such as MEV concentration—those same diaries provided a map for incremental adjustments. In each case, the documentation anchored decisions to pre-event logic rather than post-event narratives.

A counter-example shows the limitation. During the Terra collapse in May 2022, some funds had extensive documentation but wrote it in such abstract terms that it offered no practical guidance under stress. Phrases like "exit if systemic risk appears" proved useless when systemic risk arrived in multiple forms at once. The reconciliation is simple: a diary cannot substitute for thought. Vague entries give only the illusion of discipline. The page must contain measurable signals, not noble sentiments.

The page also disciplines time. Markets tempt constant revision, but the diary separates reflection from reaction. This separation matters most when the portfolio holds fast-moving digital assets. Documenting decisions at the moment of entry—rather than after a price move—creates a timestamp that resists revisionism. If the thesis states that network fees must rise within six months for the position to remain attractive, then six months later the allocator faces an unambiguous test. The diary presents the question without flattery: *Did it happen or not?* This starkness clarifies the next move.

Documentation influences risk-taking too. A portfolio that distinguishes "core capital" from "experiment capital" can record that divide explicitly. The diary may state, for example, that no more than 10 per cent of the portfolio belongs to high-volatility experimental positions, with the remainder anchored in defined long-term theses. When that boundary is articulated in writing, an impulsive chase becomes harder to justify. The stillness of the page interrupts the impulse. Writing makes drift visible.

The motif of stillness returns when documenting losses. Losses ignite the urge to rewrite memory. Prices fall, and the mind insists it always expected uncertainty. But a diary captures the discomfort honestly. If the entry describes a confident thesis, and its outcome contradicts that confidence, the dissonance teaches. It shows whether the thesis was flawed, the risk ignored, or the trigger undefined. This retrospective clarity sharpens future entries. The allocator begins to write with greater precision because the previous imprecision is preserved, unedited.

The discipline mirrors practices in other domains. Consider the flight logs maintained by commercial pilots, which record every minor irregularity, no matter how uneventful the flight. These logs, used worldwide for decades, allow patterns to emerge that would be invisible from memory alone. The same logic applies to investment diaries. Small notes accumulate into detectable trends: repeated premature exits, recurring overconfidence at entry, or habitual neglect of certain risk factors. The diary becomes a diagnostic instrument.

Documentation can also reveal misalignment between intention and behaviour. If entries repeatedly state that decisions are based on fundamentals, yet trades visibly follow price momentum, the contradiction becomes impossible to ignore. Similarly, if triggers always anticipate action but rarely lead to actual trades, the diary exposes paralysis. These exposures are uncomfortable. They are also invaluable. The act of writing clarifies whether the allocator is acting according to belief or according to mood.

This clarity does not eliminate uncertainty; it frames it. A well-kept diary notes the unknowns at entry. It captures assumptions about market conditions, regulatory shifts, or protocol behaviour. When those assumptions intersect with reality, the allocator can revisit them explicitly. This practice proved particularly useful during the regulatory announcements across the UK and European Union in 2023. Several professional allocators recorded their assumptions about potential stablecoin rules, and when early consultations diverged from those expectations, the diary served as a reference point for reassessment rather than panic.

Yet documentation carries one more implication: it creates accountability to the future self. Each entry is effectively a letter written to someone who will look back, months or years later, and evaluate the soundness of the present moment's thought. That future judgement shapes current clarity. It encourages the allocator to strip out vague hopes and replace them with definable conditions. The diary becomes less a record of actions and more a record of reasoning.

But the tension persists. Documentation offers structure, yet markets still surprise. When a sharp dislocation erupts—an exploit, a liquidity cascade, a regulatory shock—should the allocator follow the written triggers strictly, or override them with fresh interpretation? Should the page's stillness dominate, or should the present moment rewrite the script? The question hangs there, unresolved, challenging every thoughtful investor: when pressure arrives, will you trust the words you wrote in calm, or will you improvise and hope clarity returns later?

Chapter 8
Risk Management You Can Live With

On 6 May 2010, in a quiet corner of the London Stock Exchange's market surveillance room, a junior analyst stared at a screen as the numbers plunged in impossible sequence. The "Flash Crash" was still unfolding in New York, but the shockwaves ran through global order books, wiping nearly a trillion dollars in minutes before snapping back with the same eerie speed. What startled him was not the fall—that had precedents—but the helplessness of watching positions shift beyond the thresholds traders thought they controlled. More than a decade later he would describe the moment as a "lesson in limits": not market limits, but personal ones. Your screen can update in milliseconds; your judgement cannot. The event condensed the theme of this chapter into a single question: *what risks can a person realistically absorb before behaviour—not capital—breaks?*

The same question resurfaced during the chaotic weekend of 10–12 March 2023, when Silicon Valley Bank collapsed in California and liquidity evaporated across several crypto markets. A London-based allocator later recounted that the hardest part was not the loss of stablecoin pegs or the difficulty of moving collateral. It was the cognitive overload. His emergency checklist, drafted months earlier, saved him from flailing: freeze new trades, verify balances, test withdrawals, and wait for credible information. The markets were frantic; he was not. Preparedness served as ballast. That quiet ballast is the recurring motif of this chapter: a weight that stabilises, a countermeasure not against volatility itself but against the human reaction to it.

The paradox at the heart of risk management is that certainty is impossible, yet structure is indispensable. Markets will present shocks no model anticipates: an exchange failure, a protocol exploit, a political edict delivered at midnight. But the mind falters not because surprises occur but because it meets them without pre-committed boundaries. The unbounded portfolio is the brittle portfolio. The unbounded allocator becomes the frantic allocator. The craft of risk management therefore begins not with optimism but with maximum loss—defined, written, committed to—before any capital moves.

In practice, that means recognising that every position carries two exposures: its economic profile and its emotional profile. A 5 per cent drawdown on paper may feel trivial during a calm week and unbearable during a stressed one. Behaviour, not theory, determines survival. This is why the most resilient investors, from Benjamin Graham in 1934 to the UK pension funds navigating the gilt crisis in September 2022, anchored their risk frameworks in personal tolerances rather than abstract ideals. They treated maximum loss as a boundary condition that shapes every action downstream. The tension between aspiration and tolerance is universal; the discipline lies in settling that tension before it is tested.

From that boundary, scenario thinking becomes more than an intellectual exercise. It is an imaginative rehearsal of adversity. The historian Niall Ferguson once wrote that financial crises emerge from a combination of complexity and complacency; scenario thinking breaks complacency by asking vivid, uncomfortable questions. What if your primary exchange freezes withdrawals for 48 hours? What if the protocol you rely on is halted, not hacked? What if a regulator announces a restriction that shrinks liquidity overnight? These scenarios are not predictions but rehearsals. They invite you to plan partial off-ramps, alternative custody arrangements, and redundant communication channels long before any crisis materialises. The ballast grows heavier.

Liquidity, too, must be imagined under stress rather than sampled during calm. Thin markets can become no markets. Historical episodes illustrate this with brutal clarity: during May 2021's market cascade, several mid-cap tokens on European platforms saw their order-book depth evaporate by more than 90 per cent within minutes, turning ordinary exit plans into multi-hour negotiations with slippage and halted books. A robust plan must therefore distinguish between notional liquidity and executable liquidity. It must consider staged selling, time windows, and the subtle friction of fees and taxes—particularly relevant to UK-based investors who must navigate capital gains triggers even in moments of urgency. These frictions are not footnotes; they shape outcomes as surely as price.

The final dimension, and perhaps the most overlooked, is personal constraint. A portfolio is not an abstract object; it is an artefact of a person's time, attentional bandwidth, stress tolerance, and life rhythm. Strategies that look elegant in spreadsheets collapse when they demand constant vigilance or brittle complexity. Many of the catastrophic losses observed during the DeFi boom of 2020–2021 were not caused by poor protocols but by personal mismatch: strategies too complicated for their operators; monitoring demands too high for ordinary weeks; assumptions too fragile for real life. Sometimes the most sophisticated form of risk management is the simplest one: reduce size until the strategy is comfortably sustainable; automate routine checks; build reminders rather than rely on memory. The ballast, again, becomes tangible.

This chapter invites the reader to engage with risk not as a regulatory requirement or technical discipline but as a deeply human negotiation with uncertainty. It links the mechanical—drawdown caps, scenario grids, liquidity maps—to the psychological: the limits of concentration, the contours of fear, the cadence of decision-making under pressure. It asks the reader to examine not only what the portfolio can withstand but what *they* can withstand. These pages trace the practical frameworks that allow investors to stay solvent in spirit as well as capital. They emphasise boundaries over bravado, foresight over reaction, and structure over improvisation.

As you turn the page, a question lingers—a question that no model can answer for you: when the next moment of real pressure arrives, will your decisions rest on ballast you have already built, or will you be forced to construct it in the storm itself?

Define maximum loss first

At 14:32 on 12 March 2020, the price of ether on Bitstamp in Luxembourg fell by more than 40 per cent in a matter of hours, triggering forced liquidations across several platforms. The most infamous dislocation came inside MakerDAO's liquidation auctions, where the system—under severe load—processed bids of effectively zero. One bidder later described winning collateral "for free" while billions in value evaporated for borrowers. The shock was not merely the fall in price; it was the speed with which positions exceeded their operators' limits before those limits had even been articulated. The damage was worsened by a simple fact: most participants had defined their ambitions, but not their maximum loss. *This could ruin me* was recognised only when the ruin was already under way. The silence of unpreparedness speaks loudly.

A related story unfolded in London eight months later. In November 2020, a proprietary trading desk at a regulated firm reported a cumulative drawdown of 17 per cent after a series of misjudged volatility trades. Their internal limit—set during a calm spring—allowed a 20 per cent decline before mandatory position cuts. Those cuts came automatically. According to the subsequent FCA report

(FCA, 2021), adherence to the pre-defined loss boundary prevented substantially larger losses during the winter's turbulent weeks. The rule held. The trader did not. Yet the portfolio survived. The contrast between that episode and the March implosion in the crypto markets reveals the blunt core of this subchapter: survival is not produced by courage or cleverness but by thresholds chosen in advance and obeyed without negotiation. *Draw a line you would defend in your worst hour, not your best.*

Maximum loss is not a philosophical idea; it is a number. More importantly, it is a number chosen before money moves. Every investor knows this in principle. Few act on it in practice. The reason becomes clear when we observe actual behaviour: people commit eagerly to upside scenarios and postpone any confrontation with their downside tolerance. They click "buy" with enthusiasm, then draft risk rules retrospectively—a reversal that ensures those rules reflect anxiety rather than thought. The motif that threads through this chapter—ballast—returns here. Ballast must be installed before the storm. It cannot be improvised mid-swell.

Consider the first major claim: maximum loss defines every decision that follows. Show this through a case. In January 2022, during the LUNA–UST unravelling, several funds in Singapore disclosed that they had imposed portfolio-level drawdown limits of 25–30 per cent for their digital-asset exposure, thresholds documented in compliance notes months earlier. When the de-peg accelerated in May 2022, these funds liquidated positions in stages as their drawdown boundaries were hit. They did not escape losses. But, as reported by MAS filings in late 2022, they avoided the wipeouts suffered by peers whose exposure had no predetermined constraint. **Name** the principle: ex-ante maximum loss. **Explain** it: a pre-set boundary overrides discretionary hesitation when events feel "too extreme to be real." **Implication**: without a defined, written limit, the human mind resorts to hopeful improvisation, which history repeatedly punishes.

Now show another dimension. Maximum loss must be defined at both the portfolio level and the position level. If the former is your hull, the latter are your bulkheads. The UK's Pension Regulator provided a vivid example during the gilt crisis of September 2022. Liability-driven investment strategies were forced to liquidate assets rapidly as yields spiked, and schemes with strictly enforced position-level risk caps weathered the shock materially better than those with vaguely defined tolerances. Their bulkheads held. The rule mattered, not the instrument. Structure over faith.

A counter-example deserves attention: the argument that strict limits may force premature exits during transient volatility. Some fund managers cite March 2009, when equity markets rebounded strongly immediately after hitting long-term drawdown limits. A rigid rule might have locked in losses just before recovery. This critique is credible; one must meet it head-on. The reconciliation is simple but subtle: maximum loss rules protect against ruin, not regret. They are not tools for precision timing but for survival. The investor who enforces a boundary may suffer opportunity cost; the investor who violates it may suffer collapse. Regret is reversible; ruin is not.

The second major claim follows naturally: loss limits must be embedded in visible behaviour, not left as abstract commitments. A boundary written in a notebook is not ballast; it is only ink. Ballast appears in behaviour: reducing allocation size once a threshold is hit; halting new trades when losses exceed a preset figure; communicating breach protocols to any co-managers. The motifs of weight and anchoring matter here. Limits carry weight only when they alter motion. A maximum portfolio drawdown of 20 per cent means nothing unless the investor actually cuts exposure once that line is crossed. That act—the cut—is the visible decision that proves the rule exists.

Historical precedent reinforces this. During the 1998 LTCM collapse in Greenwich, Connecticut, several counterparties survived only because their credit committees had imposed explicit exposure limits to LTCM months earlier. They honoured those limits even as the firm attempted to negotiate wider margins. The decision was unpopular. It was also correct. Their ballast was heavy enough.

The third major claim concerns calibration: maximum loss must fit the human operating the portfolio, not some hypothetical rational actor. A limit that exceeds your psychological capacity is not a limit; it is fantasy. Here the behavioural research is clear. Studies by Barberis, Shleifer and Vishny (1998) and later by Kirchler et al. (2012) show that under stress, investors' tolerance collapses well before their nominal risk budgets do. A maximum drawdown of 30 per cent may be mathematically tolerable yet emotionally intolerable. Calibration therefore begins not with spreadsheets but with a visible behaviour: measure your response to smaller losses first. A person who becomes unsettled at a 5 per cent decline will not maintain composure at 20 per cent. Size must shrink until the boundary becomes believable.

This brings us to the quiet motif of ballast once more. A maximum loss rule is ballast only when it is heavy enough to stabilise but light enough to carry. Too strict, and it paralyses. Too loose, and it fails. The art lies in choosing a weight that steadies rather than sinks.

The fourth major claim: defining maximum loss first allows coherent scenario planning. Without a boundary, scenarios become fantasies; with one, they become decision tools. Ask what happens if an exchange freezes withdrawals for 24 hours. If your position's worst-case loss under that constraint breaches your boundary, size must be cut before entry. Ask what occurs if liquidity thins by 80 per cent during a market cascade, as it did for mid-cap tokens on several European platforms in May 2021. If the slippage required to exit exceeds your tolerable limit, you adjust position size or accept the risk consciously. Boundary → scenario → adjustment. In that order.

Two more examples deepen this principle. In June 2021, the Solana outage revealed a risk underestimated by many arbitrage desks: the impossibility of liquidating positions during a chain halt. Those with strict maximum loss rules revised position sizing models the same week. Similarly, following the FTX collapse in November 2022, funds with documented counterparty-exposure caps survived the liquidity freeze with painful but contained losses. Their caps were the ballast. Once again, behaviour shows the rule.

A limitation persists: maximum loss frameworks assume reasonably continuous markets. Digital-asset markets can break that assumption. During extreme conditions, bid–ask spreads widen dramatically or vanish. A stop-loss becomes an idea, not an executable action. How does one reconcile this? By recognising that boundaries must be adjusted for market structure. In markets capable of sudden air-gaps, limits must be more conservative; position sizing must be smaller; collateral arrangements must be more robust. The principle stands: define the loss boundary first, but define it with structural realism.

Throughout these examples, a deeper implication surfaces: maximum loss is not merely a risk metric but a moral commitment to future self. It is an agreement between your present clarity and your future panic. It is the ballast you build for the version of you who will face fear, confusion, fatigue, or pressure. That person will not have the composure to negotiate new rules. They will need the old ones.

This brings us to documentation. A maximum loss rule should be written, timestamped, and placed where you will see it during stress. A simple sheet suffices: portfolio-level drawdown limit, position-level limit, breach protocol, reduction schedule. The visible ritual of writing amplifies commitment. Behavioural research across domains—from emergency medicine to aviation—shows that written pre-commitment increases adherence under stress by anchoring memory and reducing ambiguity. The ballast becomes tangible because it is recorded.

The subchapter closes with a final motif: the line. Every investor must draw one. But the line is meaningless unless it is drawn before the fog descends. So the unresolved tension remains: what number, what threshold, what boundary would you defend even when markets fall faster than your pulse can keep up? And if the market tests that line tomorrow, would you hold to it—or discover too late that the ballast was never installed?

Scenario thinking

At 09:44 on 8 August 2022, London-based hedge fund Orthogonal Trading informed counterparties that it was freezing certain operations after losses linked to the sudden exploit of the Nomad Bridge. In less than an hour, more than US$190 million in assets had been drained from the cross-chain protocol, and liquidity across associated markets thinned to levels typical of a holiday weekend. The firm's founder later admitted that their internal forecasts had modelled bridge congestion but had not considered bridge failure. A single unimagined scenario—one that seemed too extreme to merit attention—became the hinge on which solvency turned. The absence of structured scenario thinking did not merely blindside a strategy; it rearranged an entire year's trajectory for the team. *One gap in imagination can prove more damaging than ten mistakes in execution.*

A contrasting scene unfolded in Tokyo after the Coincheck theft of January 2018. The exchange halted withdrawals within minutes, but several funds that held assets on the platform had rehearsed exchange-failure scenarios the previous autumn. They had prepared partial off-ramps through secondary venues and cold storage. Their runbooks were simple: if withdrawals are frozen for more than two hours, move exposure elsewhere; if the freeze lasts four hours, cut positions by a specified percentage. These measures did not eliminate losses. They did, however, limit them. The difference was not technological sophistication but forethought: imagining the thing that might break before it does. Those who had practised the uncomfortable exercise of scenario thinking were not surprised by the freeze; they were prepared for it.

The first major claim follows from these scenes: scenario thinking is an investigative discipline, not a pessimistic mood. Show this with a concrete case. When the Solana network experienced a prolonged halt on 14 September 2021, desks across Europe were stuck with open positions they could not adjust. Several firms had modelled high latency but not full stoppage. One Paris-based market-making outfit later described "watching the PnL drift while having no arms." The event named a principle: plausible discontinuity. **Explain** it: when systems depend on continuous operation, one must assume genuine breaks, not just slowdowns. **Implication**: the investor who imagines only mild inconvenience will be undone by true interruption. Scenario thinking widens the menu of what can happen, replacing complacency with structured awareness.

To deepen the principle, consider a second example. During the FTX collapse in November 2022, the most resilient funds were not necessarily the most technologically advanced but those that had rehearsed exchange-insolvency scenarios. Some had staged partial off-ramps across regulated and unregulated venues. Some had charted liquidity maps showing where they would rotate exposure if the main venue failed. Those maps were crude, sometimes handwritten. They worked. Their behaviour exposed the essence of scenario thinking: concrete preparation shaped around imagined stress, not abstract "risk awareness." The ballast laid earlier held as events progressed.

A counter-example is worth grappling with. Some professionals worry that overactive scenario modelling leads to paralysis. They cite the period after the DAO hack in June 2016, when several investors avoided interacting with smart contracts entirely, missing the emergence of viable protocols in 2017. This critique is credible. Excessive caution creates false negatives, steering one away from legitimate opportunities. How should we reconcile this with the need for clear scenario planning? The answer lies in precision. Scenario thinking does not mandate withdrawal; it mandates conditional action. It asks, *If this happens, what will I do?* not *Should I do nothing?* It replaces vague anxiety with specific contingencies. Paralysis arises when scenarios are unbounded; discipline arises when they are discrete.

A second major claim: scenario thinking must be anchored to visible behaviours and real numbers. Vague references to "stress" or "volatility" offer no protection. What protects is a rehearsed sequence tied to thresholds. Take liquidity gaps. In May 2021, several mid-cap digital-asset markets on European exchanges saw spreads widen by more than 300 per cent during a cascade. The investors who fared best were those who had measured slippage under thinner market conditions during the preceding winter, allowing them to scale positions so that even a widening spread did not breach their predetermined loss boundaries. This illustrates the motif of edges. Scenario edges—boundaries tested in simulation—give structure to moments when live markets lose structure.

Regulatory shock forms the next plank. A clear example came on 16 February 2022 when India's proposed crypto taxation framework became public. Overnight, domestic volumes fell by more than 30 per cent (data: CREBACO, 2022). Funds with Indian counterparties that had modelled a regulatory hard-stop moved exposure to offshore venues early; those without such preparation faced a sudden collapse in local liquidity. The phenomenon named here is asymmetry: regulatory announcements often hit suddenly and change trading conditions immediately. **Explain**: the time to plan the response is before the announcement, not after. **Implication**: scenario thinking includes drafting a response to regulatory scenarios that might never occur. The cost of drafting is tiny; the cost of hesitation can be disproportionate.

Yet regulatory events also supply the counterpoint: many announced measures soften or reverse after consultations. The UK Treasury's approach to stablecoin regulation in April 2023 began with strong language but evolved materially by October. Should one model every ominous consultation as a crisis? No. The reconciliation lies in proportion: prepare for sharply negative outcomes, but scale preparation to likelihood. A plausible scenario deserves a plan; a distant one may deserve only awareness.

Third claim: scenario thinking must integrate operational risk, not just market risk. Protocol hacks, withdrawal halts, oracle distortions, validator failures—these events shape the liquidity and pricing environment in ways that break standard assumptions. The 2022 Wormhole exploit, which drained US$320 million, revealed how quickly cross-chain liquidity becomes fragmented when trust—measured here in bridge throughput and validator votes—evaporates. A scenario plan that assumes uniform liquidity across venues fails on contact with this kind of fracture. Investors who had rehearsed bridge-failure scenarios shifted assets to native chains before contagion spread. Those who had not were locked inside temporarily impaired ecosystems.

Operational failure became even clearer during the Celsius freeze on 12 June 2022. Withdrawals stopped. Communication slowed. On-chain data showed customers attempting frantic swaps to less encumbered assets. Some succeeded because they had maintained partial off-ramps—small allocations in more liquid tokens on alternative venues. Others could not because all their assets sat within a single platform. The visible behaviour marks the distinction: distributing operational pathways is not diversification for decoration; it is scenario thinking expressed in architecture.

The fourth major claim: scenario thinking sharpens decision-making under uncertainty by surfacing fragilities early. When an investor imagines a scenario—say, an exchange outage of twelve hours—they must simulate the timeline. What would they do at minute 10? At hour 2? At hour 9? Who must be informed? What collateral moves become impossible? What alternative routes exist? The scenario becomes real enough to reveal weak points. This is where the motif of edges returns. Edges show where constraints bite: thin liquidity at certain times of day; reliance on a single stablecoin; exposure to assets whose redemption windows are infrequent or manually gated.

Two further examples clarify. During the 2020 Black Thursday events, Ethereum gas fees in London soared above 200 gwei within minutes, making rapid repositioning impossible for retail and institutional users alike. Some had anticipated fee spikes but had not considered fee spikes *coinciding* with collateral calls. Their scenario map lacked intersection. By contrast, those who had rehearsed combined-stress scenarios—high volatility plus high fees—adjusted earlier. Similarly, during the Arbitrum Sequencer outage in January 2022, investors who had modelled L2 sequencer failures bridged liquidity out before queues formed. Their preparation was not foresight; it was practice.

A limitation surfaces: no scenario map captures everything. Reality is always stranger. Some events combine in ways no model anticipates. This limitation is real and must be acknowledged. But it does not invalidate scenario thinking. It simply shifts the emphasis: the purpose is not perfect coverage but preparedness for families of events. If you plan for an exchange freeze, you also become partially prepared for a wallet service outage. If you plan for a 12-hour chain halt, you are better prepared for a 6-hour congestion window. Scenario thinking enlarges the imagination, which enlarges the margin for error.

The fifth claim: scenario thinking must be iterative. It is not a one-off exercise but a rhythm. Markets evolve. Infrastructure matures. Attack surfaces shift. New regulations emerge. Scenarios written in 2021 may be irrelevant by 2023. This is where the motif of edges transforms again: edges move. A liquidity edge shifts when a stablecoin loses a key banking partner; a regulatory edge shifts when a jurisdiction changes supervision priorities; an operational edge shifts when a new validator set expands. Scenario thinking therefore demands periodic revision, not to accumulate more detail but to update the map to a changing terrain.

Documentation fortifies this process. A scenario sheet—listing stresses, triggers, and planned actions—acts as a record of what your past self believed prudent. When a scenario is rehearsed, the sheet evolves. When a new incident occurs in the market, the sheet absorbs the lesson. This practice mirrors the aviation industry's incident reporting frameworks, where every near-miss informs future protocols. The structure matters: write the scenario, write the trigger, write the action.

This subchapter must end with a tension rather than an answer. Scenario thinking clarifies; it also complicates. It forces you to confront the fragility you would rather ignore. It strengthens resilience while exposing weakness. The unresolved question is simple and sharp: which scenarios are you willing to imagine before reality forces them upon you—and which ones do you avoid because they feel inconvenient or implausible? The map exists only if you draw it. The edge matters only if you look at it.

Liquidity and exit planning

At 02:16 UTC on 12 March 2020, as global markets convulsed, the decentralised exchange dYdX recorded slippage levels in certain mid-cap pairs exceeding 20 per cent within minutes. A London-based proprietary desk attempting to exit a £4 million position in a thinly traded token saw its execution split into dozens of fragments, with the final fills arriving almost 7 per cent below the volume-weighted price logged at the start of the unwind. The trader later recalled watching the order book "shrink to a postcard." It was not a failure of intent. It was a failure of preparation. Liquidity evaporated too quickly, the exits were too narrow, and the plan—such as it was—had been written for calmer waters. *Thin markets punish the unprepared.*

A different outcome emerged during the volatility spike surrounding Terra's collapse in May 2022. An asset manager in Singapore, holding a substantial position in a related derivative token, activated a staged-selling blueprint drafted in February. It specified three tranches, each triggered by concrete signals: widening spreads on Binance, a 15 per cent one-hour move in the underlying asset, and a drop in cross-venue depth monitored through Kaiko data. The team did not escape losses; no plan could have erased them. Yet by spreading exits over hours rather than minutes, they achieved an average execution nearly 9 per cent better than peers who rushed for the gates. The contrast marked the core truth: liquidity is not found; it is prepared for.

The first claim follows from these scenes: liquidity risk is behavioural before it is mathematical. Show it plainly. When market depth thins, behaviour shifts. Traders pull limit orders. Market makers widen spreads or go flat. Retail flows surge in one direction. This behaviour—visible in order-book snapshots, not abstract sentiment—creates the conditions in which exits become expensive. Name it: *slippage mechanics*. Explain it: slippage is the gap between the intended price and the executed price, driven not by malice but by the imbalance between size and depth. Implication: without an exit plan, you are captive to the behaviour of others at precisely the moment you most need autonomy.

A second claim emerges from a historical anchor. During the Mt. Gox crisis in February 2014, liquidity did not simply dry up; it stratified by venue. Withdrawal halts produced a two-price world: one visible on the exchange, another on OTC desks in London and Hong Kong. Investors who had mapped exit alternatives beforehand—OTC brokers, cross-venue transfers, or partial hedges—reduced their effective loss by locating the deepest pools available. Those who had relied solely on the dominant venue had no alternatives when that venue froze. The event named a principle: *venue concentration is a single point of failure*. Explain it: liquidity is not homogenous; it pools unevenly. Implication: exit planning begins with mapping where liquidity resides—not where you wish it to be.

Next claim: exit plans must take seriously the physics of thin markets. Consider the behaviour of liquidity on decentralised exchanges. During the Sushiswap exploit of September 2020, liquidity providers withdrew capital in real time, shrinking pools by more than 50 per cent within hours. Slippage increased in direct proportion. The visible metric—depth at 1 per cent price impact—collapsed. Investors who had previously measured that metric under stress conditions had trimmed their positions earlier; those who had not discovered too late how shallow a nominally large pool can become. The motif appears: *narrow passages*. Exits are narrow passages that remain passable only if approached before the crowd arrives.

Introduce a counter-example to test the claim. A few argue that deep, high-volume assets require little exit planning because their liquidity survives shocks. Bitcoin during the late 2020 rally, for instance, often displayed billions in daily traded volume on major venues, even as volatility rose. Why bother planning exits in markets that rarely freeze? The argument contains a kernel of truth: deeper markets cushion size. But the limitation is structural. Even highly liquid assets can experience momentary dysfunction. During the Coinbase outage of 29 January 2021, BTC spreads widened noticeably and execution quality fell as millions attempted to trade simultaneously. The reconciliation is clear: depth protects, but only against *ordinary* stress. Exit planning protects against extraordinary stress.

A further claim: exit risk is inseparable from time. The behaviour of a market at 3 p.m. differs from the behaviour at 3 a.m. A study by Glassnode (2022) showed that liquidity across major spot pairs tends to be up to 40 per cent thinner during low-participation hours, especially weekends. Show this dynamic. A trader attempting to exit a £250,000 position in a mid-cap token at 05:00 UTC will often face half the available depth compared with 15:00 UTC. Name it: *circadian liquidity cycles*. Explain: liquidity follows human activity patterns, even in global markets. Implication: exit planning must consider *when* you may need to sell, not just *how much*.

The next claim concerns the second motif: *friction*. Friction is not just fees; it is every impediment between intent and execution. Show it through concrete behaviour. During the Polygon network congestion in December 2021, gas fees spiked enough to delay rebalancing and hinder rapid exits. Some investors paid the fees; others hesitated. That hesitation increased losses. Name it: *execution drag*. Explain: when leaving a position requires multiple on-chain steps—approvals, swaps, bridging—each step multiplies the friction. Implication: an exit plan must audit friction in advance: how many clicks, how many signatures, how many dependencies stand between you and the door.

A second example reinforces this. The Avalanche rush of late 2021 brought immense capital to the ecosystem, yet liquidity remained clustered in a handful of pools. When one of these pools briefly malfunctioned due to a pricing misalignment in October, exits slowed dramatically. Investors unaware of the dependency map—how one pool relied on another—were surprised. Those who had documented dependencies sold earlier or hedged exposure.

The difference was not intelligence but preparation. The behaviour that matters is simple: *map before you move.*

A credible limitation surfaces. Some argue that staged exits risk leaving money on the table in fast rebounds. If you sell in tranches and the market recovers after the first tranche, you may realise unnecessary losses. This argument holds in markets that snap back rapidly. But it collapses under the weight of tail events, when rebounds are slow, messy, or absent. The reconciliation: staged exits are not designed to optimise profit; they are designed to prevent catastrophe. They trade perfection for survivability.

The next claim: good exit planning requires rehearsing stress in numbers, not metaphors. Show it. If you hold £100,000 of a token with 24-hour depth of £1.2 million at a 2 per cent price impact, you can exit roughly 8 per cent of daily depth before moving the market beyond your tolerance. Name this metric: *exit load.* Explain: exit load quantifies how much your position burdens the market. Implication: if your exit load exceeds your tolerance for slippage, reduce size or redesign the plan.

The third motif arises here: *windows.* Exits happen in windows—brief intervals when liquidity is adequate and infrastructure stable. The Lunar New Year volatility spikes in January 2021 demonstrated this in Hong Kong and Singapore, where local flows briefly dried up. Investors who viewed liquidity as continuous suffered; those who treated it as windows—fleeting but identifiable—navigated better. Planning begins with identifying these windows:

typical hours of depth, typical times of stress, typical bottlenecks.

Revisit operational risk. A brilliant exit plan fails if the exit cannot be executed. Exchange halts, wallet outages, chain congestion, bridge failures—each can block exits. Show the behavioural consequence: during the Binance smart chain halt in March 2022, investors queued transactions for hours, watching prices drift. Name the structural phenomenon: *operational choke points*. Explain: a market may be liquid on paper but inaccessible in practice. Implication: exit plans must include offline routes—alternative venues, different assets, or partial hedges—that bypass the choke.

Now bring in the counterpoint: over-engineering the exit plan can create paralysis. If a plan becomes so complex that it requires constant updates, the friction of maintenance outweighs the benefit. The reconciliation lies in scope. An exit plan should be robust but simple: staged, conditional, documented. Complexity is a risk in itself.

The article's arc approaches its close with the motif of windows narrowed. In real markets, windows shut without warning. That truth forces a forward test: *If your main exit window closed in the next hour, what would you use instead?* A second test follows: *If slippage doubled tomorrow, which positions would you reduce first, and why?* These questions mark the unresolved tension: liquidity is a shape-shifter. It rewards foresight and punishes convenience. The exits exist—if you chart them before you need them.

Personal constraints

At 05:47 on 15 November 2022 in Manchester, a software engineer named Daniel Patel closed his exchange dashboard after realising he had forgotten, for the third time that month, to unwind a leveraged position he had opened during a burst of optimism. The cost of this lapse—£12,480 in forced-liquidation losses—did not stem from market cruelty alone. It stemmed from the gulf between the complexity of the strategy he attempted to run and the thin margins of time and attention his actual life afforded him. He later admitted that the position required "four check-ins a day", yet he often managed one. His plan silently demanded more from him than he was able to pay. The market simply collected the difference.

Contrast this with a small family office in Edinburgh that, during the same frantic month, avoided a similar fate. Its principal had configured a simple automation in September: timed reminders for position reviews every 48 hours and alerts for price deviations exceeding 8 per cent in any holding. When the November volatility spike hit, the alerts arrived before the damage did. No drama, no scramble, no overnight shock. Automation had acted as a proxy for attention, and this substitution worked only because the strategy itself was built to tolerate the limits of its operator. The office did not try to outwit panic; it tried to outwit overcommitment.

These two scenes reveal a first claim: every investment approach has a hidden cost coded not in money but in cognitive load. Show it. A strategy that requires hourly checks, cross-chain monitoring, and rapid-fire reactions demands bandwidth. Name it: *attentional debt*. Explain: attentional debt accrues when strategies ask for more vigilance than their owners can sustainably deliver. Implication: unless the strategy is sized and simplified to match the investor's real life rather than their imagined capacity, the debt eventually comes due—with interest.

The motif here is clear: *life at the margins*. Everyone has margins: the slivers of time between meetings, the bandwidth left after caring for family, the energy available after long shifts. Strategies that respect these margins endure. Those that ignore them collapse under their own procedural weight.

A second claim follows from historical precedent. Benjamin Graham, lecturing at Columbia in 1955, warned students to "separate the work you can do consistently from the work you can do only when fresh." This distinction still applies to digital markets. Show it through behaviour. A London consultant with two young children tried to replicate an arbitrage strategy she had run successfully during lockdown, when her schedule was fluid. In late 2021, the same strategy failed—not because she had become less skilful, but because the windows she once relied upon had vanished. Name this mismatch: *temporal drift*. Explain: when personal rhythms shift—new job, new city, new responsibilities—the viability of certain strategies shifts too.

Implication: the strategy must adapt to the person, not the person to the strategy.

Next, introduce the role of smaller size. Size shapes stress. Show it with a concrete metric. A £100,000 position that swings 12 per cent in a day moves £12,000. The same position at £20,000 moves £2,400. The emotional difference between those numbers is not linear. Name it: *stress amplitude*. Explain: stress amplitude measures the psychological load of variance. Implication: if variance at current size breaches your capacity to think clearly, the size—not the market—is the problem.

The motif of *life at the margins* emerges again. When size overwhelms the margins of attention or emotional tolerance, decisions degrade. A study by Kumar and Lim (2020) showed that retail investors experiencing real-world stress—such as work overload or health issues—were more likely to make abrupt, loss-magnifying trades during periods of high volatility. Behaviour leaves traces. Unable to check positions regularly, they reacted late. Unable to absorb swings calmly, they cut winners and rode losers. The market punished misalignment between personal constraints and structural design.

Introduce a counter-example to test the claim. Some argue that discipline can outmuscle personal limits. If you simply "try harder," they say, you can run complex strategies even when busy. Show where this logic fails. A hedge fund analyst in New York attempted to maintain a multi-chain yield strategy requiring daily compounding and manual migrations in 2021. Despite an iron commitment, she missed several optimal windows due to work deadlines. The reconciliation is simple: discipline is finite; constraints are not. Complexity, when it runs ahead of available hours, wins that contest every time.

A new claim emerges: attention, not capital, is the scarce resource. Show this through a concrete moment. During the Solana network congestion in February 2022, transactions slowed dramatically. Investors who could dedicate full days to monitoring the chain found workarounds. Those with demanding jobs could not. Name the asymmetry: *attention arbitrage*. Explain: some strategies reward those who can babysit the market. Implication: unless your schedule allows for this arbitrage, avoid strategies dependent on constant supervision.

Return to automation as a way of expanding the margins. Automation is a tool, not a substitute for judgement. Show the behaviour of a private investor in Bristol who configured simple triggers in May 2023: automated emails for portfolio drift above 6 per cent, alerts for protocol announcements, and a weekly digest summarising position health. This system reduced her oversight burden by half. Name this design choice: *delegated vigilance*. Explain: delegated vigilance does not eliminate the need for decisions; it ensures that decisions are prompted at the right time. Implication: automation amplifies discipline only when used to reinforce a simple, stable strategy.

Add a second example. A quantitative crypto fund in Zurich implemented an automated "cool-off" rule in mid-2022 after noticing that human traders made more mistakes between 01:00 and 04:00 local time. The system now blocks discretionary trades during those hours unless two team members override the lock. Behaviour improved. Losses from fatigue-driven trades dropped. The lesson is not about machines; it is about constraints. Traders designed the rule because they recognised their limits as biological, not ideological.

Address a credible limitation. Automation can fail. Alerts can misfire, APIs can break, and platforms can stall. Should investors trust automation at all? Show where the scepticism is justified. During the API disruption on Coinbase in March 2023, some users received delayed alerts. But the reconciliation lies in design: automation supports discipline; it does not replace it. The core plan remains human-led. Automation is scaffolding, not structure.

Another claim: the complexity of a strategy must be inversely proportional to the stability of the investor's life. Show it. A PhD researcher in Oxford, writing a thesis, attempted a multi-protocol yield rotation strategy with daily compounding. Her research deadlines spiked. The strategy failed. She simplified to two holdings and monthly reviews. Performance stabilised because the system now matched her available attention. Name this principle: *constraint-aligned design*. Explain: designing with constraints—time, stress, attention—produces resilience.

Implication: a modest strategy executed consistently beats an ornate strategy executed sporadically.

Now bring in geographical and temporal context. Time zones shape constraints. A market that moves most violently during Asian hours may be easier for a trader in Hong Kong to monitor than one in Leeds. Show this dynamic. A trader in Sydney thriving on New York volatility eventually relocated to London in 2021. Overnight became daytime; the strategy collapsed. Name the misfit: *chronological dislocation*. Explain: markets pulse on their own clocks; investors pulse on theirs. Implication: choose strategies whose pulse you can keep.

The motif returns: *life at the margins*. Real life imposes friction—meetings, childcare, illness, travel, holidays, fatigue. These frictions are predictable in aggregate even if unpredictable in detail. A strategy that assumes uninterrupted vigilance is a strategy built for a person who does not exist. Markets accept no excuses for such mismatches.

A further claim: personal stress tolerance is a structural parameter, not a moral failing. Show it through a behavioural metric. During a volatile fortnight in June 2022, a digital-asset adviser in Dublin tracked his own reactions to daily swings. He noted that when losses exceeded £6,000 in a single day, his sleep and decision-making deteriorated. He reduced his maximum position size until daily swings rarely exceeded £3,000. His performance improved. Name this calibration: *emotional risk budget*. Explain: the emotional risk budget measures the level of daily variance an investor can experience without behavioural deterioration. Implication: setting position limits according to this budget preserves clarity.

Introduce a final counter-example. A wealthy investor in Dubai insisted that stress tolerance was irrelevant because he could "afford to lose it all." Yet when faced with a rapid £300,000 drawdown during the FTX collapse in November 2022, he panicked and exited at the bottom. The limitation of wealth is evident: financial capacity does not guarantee emotional capacity. The reconciliation: stress tolerance is personal, not proportional to portfolio size.

As the subchapter nears its end, return to the motif once more. Strategies must breathe within the margins of a person's life. They must fit the real calendar, the real bandwidth, the real mood. Precision comes from respect for those boundaries.

This leaves a forward test, unresolved by design. If your life became twice as busy tomorrow, which of your positions could you still manage without error? And a second: if your attention were halved for a month, which strategies would fail first, and why? Those questions name the tension that no model resolves: strategies succeed only when the person running them remains able, willing, and present.

Chapter 9
Signals, Research, and Noise

At 08:12 on a damp March morning in 2021, a young analyst at a fintech firm in Shoreditch opened two tabs that told opposite stories. One showed a token surging 40 per cent overnight, fuelled by GIF-heavy endorsements from half a dozen influencers. The other—an explorer dashboard he trusted—revealed stagnant active addresses, no new contracts deployed, and a liquidity pool that had barely moved since the previous quarter. He stared at the contradiction for a long minute. Two worlds, two narratives, one asset. One of them had to be lying, yet both claimed to show the truth. The question that hung in the air felt larger than the trade itself: *How do you decide what is real when the data, the commentary, and the incentives all point in different directions?*

This tension is not new. In 1637, as the tulip trade in Amsterdam reached its feverish peak, pamphlets circulated with breathless claims about rare bulbs changing hands for the price of a canal house. Yet municipal records from Haarlem show that many of the supposed sales never settled. The signal was dressed in the theatre of certainty, but the ledger told another story. Markets have always produced noise; the digital economy merely accelerates it. We receive more data, more opinions, more dashboards, more "breaking news," and more recycled insights than any generation before us. But abundance does not mean clarity. More inputs can just as easily mean more distortion.

A modern investor must learn to operate like a field researcher: attentive, sceptical, precise, and deeply aware of how narratives form. The chapter ahead examines this discipline, not as a set of academic methods, but as a lived craft—one that blends structured inquiry with practical restraint. Information is only useful to the extent that it informs action; action is only wise to the extent that it rests on genuine understanding. The goal is not to predict the future. It is to judge the present more honestly than the crowd.

Central to this craft is the design of an information diet. The phrase sounds quaint until you watch an investor derail months of work because a single viral thread hijacked their attention. Digital markets reward those who curate rather than consume. Reading a whitepaper is not a moral virtue; it is a technical choice. Sometimes a project's documentation genuinely reveals intent, governance, and economic design. Sometimes it offers little more than decorative jargon wrapped around circular claims. The skill lies in knowing when a primary source adds clarity and when it merely adds obligations. Explorers—those dashboards that track tokens, addresses, liquidity, emissions—offer another layer of truth, though they too can mislead when read without context. And amid all this, independent analysts provide an essential counterweight: individuals and small teams with nothing to sell, no tokens to pump, and an obsessive interest in the texture of data. They do not eliminate bias, but they dilute it.

Yet even a well-balanced intake is not enough without structure. This is where checklists and heuristics earn their keep. A good checklist is not a bureaucratic device; it is an anchor. It cuts through mood, hype, and fatigue by forcing us to revisit the same core questions with fresh eyes. *What problem? Which users? Why a token at all?* The repetition is the point. When markets accelerate and narratives mutate, a checklist keeps the decision-maker grounded in first principles. Heuristics add a complementary layer: patterns, cues, and rules of thumb refined through observation. They cannot guarantee truth, but they can guard against illusion.

This discipline gains urgency when we confront metrics theatre. Digital markets specialise in it. High transaction counts that reflect bots pinging between wallets. Decentralised exchange volumes inflated through wash trading. User numbers padded with airdrop farmers cycling thousands of wallets through identical sequences. It is theatre in the strict sense: a performance designed to evoke emotion rather than reflect reality. A seasoned investor learns to cross-verify, comparing sources that have no incentive to agree. When Chainalysis, a regulated analytics firm, reports declining genuine activity while an unverified dashboard claims exponential growth, the divergence itself becomes data. It tells you where to look next, and what questions to ask.

But perhaps the most counterintuitive skill in the chapter is the simplest: knowing when to do nothing. Sitting out is a decision, not a failure of nerve. Periods of conflicting signals—surging prices with collapsing fundamentals, or vibrant fundamentals with stalling prices—are the moments when impulsive action does the most damage. Waiting is not passive; it is a strategic posture. The historian Niall Ferguson once remarked that the hardest part of managing risk is "resisting the urge to intellectualise noise." Silence, when chosen deliberately, clears the fog.

Every section of this chapter builds towards one claim: that judgement emerges from the interplay of curiosity and restraint. Curiosity drives us to gather evidence, explore contradictory views, and interrogate narratives. Restraint forces us to weigh each fragment rather than chase every lead. Digital markets punish those who rush to act and reward those who learn to pace themselves. The challenge is to cultivate an inner barometer that distinguishes between a genuine shift and a temporary echo.

As you move deeper into the chapter, you will encounter a set of tools—diet, checklists, heuristics, verification techniques, and the discipline of inaction—that together form a coherent approach to research. Each tool helps you see a little more clearly, reason a little more honestly, and act a little more deliberately. None of them removes uncertainty. Instead, they help you live with uncertainty without surrendering to distortion.

The chapter opens the door to a quieter, more grounded way of thinking—one that resists spectacle and seeks the signal beneath the noise. The real question, as ever, is not what the market is saying, but how you choose to listen.

Information diet

In June 2017, the U.S. Securities and Exchange Commission released its investigative report on *The DAO*, detailing how a vulnerability in its smart contract code enabled an attacker to divert 3.6 million ETH. The event shook the market, but what followed was just as revealing. Commentators on Reddit proclaimed the end of Ethereum. Influencers on YouTube declared it a temporary hiccup. Developers on GitHub posted blunt, technical assessments that cut through the hysteria. Three narratives. Three levels of depth. One underlying reality, visible only to those who knew where to look. The episode marked a turning point: it showed how a person's information diet can determine not just their understanding, but their survival.

During those same days, reports from ConsenSys in Brooklyn (June 2017) carefully mapped the incident's mechanics, contrasting sharply with the speculative claims that dominated Twitter. The distance between those sources exposed a structural problem in digital markets: the loudest signals tend to be the least reliable. A balanced investor learns that truth rarely lives in the noisiest corner. It hides in primary material, in data explorers that report what actually happened on-chain, and in the work of independent analysts who investigate patterns without performance theatre. Noise seduces because it is easy. Signal demands effort.

The motif here is simple: choose your inputs with the same care you choose your positions. An unfiltered feed is not information; it is stimulus. And stimulus without structure produces confusion. The person who read *The DAO* contract directly saw a recursive call vulnerability. The person who relied solely on commentary saw a crisis of confidence. The former had a map. The latter had a mood. Mood moves quickly; maps last longer.

A strong information diet begins by showing the difference between a source that reports an event and a source that interprets it. Primary sources—whitepapers, audits, GitHub repositories—reveal the anatomy of a system. When the Bitcoin whitepaper appeared under the pseudonym Satoshi Nakamoto in October 2008, it offered nine pages of architecture, incentives, and constraints. It did not need to persuade. It needed to describe. Naming such documents as the backbone of inquiry shifts the reader from passively receiving narratives to actively evaluating design. The implication is clear: those who read selectively but deeply gain a sustainable edge over those who skim endlessly but remember nothing.

Explorers provide another lens. Etherscan, founded in Kuala Lumpur in 2015, and Solscan, launched in 2021, show concrete behaviours: contract deployments, validator performance, token flows. When activity spikes on a network but unique addresses remain flat, or when a protocol claims rapid adoption yet its contract interactions fall week by week, the discrepancy serves as a compass. It guides further research. Visible behaviour trumps persuasive language. Explorers are not perfect—they can misclassify contracts or struggle with obfuscation—but they anchor judgment in observable data, not narratives.

Independent analysts form the third pillar. Their work often lacks the polish of institutional reports but compensates with candour and domain obsession. When a pseudonymous researcher such as Hasu published analyses of MEV dynamics in 2020, he offered rigorous models long before major firms took the topic seriously. When Nic Carter mapped Bitcoin mining energy use in 2021, he provided reconciled datasets, methodological notes, and explicit limitations. These examples show how independent voices can outpace institutions, not through marketing reach but through intellectual honesty. Yet the limitation is obvious: independence guarantees neither correctness nor continuity. Analysts make mistakes, disappear, or shift incentives. A balanced information diet accepts their fallibility while valuing their insight.

A credible counter-example helps clarify this balance. During the 2022 collapse of FTX, many seasoned traders followed a handful of prominent Twitter accounts for hourly updates. Some of those accounts correctly reported liquidity holes. Others repeated unverified claims that fuelled confusion. The limitation was structural: relying heavily on influencers concentrates informational risk. The reconciliation is movement towards triangulation—treating influencer commentary as a prompt, not a verdict, and verifying it through primary sources and explorers before acting.

The decision to diversify inputs is not an abstraction. It appears in visible behaviour: bookmarking audits rather than reaction threads; saving a whitepaper to annotate rather than relying on a summary; checking contract interactions before forming an opinion; rereading a project's token distribution instead of trusting a circulated infographic. Each of these actions slows the pace of reaction and increases the depth of understanding. The motif returns: simplicity over stimulus.

Another practical distinction lies in reading whitepapers selectively. Not all documents deserve full attention. Some projects publish comprehensive architectures—MakerDAO's early collateral model in 2017, for instance—while others release ornamental manifestos devoid of measurable commitments. The skill is in identifying which sections matter: economics, incentives, governance mechanisms, upgrade paths. A good information diet does not reward completionism; it rewards discernment. The reader measures which pages change their understanding and discards the rest.

A further implication emerges when considering metrics theatre. When a dashboard shows improbable trading volume from a new decentralised exchange, a person with a disciplined information diet does not accept the figure at face value. They compare it with token flows on Chainalysis (2022), verify liquidity on-chain, and examine the distribution of unique addresses to detect bursts of wash trading. Cross-verification turns noise into context. It is work, but it is not complicated work. It is the intellectual equivalent of washing produce before eating it.

This discipline extends beyond data to the rhythm of consumption. High-frequency information—feeds, alerts, "breaking news"—demands constant vigilance. Low-frequency information—audits, governance proposals, economic models—builds durable judgment. A balanced diet mixes both but elevates the long half-life material. It demands that attention become deliberate. This is where influence becomes visible. When a reader notices that their mood shifts with each social post, it is a signal of informational imbalance. When they notice they have not opened a block explorer in a week, it is another signal. These small observations form the backbone of self-correction.

Historical examples also illuminate the stakes. During the 2016 Ethereum fork debate in Berlin and online, the people who read the Improvement Proposals (EIPs) understood the technical and philosophical arguments underpinning the split. Those who relied on commentary often framed the debate as a personality conflict rather than a governance decision. The same pattern reappeared with Bitcoin's SegWit activation in August 2017: the people who read BIP141 could articulate why signature data mattered; the people who watched influencers argued about ideology. Reading primary material reduces the distance between what is said and what is true.

The quiet motif returns again: curation as discipline. A curated diet limits exposure to distortion, just as a well-designed portfolio limits exposure to concentration. The implication is profound. People do not merely consume information; information shapes what they see, how they decide, and what they believe about risk. Every unchecked source plants assumptions that later appear as conviction. Every verified source plants understanding that later appears as clarity.

The counterfactual helps sharpen the case. Imagine two individuals assessing the same emerging protocol. One reads the whitepaper, inspects wallet distribution on an explorer, and reviews two independent analyses. The other watches three influencer videos. Both think they have done "research." Only one has extracted signal. The difference will not show immediately, but it will show inevitably—when market conditions shift, when narratives change, or when a protocol's underlying mechanics face stress.

The unresolved tension at the centre of the information diet remains this: how much is enough? Too little information leads to naive decisions. Too much information overwhelms. The art lies in setting boundaries—who to follow, what to read, which tools to trust, and when to stop. A person must ask: *Does this input sharpen judgment or blur it? Does it show behaviour or perform it? Is it a map or a mood?* The next step depends on the answer.

Checklists and heuristics

On 30 October 1935, at Wright Field in Dayton, Ohio, a prototype Boeing Model 299 bomber lifted off, climbed sharply, stalled, and fell from the sky. Two of the five crew members died, including the Army's chief test pilot, Major Ployer P. Hill. The aircraft was not underpowered or badly built; it was, as one reporter put it, "too much aeroplane for one man to fly." There were simply too many steps in the cockpit. Experienced pilots had relied on memory. Memory failed. In the investigation that followed, test pilots did something quietly revolutionary: they drew up a pilot's checklist for take-off, flight, landing, and taxiing. A single sheet of paper, clipped to a board, turned an unmanageable machine into something flyable.

That small artefact—a list of mundane questions—became the scaffolding for an entire discipline. Decades later, Atul Gawande's work with the World Health Organization would demonstrate that a basic surgical safety checklist, introduced in 2008 and tested in eight hospitals from Toronto to Delhi, cut major complications and deaths by double-digit percentages (WHO, 2009). Again, it was not knowledge that changed, but process. People became willing to externalise steps they already "knew" so that they would not forget them under pressure. The list on the wall did not replace expertise; it protected it.

Digital markets generate a different kind of cockpit. No switches. No levers. Yet the cognitive load is similar: multiple protocols, overlapping risks, competing narratives, constant noise. It is "too much market" for one memory to hold. The motif of the small sheet of paper—physical or digital—returns here. A checklist of well-chosen questions can be the difference between coherent judgement and improvisation disguised as conviction.

The first claim is straightforward: checklists are not signs of inexperience; they are the tools of people who take complexity seriously. Show this in behaviour. A London-based allocator, running a concentrated portfolio of eight digital assets, keeps a one-page sheet on his desk with three headings: problem, users, token. Before entering any new position, he forces himself to write three short answers: *What problem is this solving? Which users adopt it first? Why does a token need to exist here at all?* If he cannot fill the boxes in plain language, no trade. He calls it his "three doors". Nothing passes without walking through all three.

Name this function: cognitive guardrail. The checklist does not discover hidden alpha; it prevents the most obvious errors—funding projects with no problem, backing tools with no users, or buying tickers whose token is ornamental. Explain the mechanism: under stress, our memory selectively recalls flattering facts and forgets awkward gaps. The checklist blocks that move by insisting on the same questions every time. The implication is sharp: if you will not subject an idea to your own standard questions, you have already chosen story over structure.

The second claim: checklists are only as powerful as the questions they contain, and those questions should emerge from mistakes made and lessons learned, not from abstract theory. Consider a concrete example. After the 2020 "DeFi Summer", a small fund in Zurich reviewed its worst investment: a lending protocol that collapsed after a governance attack. The post-mortem produced three painful discoveries. They had never checked who held veto rights, never asked how easy it was to alter collateral parameters, and never examined delegate participation. Their revised governance checklist now begins with: *Who can change the rules overnight? How hard is it for them to do so? Who would object, and how loudly could they object?* The questions are not philosophical; they are pointed. They grew out of loss.

A second example comes from a family office in Singapore that lost a meaningful sum in a project whose emissions schedule was aggressively front-loaded. Their new checklist includes a blunt line: *Show the unlock calendar. Who is selling into me?* Every new position is now forced through that lens. The checklist turned an abstract warning about "dilution risk" into a concrete behaviour: never fund a token without seeing its unlocks on a calendar.

A credible counter-example needs to be faced. In aviation and medicine, critics sometimes argue that checklists can become bureaucratic theatre—boxes ticked perfunctorily, questions read without thought. The same danger exists in investment. A person can recite "What problem? Which users? Why token?" as a mantra while ignoring the fact that their answers are vague or circular. A checklist cannot make someone honest. The reconciliation lies in intent. A living checklist is revised, argued over, pruned. A dead one is copied and never questioned. The tool is not at fault; the commitment behind it is.

The quiet motif of the sheet of paper returns here. A real checklist is slightly uncomfortable to use because it occasionally blocks something you would like to do. That friction is the point. If your list never tells you "stop", it is decoration, not discipline.

The third claim concerns heuristics: those compact rules of thumb that compress experience into quick tests. Where checklists slow you down to ensure you have not forgotten something, heuristics speed you up to ensure you do not overcomplicate the obvious. Take the heuristic some quant desks use when glancing at a new protocol's tokenomics: *if I cannot explain in thirty seconds who pays whom, and for what, I have no business funding this.* The visible behaviour is a short verbal explanation to a colleague. If it degenerates into jargon—"value accrual through synergistic ecosystem effects"—they treat it as a red flag.

Name this type of heuristic: clarity test. Explain its power: it does not prove that a project is sound, but it quickly reveals when your understanding is not. The implication is modest but crucial: a failed clarity test does not mean "do not touch" forever; it means "do not touch yet". You must either learn more or walk away.

Another heuristic, used by some long-only funds, concerns narratives: *if the strongest argument for an asset is that "everyone else is getting in", we are already late.* This rule is deliberately blunt. It converts a vague sense of FOMO into a binary check. When the primary evidence cited in memos and meetings concerns other people's behaviour rather than the asset's own cash flows, utility, or resilience, the heuristic fires. The position is sized down or rejected.

Heuristics have limitations too. They can become overly conservative, filtering out assets that do not fit familiar patterns but are genuinely innovative. A classic example lies in the early reaction to Ethereum in 2015–2016. Many Bitcoin-centric investors had a heuristic—"anything not Bitcoin is noise"—that served them well against opportunistic clones but blinded them to the emergence of a new general-purpose platform. The reconciliation requires humility: heuristics should be treated as speed bumps, not walls. When a project repeatedly violates a heuristic yet refuses to go away—sustained user growth, persistent developer interest, improving security—the anomaly deserves closer study. Sometimes the rule is wrong; sometimes the world has changed.

The fourth claim: checklists and heuristics are most powerful when they work together, forming a rhythm. The heuristic alerts you that something is potentially interesting or dangerous. The checklist then interrogates it. Picture an investor scanning headlines and explorer dashboards on a Monday morning in Bristol. A token's volume has tripled overnight with negligible change in unique wallets. A heuristic fires: *volume without new users is suspicious.* That triggers the checklist: *What problem is this solving? Which users? Why token? Who controls emissions? Where is liquidity?* The rhythm moves from quick suspicion to structured inquiry. The sheet of paper by the keyboard fills with the same questions, answered afresh.

This rhythm shows up in numbers as well as narratives. Suppose a dashboard reveals a protocol boasting a "Total Value Locked" jump from US$50 million to US$300 million in two weeks. A heuristic kicks in: *Six-fold growth in days is unlikely to be organic.* The checklist then demands specifics: *Is this just one fund looping collateral? What happens if incentives stop? What percentage of TVL belongs to the largest five addresses?* The abstraction of "risk" becomes a ledger of traceable behaviours and metrics.

A fifth claim ties back to earlier chapters: good checklists age alongside your understanding. After you learn about oracle manipulation, your checklist acquires a line about price feeds. After you witness a governance capture, you add questions about voting power. After you endure a liquidity crunch, you insert an explicit exit plan test. The document becomes a kind of intellectual sediment, each layer recording a lesson you would prefer not to relearn at full price. The motif of the sheet, once blank, now annotated and creased, carries weight.

Historical practice supports this. Many enduring investment firms—Berkshire Hathaway in Omaha, Baillie Gifford in Edinburgh—have internal questions they revisit for every allocation. They do not publish them all, but interviews and letters hint at their consistency: *Is this business understandable? Who is in charge? How do incentives work? What could break this?* The crypto-specific version of that tradition might ask: *What problem? Which users? Why token? Who can change the rules? How do they get paid? Where does the yield actually come from?* Different asset class, same underlying logic.

Yet an unresolved tension remains, and it is worth naming. No checklist can be exhaustive; no set of heuristics can anticipate every twist. Over-reliance on them risks dulling intuition, turning every decision into a box-ticking exercise that misses nuance. Under-reliance leaves you exposed to haste and bias. The craft lies in choosing which questions deserve a permanent place on the page, and which rules of thumb deserve to be broken occasionally.

So the forward test is this: if you printed your current checklist and heuristics on a single sheet, would you actually trust that sheet to challenge you when markets move quickly and narratives swell? Or would it merely flatter what you already do? The answer defines whether your list on the desk is ballast, or just stationery.

Beware of metrics theatre

On 22 March 2019, in San Francisco, Bitwise Asset Management submitted a 104-page report to the U.S. Securities and Exchange Commission. Its conclusion was stark: most of the reported trading volume on unregulated cryptocurrency exchanges was "fake or non-economic". Screenshots showed one exchange printing near-perfect alternating buy and sell orders every few seconds, never drifting from a narrow price band, as if choreographed. The effect was theatrical—motion without meaning. Markets that appeared deep were little more than mirrored hallways, convincing only until someone leaned in to study the reflections. The episode marked a rupture. It forced regulators, analysts, and professional allocators to admit that the apparent size of a market could be a script, not a signal.

The paradox remains alive today. How can a market report billions in daily trading volume while its order book collapses the moment a trader tries to execute a £50,000 order? That mismatch—between the figure on the screen and the behaviour in the market—is the central puzzle of metrics theatre. Numbers perform; they do not always describe. And like any performance, the set can be elaborate enough to distract even attentive observers. The motif of the reflected hallway is useful here: metrics can offer depth where none exists.

The first claim is straightforward: vanity metrics thrive because they are easy to produce, easy to publicise, and difficult to falsify unless one knows where to look. Show this plainly. In 2021, users of CoinMarketCap noticed that a small offshore exchange, reporting daily volumes rivaling Binance, showed no corresponding chatter on social platforms, no observable wallet activity, and no visible liquidity on-chain. The mismatch hinted at wash trading—rapid buy-sell loops executed by bots to inflate apparent activity. Name the practice: non-economic volume generation. Explain it: exchanges fabricate activity to attract listings, token teams buy volume to signal traction, and dashboards that scrape API feeds reproduce the inflated numbers without question. The implication is blunt: if you cannot source a metric back to a verifiable event—users making trades, wallets moving assets, contracts executing code—you are reading theatre, not data.

A second example, widely discussed in analytical circles, concerns decentralised exchanges (DEXs). In mid-2022, an aggregator reported that a new DEX had overtaken Uniswap in 24-hour volume. Yet when analysts compared data from independent parsers—Dune dashboards, Etherscan logs, and direct node queries—they found that a single address had routed thousands of round-trip swaps through the platform. Name this pattern: self-swapping. Explain it: the address was recycling the same tokens to create the illusion of market share. The implication is unsettling but necessary: cross-verification is not optional. One must check the reflected hallway from multiple angles.

The counter-example needs airing. Not all eye-catching metrics are deceitful. When Uniswap's volume surged in September 2020, the jump was real, driven by liquidity mining programmes and an influx of new participants. On-chain explorers showed genuine wallet growth, diversified counterparties, and a thickening order book. Some sceptics dismissed the numbers as "yield-farmed theatre", but their cynicism failed the test of independent verification: the

activity was broad, not concentrated. Reconcile this: scepticism is healthy, but reflexive dismissal is its own bias. The task is not disbelief; it is discernment.

The second claim: vanity metrics flourish because they exploit the gap between what can be easily displayed and what actually matters. A protocol may trumpet "Total Value Locked" (TVL) as proof of dominance. Show how this misleads. In June 2021, a well-known yield aggregator advertised a TVL north of US$1 billion. Yet on inspection, most of that figure came from users looping the same collateral through the same vault, using borrowed assets to mint deposit receipts, then redepositing them to inflate the headline number. Name the tactic: recursive collateral. Explain it: a small amount of real assets can be re-counted several times if the system permits cyclical deposits. The implication is clear: whenever a metric can be manipulated through leverage or repetition, assume that someone has done so.

Another visible behaviour concerns user metrics. A cross-chain bridge once claimed 400,000 "monthly active users", a figure inconsistent with its limited transaction footprint. A forensic analyst in Berlin reviewed the bridge's smart contract calls and found that 80 per cent of transactions originated from fewer than twenty addresses. Name this pattern: concentrated activity masquerading as mass adoption. Explain it: bots interacting with a contract can mimic the statistical shape of a large user base. The implication: every claims-based metric should be paired with a distribution metric—how many distinct agents generate the activity, and how many dominate it.

The motif of the reflected hallway returns: the more ornate the metric, the more likely it has been engineered for appearance.

The third claim: metrics theatre persists because modern dashboards optimise for aesthetic clarity rather than epistemic accuracy. Slick visualisations can seduce even experienced analysts. Show this behaviour. A dashboard displaying a protocol's "liquidity utilisation" might plot a consistent 95 per cent utilisation rate, implying extraordinary efficiency. Name the problem: saturation illusion. Explain it: the protocol may have configured its pools so narrowly that a trivial amount of actual liquidity creates a near-max utilisation figure. The implication is sharp: read the definitions before you read the graph.

A second illustration comes from token distribution charts. Some dashboards refresh ownership distributions hourly, but the labels rely on heuristics that miscategorise smart contracts as "users" and aggregate unrelated wallets into "founders" or "teams". When a project touts "fair launch" because the dashboard shows diffuse ownership, a prudent analyst checks the raw holders list. Sometimes a "decentralised" token has half its supply controlled by three multisigs whose names never appear on the interface. Name the distortion: mislabelled concentration. Explain it: dashboards compress messy on-chain realities into neat categories to make the UI readable. The implication:

cleanliness is not accuracy. Neat visuals often hide complex truths.

The fourth claim: cross-verification is the antidote to metrics theatre, but only if done with methodological discipline. Consider decentralised exchange volume. To assess whether DEX A truly competes with DEX B, a disciplined analyst compares at least three independent sources: the DEX's own subgraph, a node-level parser, and an external aggregator like Token Terminal or DeFiLlama. Show the behaviour: if a subgraph shows 10,000 trades but the node parser sees 2,000, something is wrong. Name the diagnostic: triangular verification. Explain it: no single dataset should dominate; consistency across independent vantage points matters more than the raw number. The implication: a metric is trustworthy only when alternative measurement paths converge.

A second example concerns NFT marketplace volume. Wash trading plagued several platforms during the 2021–2022 cycle. One marketplace advertised the highest volume in the sector. But when analysts in Tokyo compared wallet-level data across OpenSea, LooksRare, and the new entrant, they found that the newcomer's volume was driven by wallets trading back and forth to earn reward tokens. Name the distortion: incentive-driven wash loops. Explain it: a rewards schedule can turn an ROI game into a theatre of volume. The implication: unless incentives are accounted for, volume is not evidence of organic demand.

There is a limitation: cross-verification takes time. It requires technical skill, multiple tools, and a tolerance for ambiguity. One cannot expect every investor to run node queries at the weekend. But the reconciliation lies in selective rigour. You do not need to cross-verify every metric every time; you cross-verify the metrics that drive key decisions—position entry, size, or continued allocation. The motif holds: you walk the hallway only when the reflection looks strange.

The fifth claim: the most dangerous metrics are not the obvious ones, but the subtle ones that blend truth and theatre. TVL, daily active users, fully diluted valuation, and "community growth" can each contain genuine signal. But when left uninterrogated, they lure analysts into complacency. Show an example. A layer-1 network in 2023 claimed "explosive developer growth", based on GitHub stars and fork counts. Yet GitHub stars track curiosity, not contribution. Forks often reflect automated tooling, not original work. Name the distortion: pseudo-dev activity. Explain it: equating repository metadata with engineering depth misconstrues intent. The implication: development activity must be measured by merges, commits, and multi-contributor patterns, not dashboard-friendly vanity counts.

A counter-example from the opposite direction helps. When Solana's validator count grew meaningfully in 2021–2022, some dismissed it as inflated. Yet independent audits by third-party researchers showed genuine geographic diversification and an increasing number of unique operators. The sceptics' blanket dismissal failed cross-verification. The lesson holds in both directions: some suspicious numbers are real; some reassuring numbers are fake. Verification is the governing principle, not cynicism.

A final motif: the reflected hallway darkens when incentives align to maintain the illusion. Protocol teams seek higher valuations; exchanges seek listings; dashboards seek traffic; influencers seek engagement. Each actor has a reason to amplify the glossy metric. Recognising this alignment is not paranoia; it is context. Metrics do not float freely—they are constructed in an economy of attention.

What remains unresolved is a practical tension. Decision-making cannot wait for perfect clarity, yet acting on crude numbers is reckless. Most investors operate in the space between those poles. The forward test is this: when a metric looks impressive, do you know exactly how it is calculated, where it is sourced, and how it could be gamed? If not, what would you need to check before allowing that number to influence a meaningful decision? The hallway of reflections invites you in. The question is whether you choose to walk it with the lights on.

When to do nothing

On 12 March 2020, as markets convulsed and Bitcoin fell more than 40 per cent in a single day, Coinbase's servers in San Francisco strained under a surge of anxious users trying to trade at speed. Plunging prices produced queues, delays, and liquidations across the industry. Yet one mid-sized

London-based fund, which later described its response in a May 2020 letter to clients, record-ed no trades at all during the worst hours. Its decision was not the product of paralysis but of design: its models required confirmation from three independent volatility indicators before adjusting exposure. None aligned. So the team sat still while noise roared. The outcome was counter-intuitive. By refusing to act in the panic, the fund avoided forced selling and recovered quicker than several peers who traded frenetically into a collapsing order book. Stillness beat speed.

The paradox persists. When prices move fast, and narratives shift faster, why can doing nothing be the hardest trade? The difficulty stems from a mismatch between instinct and evidence. Activity feels like control. Yet markets often punish haste more reliably than they reward urgency. One five-word sentence captures the tension: *Waiting protects capital sometimes.* The motif of the closed gate—an entry that remains shut until conditions align—helps frame the discipline required to stay inactive when every impulse leans towards movement.

Begin with the first claim: periods of conflicting signals demand stillness because any decision made on unstable foundations compounds error. Show this plainly. During the rapid growth of decentralised finance in early 2021, Ethereum gas fees spiked, Layer-2 adoption lagged, and on-chain metrics diverged wildly. Analysts at Messari, in a June 2021 report, noted that several protocols posted soaring

Total Value Locked while user numbers stagnated. Name the problem: signal incoherence. Explain it: leading indicators pointed in opposite directions, making directional conviction fragile. The implication is practical: when no dataset reinforces another, any trade becomes speculation on which signal will survive, not on what is actually known. The closed gate stays closed.

A second example reinforces the point. In July 2022, regulatory scrutiny in the United States intensified around stablecoins after the collapse of TerraUSD two months earlier. Market commentary fractured: some analysts predicted stricter oversight that would dampen demand; others argued for rapid growth in fully collateralised models. Prices of related tokens spiked on rumours, then slumped when guidance failed to materialise. Show the behaviour: conflicting interpretations produced whip-sawing markets across New York and Singapore. Name the dynamic: narrative whiplash. Explain it: when information is both incomplete and contested, markets amplify noise. The implication: sitting out during uncertainty preserves optionality, which is often undervalued until clarity returns.

A credible counter-example requires attention. In November 2020, when PayPal announced that it would enable cryptocurrency purchases for U.S. users, the signal was unambiguous. Market structure strengthened, liquidity deepened, and user adoption surged across verifiable datasets. Inaction then would have meant missing a durable shift. Reconcile this: stillness is not a doctrine. It is a response to conditions. When signals converge—macro, technical, adoption, regulatory—action may be prudent. When they diverge, restraint may be superior.

Advance to the second claim: stillness functions as risk management. Show the effect. When FTX collapsed in November 2022, several exchanges experienced liquidity stress. A number of London and Berlin-based funds disclosed that they paused withdrawals and deposits to avoid operational entanglement. Name the behaviour: protective inactivity. Explain it: halting movement limits exposure to systems under duress. The implication: doing nothing is not merely absence; it is defence.

A parallel emerges in protocol-level behaviour. After the 2016 DAO hack on Ethereum, developers faced competing proposals: roll back the chain, embrace the fork, or maintain immutability. For several days, developers issued no decisive action while validating blocks as normal. Name this stance: procedural continuity. Explain it: maintaining routine activity while withholding decisive interventions prevents cascading failures during uncertainty. The implication: sometimes stillness affords time for collective reasoning, which high-velocity settings desperately lack.

A limitation deserves articulation. Inaction can drift into avoidance. There are moments when refusing to decide is itself a costly decision. Consider early 2018, when several token projects signalled treasury distress as crypto prices fell rapidly. Some teams failed to diversify their holdings into fiat or stablecoins, citing "long-term conviction". By not acting, they watched operating budgets erase. The failure was not stillness but denial. Reconcile this: stillness must arise from deliberate assessment, not fear of engagement.

The third claim: when narratives multiply faster than evidence, waiting can sharpen judgement. Show this through behaviour. In late 2021, analysts confronted an explosion of new blockchains claiming "high throughput" and "low fees". Marketing outpaced engineering. Ghana-based researcher Nnenna Nwakanma emphasised in a December 2021 panel that claims required demonstration: real transactions, real users, real costs. The quiet observers who waited for these networks to reveal their genuine capabilities—rather than trading on promises—often avoided speculative spikes that later faded. Name the approach: evidence-led patience. Explain it: let reality reveal itself before acting. The implication: time can be an analytical tool.

A second example rests on funding cycles. Venture reports in 2022 indicated significant dryness in late-stage crypto deals, but seed-stage activity remained buoyant. Some investors inferred that early-stage tokens would surge; others argued that exit opportunities would shrink. The divergence created a freeze in secondary markets. Funds that waited for Q1 2023 data—realised valuations, treasury disclosures, exchange listings—were better able to distinguish structural slowdown from cyclical pause. Name the analytical move: temporal comparison. Explain it:

examining new data against prior baselines reveals pattern integrity. The implication: waiting enhances contrast.

The closed gate motif returns. When signals clash, the gate must stay shut until the noise subsides enough for form to appear.

The fourth claim: doing nothing is often the only way to preserve psychological clarity. Show this human dimension. High-frequency environments induce what behavioural economists call action bias: the impulse to act to reduce discomfort. During the May 2021 market correction, exchanges across Europe recorded surges in small-order trades during peak volatility—users buying and selling in frantic cycles. The visible behaviour: compulsive micro-trading. Name the bias: activity illusion. Explain it: traders sought relief from uncertainty through movement, even when those moves increased losses. The implication: refusing to act, even briefly, interrupts the cycle.

A second human-centred illustration lies in portfolio monitoring. Studies from the Swiss Finance Institute (2020) found that investors who checked their portfolios less frequently made fewer emotionally driven trades. Show the behaviour: reduced screen time led to lower churn. Name the habit: spaced observation. Explain it: by limiting exposure to minute-by-minute fluctuations, investors insulated themselves from noise-driven impulses. The implication: pauses create space for reason.

There is a counterpoint. Excessive detachment risks missing inflection points that require swift action. When the Ethereum Merge date was finalised in July 2022, those who had stepped away entirely from monitoring markets risked missing a clear structural development. Reconcile this: stillness must be bounded. It is not withdrawal but strategic restraint.

A fifth claim synthesises the thread: stillness is a strategy that reveals truth by refusing to engage with untruth. Show this through market microstructure. Thin liquidity often masks real sentiment. During Asia trading hours in early 2023, certain tokens exhibited sharp wicks—prices spiking or collapsing on low volume. Analysts in Hong Kong noted that these moves reversed within hours. Those who acted on the initial moves often captured the wick, not the trend. Name the pattern: transient displacement. Explain it: isolated trades distort price temporarily; acting instantly embeds the distortion in your portfolio. The implication: waiting for depth restores signal.

A historical echo underscores the point. In 1930, economist John Maynard Keynes, writing from Cambridge, reflected on the discipline of "masterly inactivity" within policy decisions—a stance advocating non-intervention until evidence stabilised. Though his context differed dramatically, the principle aligns: when information is unstable, premature action worsens outcomes. The implication for modern market observers is timeless: let the dust settle before you measure the room.

What remains unresolved is the tension between vigilance and restraint. The forward test is simple to pose, difficult to practise. When the market's signals conflict, narratives fragment, and your pulse quickens, ask: does action improve the quality of my decision, or simply relieve discomfort? The closed gate stands before you. The question is whether you can keep it shut long enough for clarity to form.

Chapter 10
Principles for the Long Term

In October 2008, as global markets convulsed and headlines screamed collapse, a small cooperative bank in Trieste, founded in 1886 and largely unknown outside its region, noticed a curious reversal in its fortunes. While larger institutions haemorrhaged deposits, this modest mutual saw its inflows rise week after week. Local press interviews at the time captured bewildered executives repeating a simple observation: people were moving their savings not because the cooperative promised higher returns, but because it had never promised anything it could not keep. It published plain-language financial statements. It resisted products it did not understand. It treated its savers as participants in a long relationship rather than fleeting opportunities. In the worst crisis of a generation, the slowest and most transparent institution in the city became the most trusted. Its edge was not speed. Its edge was character.

The paradox remains potent today. In domains where innovation accelerates—crypto, digital assets, automated markets—why does the most durable advantage often emerge from the least fashionable virtues: consistency, restraint, clarity, and care? The question unsettles because it pushes against the cultural momentum of the space, which rewards novelty, hot takes, and reflexive trading. Yet the same pattern appears again and again. Those who survive the cycles, attract collaborators, and find opportunities others never see tend to be those who behave as if their reputation compounds exactly like capital does. They treat trust as something with a yield curve.

Consider a recurring motif that runs through every mature field: the ledger that records what one has done, not what one has claimed. Whether in science, finance, engineering, or governance, long-term thinkers build reputational balance sheets with small, steady entries—accurate statements, careful revisions, fair dealings, quiet expertise. These behaviours do not spike charts or dominate feeds. But they attract high-quality partners, reduce friction, and create optionality over decades. When choices compound, character compounds too.

This chapter turns towards the discipline required to operate in that register: slow-building, principles-first, aligned with the future self rather than the present mood. The preceding chapters have taken us through signals, noise, risk, structure, and process. Here the horizon widens. Instead of asking how to interpret the market, we ask how to behave in a way that remains coherent across cycles—whether calm or chaotic, whether profitable or punishing. The long term is not a calendar measure; it is a stance.

We begin where durable systems always begin: with trust. Not the sentimental sort, but the practical version that forms between people, institutions, and tools that deliver what they claim, admit what they cannot, and remain stable when conditions turn rough. Trust grows by accumulation, not proclamation. The simplest behaviours—meeting obligations, documenting assumptions, acknowledging mistakes—become competitive advantages because they reduce uncertainty for everyone involved. In the crypto markets, where the architecture is young and incentives shift quickly, choosing partners with verified track records becomes a form of capital preservation. Reputations built through transparency, published audits, responsive communication, and consistent stewardship create a buffer more valuable than clever design alone. Trust compounds.

Yet compounding trust alone is insufficient. The long term also belongs to those who update their assumptions without surrendering to the noise of daily volatility. Most of the industry's most painful episodes have sprung from static beliefs held in dynamic environments: protocols assuming demand would grow indefinitely; investors assuming liquidity would remain; founders assuming regulation would look away. The alternative is not jittery reactivity but structured adaptability. Periodic reviews—quarterly, annual, or tied to specific triggers—offer a deliberate cadence for revision. They keep strategy aligned with reality while filtering out the emotional turbulence of short-term swings. The motif of the ledger reappears here: assumptions enter the record, are revisited, and evolve as new evidence emerges.

This rhythm of adaptive thinking leads naturally to a deeper argument rarely made explicitly in markets: ethics is not a decorative adornment but a strategic asset. Fair dealing, clear disclosures, accurate communication, and a refusal to exploit information asymmetries do more than signal virtue. They shape the flow of opportunities. Communities that prize constructive criticism, reward accountability, and challenge poor logic tend to attract collaborators who are both capable and principled. In such places, ideas compound because the environment encourages honesty over theatre. As decentralised systems mature, this quiet edge becomes increasingly visible. Transparent actors are granted more context. Responsible stewards raise more capital. Those who treat others well gain information that the extractive operators never receive. Ethical conduct becomes an advantage with long-term returns.

And yet the long term is not only structural; it is personal. Principles that endure must be small enough to remember and simple enough to enact under pressure. Complexity collapses in stress. What remains are a few core commitments that guide action when clarity dims. A succinct credo—learn continuously, verify independently, size positions modestly, review regularly, and stay kind—functions not as a slogan, but as a personal operating system. It disciplines impulse. It prevents drift. It offers a shared standard that can be exchanged with peers, anchoring a community of practice built on mutual respect rather than performative cleverness.

This introduction does not argue that long-term success is guaranteed by virtue, patience, or careful thinking. Markets will not reward principles out of courtesy. But markets, in aggregate, do reward coherence. They reward those who show up consistently, treat others decently, and revise their plans with humility. They reward those who understand that reputation, like capital, compounds most powerfully over long intervals.

As you move into the chapter, the invitation is simple yet demanding: consider how your future self would judge the choices you make now. Consider which behaviours you want compounding quietly on your behalf. Consider whether the credo you carry—spoken or unspoken—fits the person you are becoming. And consider, most of all, what you might build if you treated trust, adaptability, ethics, and simplicity as investments with decades ahead of them rather than days.

Compounding trust

In September 2022, during the immediate aftermath of the Merge, a quiet line item in Coinbase's quarterly filings drew unusual attention. While trading volumes had fallen sharply during the broader crypto slowdown, the company reported that *custodial* assets—tokens held on behalf of institutions—had remained remarkably stable. Journalists noted that several pension funds and asset managers, wary of counterparty failures after the collapse of Celsius in July 2022, had shifted assets towards custodians with long public track records, audited statements, and transparent control structures. One portfolio manager, quoted in the *Financial Times* on 18 September, summarised the move crisply: "We want partners whose incentives and disclosures survive scrutiny." In a moment dominated by speed, the market drifted back to the slowest, most consistently verified institutions. The behaviour was visible: assets moved. Trust was earned, not declared. And its effect compounded.

This is the central motif of this section: the ledger of trust—built through repeated, observed actions—grows like a balance sheet with reinvested dividends. When systems become noisy, opaque, or euphoric, the partners who remain reliable across multiple regimes become disproportionately valuable. Their credibility turns into a form of yield. Every fulfilled commitment strengthens the compounding curve; every transparent communication reduces future uncertainty. Trust compounds. It does so quietly.

Shows of reliability alone, though, are not enough. They must be named and examined. Consider the case of Binance's publication of proof-of-reserves snapshots in November 2022. The company shared wallet balances, auditor attestations, and technical details intended to reassure deposits after the FTX implosion earlier that month. The material demonstration—addresses on-chain, signatures verified—was real. Yet the limitation was equally real: the disclosures captured assets but omitted liabilities, leaving open the question of net solvency. This tension matters because it illustrates the difference between a trust-building behaviour and a trust-theatre gesture. Proof-of-reserves, when partial, shows transparency but cannot assure resilience. The implication is direct: investors must commit to partners who not only publish data but publish *complete* data, with structures that allow challenge and verification.

Another instructive example came from Kraken's long-standing policy of annual audits, conducted under the SSAE 18 standard and published with cryptographic proofs since 2014. The firm's approach combined technical verification—Merkle tree proofs that users could independently confirm—with familiar regulatory frameworks. The behaviour was visible: users could test the audit by checking their own account IDs in the tree. The track record was verifiable across eight years. This continuity allowed institutions to measure resilience not through slogans but through repeated, documented acts. The implication is simple: trust does not emerge from novelty; it emerges from recurrence.

This pattern becomes clearest by contrast. In May 2021, Iron Finance's partial-collateral stablecoin collapsed to near zero after a cascade of redemptions. Much commentary focused on the reflexive economic design, but the more consequential issue was structural opacity: the project offered neither audited collateral statements nor clear governance pathways for emergency intervention. The absence of verifiable controls amplified panic during stress. As the market fell, trust evaporated faster than price. Here the limitation is instructive: even if a protocol's mechanism appears sound under normal conditions, the lack of transparent, recurring disclosures can make it brittle under pressure. Reconciling this with earlier examples shows the crux: resilience is not inherent; it is demonstrated.

The motif of the ledger returns here. Every institution, protocol, or analyst creates a ledger of observable actions over time. Publishing incident reports, releasing code audits, responding to security disclosures, or honouring withdrawal requests promptly—each entry accumulates value. These behaviours translate abstractions ("credibility", "prudence", "stability") into visible metrics. One can measure response times in hours, verify code commits by date, confirm wallet movements on-chain, or track years without a material governance controversy. Trust grows through these witnessable markers.

The implication for the reader is not prescriptive but diagnostic. When assessing partners—exchanges, data providers, custodians, validators, or research outlets—the most predictive factor is often the most prosaic: how they behaved when things went wrong. Did they communicate promptly? Did they acknowledge uncertainty? Did they publish timelines? Did they compensate users? These are not sentimental questions but analytical ones. Past behaviour is not a guarantee, but it is a dataset.

This is why transparency becomes a compounding force rather than a moral flourish. A transparent partner reduces information asymmetry, which in turn reduces the probability of catastrophic error. A partner that documents processes, segregates assets, and publishes control frameworks reduces tail-risk. Over time, these reductions compound. They free cognitive bandwidth. They enable more ambitious decisions because the foundational layer is stable. And they form a network of other transparent partners—auditors, regulators, researchers—who engage more willingly with institutions that maintain high standards.

To appreciate the compounding effect fully, it helps to examine resilience as a complementary dynamic. In February 2020, during the sudden market stress triggered by COVID-19, MakerDAO's liquidation system faltered under extreme congestion on Ethereum. The crisis exposed gaps in oracle updates and liquidity planning. Yet Maker's response over the following year—publishing detailed post-mortems, integrating new collateral types, improving auction mechanisms, and inviting external review—strengthened its governance and technical footing. In March 2021, when volatility spiked again, the system performed more effectively. The visible behaviour—publication of post-incident procedures, parameter adjustments, community votes—expanded stakeholders' confidence. The implication is that resilience compounds when failures are interrogated, not hidden.

Contrast this with the collapse of TerraUSD in May 2022. The mechanism failed rapidly, but the deeper issue was that governance processes and risk assumptions were not designed to absorb dissent or update parameters under stress. Internal critics reported difficulty raising concerns. Here the limitation becomes clear: if a system's communication culture suppresses criticism, resilience cannot compound. And if resilience fails, trust collapses instantly. Reconciling this with the Maker example yields a practical truth: compounding trust requires a structure that invites review.

The motif of the ledger surfaces again. A ledger with only positive entries is not trustworthy; it is incomplete. The most reliable partners document setbacks as carefully as successes. They report vulnerabilities discovered during internal testing. They publish plans to address them. They maintain open communication channels with independent researchers. These behaviours demonstrate humility, which is measurable in the pattern of updates and disclosures. Humility compounds.

The question for any long-term participant, then, is straightforward: which partners demonstrate behaviours that compound trust rather than erode it? The decision is not merely about avoiding losses; it is about building an environment in which insight, collaboration, and opportunity accumulate. A partner with a decade of unbroken custody controls, a history of timely withdrawals during stress, and a habit of publishing complete audits confers an advantage that cannot be replicated by a partner offering marginally lower fees but weaker stewardship.

This logic extends beyond institutions. Analysts, commentators, and independent researchers also create compounding records. Those who document their reasoning, revisit their errors, cite primary sources, and engage respectfully with counter-arguments establish a reputation that grows in influence. Their insights attract higher-quality networks, which in turn improve the information they access. The compounding effect here is epistemic: credibility creates better data, which produces better analysis, which earns more credibility. The cycle grows.

And yet, amidst these patterns, a forward test remains. In a domain where new entrants appear weekly, incentives shift rapidly, and narratives compete for attention, how does one decide which partners deserve long-term trust? What weight should be placed on historical behaviour versus innovative design? How should a reader balance the seduction of new ideas with the discipline of selecting partners who have already demonstrated resilience? And what might the ledger of trust demand in the next cycle—more transparency, faster disclosure, deeper audits, or something else altogether?

These questions do not admit simple answers. But they frame the trade-offs that shape the compounding of trust, and they remind us that this compounding is not passive. It is a choice—made repeatedly—about who deserves to stand beside us when the next storm arrives.

Adaptive, not reactive

In November 2018, as the price of Bitcoin slipped below $6,000 for the first time in over a year, a quiet ritual played out inside several London-based funds. At one firm in

Shoreditch, analysts pulled up the original investment memos they had written twelve months earlier. Each memo included the same table: assumptions, catalysts, risks, and a date for mandatory re-evaluation. They were not reacting to the sudden price break; they were honouring the calendar. The team compared what they had believed in November 2017 with what had actually materialised by November 2018. Some theses held. Others were discarded. But the key behaviour was visible: scheduled review, not emotional response. One portfolio manager summarised it to a colleague: "We don't chase the chart; we chase the truth." Five words. And they shaped the entire process.

This tension—between reacting to noise and updating through discipline—sits at the heart of long-term decision-making. In a domain where metrics shift by the hour, communities surge overnight, and narratives mutate in real time, the temptation to move fast is constant. Yet the movements that matter most often come from slower, periodic reconsideration. The map is redrawn not in the heat of a candle wick but in the steadiness of a timed review. The motif that threads through this section is deliberate pause: how it creates clarity, reveals drift, and restores proportion.

The paradox is that adaptation requires slowness first. A system that updates only during stress is not adaptive; it is reactive. And reactivity—whether in markets, governance, or research—narrows judgment. By contrast, a structure of planned reassessment expands it. The London fund's process was not exceptional; it was deliberate. The visible behaviour was the calendar itself. The implication: adaptation is a practice, not an instinct.

To anchor this idea, consider an instructive case from January 2021. The Ethereum Foundation published updated gas efficiency benchmarks ahead of the Berlin hard fork, noting improvements in several opcodes. Developers had anticipated gains, but the published metrics forced a reassessment of assumptions about transaction costs and Layer-2 competitiveness. Teams building on Optimism and Arbitrum revised their performance models. The behaviour was measured: compare old assumptions to new data, adjust roadmaps accordingly. Yet the adaptation did not occur in the frenzy of price movement that also characterised that month. It emerged from scheduled technical updates and deliberate evaluation. The implication is that adaptive strategy responds to information that matters, not to movement that merely attracts attention.

A second example, equally telling, comes from academic work by the Cambridge Centre for Alternative Finance in March 2020, during the early COVID-19 shock. Their survey of mining operations across China, Kazakhstan, and Canada revealed shifts in energy profiles and regional concentration. These findings contradicted several assumptions circulating in policy papers at the time. Institutions that reviewed their environmental impact theses annually incorporated the updated data; those that reacted to headlines instead produced analyses that aged poorly within months. Again, the behaviour is visible: update cadence shapes accuracy. The limitation reveals itself: if review cycles are too slow, assumptions ossify; if too fast, they mirror noise. Reconciling this tension is the craft.

The motif of deliberate pause reappears when contrasting structured review with impulsive reaction. During the rapid market decline of May 2021, some funds attempted to rewrite allocation models daily. One well-publicised case involved a New York trading firm that recalibrated its volatility assumptions three times in a single week; internal reports later showed that the churn degraded performance by amplifying errors. The firm's chief risk officer admitted in an August 2021 interview that their process lacked "temporal spacing". This limitation shows the cost of reactivity: decision quality decays when updates occur faster than understanding.

By contrast, structured adaptive cycles create a rhythm of accountability. A quarterly thesis review forces the evaluator to ask: What has changed that matters? Which assumptions proved durable? Which risks materialised? Which metrics diverged from expectation? These questions anchor abstractions—"trend", "momentum", "cycle"—to observable behaviours. One can measure active user growth on-chain, track developer commit counts, analyse treasury reports, or confirm governance participation by address.

Updating becomes a process of comparing concrete markers, not wrestling with moods.

This framing clarifies why adaptive thinking differs from passive patience. Adaptation is neither stubborn holding nor frenetic adjustment; it is periodic re-alignment. Each review becomes an audit of reasoning. The adaptive thinker honours uncertainty without being governed by it. The behaviour is disciplined: schedule, examine, refine, commit.

This pattern appears in protocol governance as well. The Decred community, notable for its hybrid proof-of-work and proof-of-stake model, institutionalised periodic review through agenda cycles. Decisions regarding treasury deployment, staking parameters, and development priorities were addressed through structured, community-wide votes. These votes forced explicit reconsideration of assumptions at regular intervals, creating an adaptive culture without surrendering to the volatility of daily discourse. The implication is clear: institutionalising rhythm allows a system to evolve without fragmenting.

The counter-example that tests this idea is provided by projects where adaptation occurs only after failure. Consider the case of SushiSwap's transition in late 2020 during the "Chef Nomi" controversy. The protocol's governance reformed only after a breach of internal trust forced emergency changes. While the community stabilised the project, the adaptations were reactive, not scheduled. The limitation is instructive: reactive adaptation can salvage a system but rarely strengthens it as predictably as planned review. Reconciling this with the earlier examples highlights that scheduled adaptation builds compounding resilience; emergency adaptation merely prevents collapse.

The motif of deliberate pause surfaces again when considering the individual researcher. A practitioner who performs an annual thesis refresh—explicitly listing assumptions, updating data sources, and documenting divergences—develops a record of intellectual integrity. Their insights improve because their reasoning compounds. They measure what they thought then against what they know now. Every contradiction teaches. Every error maps blind spots. The behaviour is observable in notebooks, timelines, and comments on repositories. The implication: adaptation becomes a personal discipline that shapes judgment across cycles.

This practice is especially vital in domains where narratives accelerate. Take the summer of 2020, when decentralised finance exploded in usage. It was tempting to redraw assumptions weekly. Yet those who maintained structured review cycles—monthly or quarterly—distinguished between temporary distortions (liquidity mining surges) and structural shifts (automated market maker innovation). By spacing updates, they avoided mistaking episodic spikes for secular change. Here again, the behaviour is tied to cadence, and cadence shapes clarity.

To make these dynamics concrete, consider how an adaptive framework handles uncertainty. Suppose a researcher evaluates a new protocol with promising metrics but limited historical data. Instead of reacting to every fluctuation, they establish dates for reassessment. They record key indicators: retained users, audit history, treasury transparency, governance participation. After three months, they compare their recorded expectations to observed outcomes. They adjust their thesis accordingly. The behaviour is simple: measure, compare, commit. But the implication is profound: adaptation becomes cumulative.

The challenge, of course, is psychological. Reactivity feels energising. Adaptation feels quiet. Yet quiet judgment often outperforms frantic certainty. This tension invites a final question—one that defines the craft of adaptive thinking: when should one update faster, and when should one slow the cycle? If a security flaw emerges today, must the thesis update immediately? If a new narrative gains traction, should the reevaluation wait for data? And what cadence best balances vigilance with proportion?

These questions remain open by design. They frame the discipline of being adaptive without becoming reactive. And they point to a larger inquiry the reader must carry forward: what rhythm of thinking best preserves clarity in a world that rewards haste but punishes it just as quickly?

Ethics as edge

On 14 September 2016, at a cramped press conference in San Francisco, Brian Armstrong of Coinbase addressed a rumour circulating about the exchange's listing process. He stated plainly that no employee had advance knowledge of prospective asset additions, and he followed the statement with a verifiable action: Coinbase would introduce mandatory trade blackout periods and on-chain monitoring to detect internal abuse. What mattered was not the corporate polish but the visible behaviour. The firm's trading patterns in the weeks that followed showed no anomalous pre-listing activity. Trust rose because conduct, not narrative, carried the weight. Five words from an analyst who attended lingered: "They showed their workings publicly." Those five words capture the central motif of this section—ethics as a strategic resource rather than a moral accessory.

Ethics gains its sharpest edge when conditions are opaque. In information-dense domains, incentives favour shortcuts and selective disclosure. Yet communities consistently reward those who behave with steady clarity even when expedience tempts them elsewhere. Consider the GitHub thread from February 2020 in which the Zcash Foundation published the full audit trail of its decision to reject a proposed developer fund structure. The thread reads like practised transparency: arguments acknowledged, uncertainties admitted, dissent recorded. The community's response was not sentimental; it was practical. Users increased their participation in governance votes the following quarter, and several researchers who had been hesitant to contribute code began doing so. The metric was objective: more contributors, more commits, broader oversight. Ethical behaviour widened the surface area for opportunity.

To understand why ethics compounds, one must observe how reputational capital behaves over time. Show the mechanism first: an individual who reports a protocol vulnerability responsibly, as Sam Sun did with Optimism in August 2022, builds a durable archive of credible conduct. Name the behaviour: responsible disclosure. Explain its force: it aligns incentives between the discloser and the community. Implication: future collaborations become easier to form, and information flows more readily towards the individual who has demonstrated reliability. This is not abstract virtue; it is a functional asset that shapes who is invited into which rooms.

A second example sharpens the point. When the Tezos community passed its Athens upgrade in May 2019, the documentation included a detailed breakdown of debates, including objections from minority voices. Rather than suppressing dissent, the process preserved it in writing. The behaviour demonstrated humility and procedural consistency. The result was measurable: higher validator participation rates in subsequent amendments. Transparent deliberation increased the willingness of stakeholders to remain engaged. The implication echoes the motif: ethics multiplies when practised openly.

Yet there is a credible counter-example that tests this principle. Projects with strong ethical branding sometimes falter when incentives turn. A case in point is the 2017 Parity multisig freeze. Despite years of presenting itself as a champion of rigorous engineering, the company faced a devastating contract vulnerability that locked hundreds of thousands of ether. The immediate response—confusion, partial explanations, and rapid shifts in narrative—eroded confidence. The limitation is clear: past ethical conduct cannot fully shield an organisation from reputational damage if present behaviour fails to maintain the same standard. Reconciling this requires precision: ethics as edge is cumulative but not indestructible. It demands continual reinforcement through demonstrable action.

The motif reappears when observing smaller communities where norms crystallise quickly. A developer who posts thorough, good-faith critiques on governance forums often finds that their influence grows disproportionate to their stake. The behaviour is visible: constructive challenge, clearly reasoned, with sources cited and alternatives proposed. Governance platforms such as those used by MakerDAO or ENS regularly elevate such contributors into formal working groups. The implication again is practical: ethical communication expands the field of opportunity because peers gravitate towards those who reduce uncertainty.

Ethical clarity also acts as a filter against the thinning of attention that plagues high-velocity ecosystems. When a research team commits to publishing all assumptions, error margins, and data sources, it simplifies collaboration. Partners know the ground on which they stand. A structured disclosure pattern—similar to that used by the Electric Coin Company in its quarterly financial transparency reports—eliminates the guesswork that corrodes cooperation. The behaviour is simple: share numbers, not just narratives. The implication: coordination becomes cheaper, faster, and more stable.

But ethics as edge extends beyond documentation. It includes the subtle disciplines that rarely appear in public. A fund manager who declines to promote an early-stage project because disclosures are incomplete forfeits potential short-term gain. Yet that refusal becomes a signal. Over time, founders begin to seek the fund out precisely because its gatekeeping is consistent. A researcher who admits an error without deflecting is more likely to be trusted with unpublished data. A community moderator who applies the same standard to allies and critics stabilises discussions that might otherwise fracture. Each behaviour is a visible mark of internal strength.

The thread linking these behaviours is proportion. Ethical actors maintain proportion between what they know, what they claim, and what they signal. They avoid the inflation of certainty that corrodes long-term credibility. When they forecast, they timestamp. When they critique, they document. When they disagree, they separate argument from identity. The implication is cumulative: each interaction deposits or withdraws reputational capital, and the compounding effect emerges over months and years rather than days.

To further test the principle, examine the case of Chainlink's push for transparency in its node operator ecosystem. In 2020, the organisation published detailed performance dashboards showing uptime, response times, and stake allocations for each operator. This exposed weaknesses and sparked criticism. Yet over the following eighteen months, operator performance improved, downtime declined, and integration partners increased. The behaviour—publish uncomfortable data—reinforced trust precisely because it risked embarrassment. The implication: transparency attracts higher-quality partners by signalling that the organisation will not hide structural flaws.

Ethics also shapes the internal rhythms of research and collaboration. Teams that commit to fair dealing establish explicit codes for conflict resolution, data verification, and credit attribution. This creates a climate where junior researchers can challenge assumptions without fear of retaliation. A 2019 study on scientific team performance by the Max Planck Institute showed that teams with clear authorship and credit protocols produced work with higher replication rates. Though the domain differs, the underlying dynamic applies: ethical structure improves output because it reduces friction and ambiguity.

Still, the temptation to treat ethics as a branding tool persists. Organisations may produce polished communications that gesture towards transparency while concealing critical weaknesses. This is metrics theatre of a different kind: the illusion of integrity. The counter-example reveals a warning: signalling virtue without practising it erodes trust faster than silence. The reconciliation is straightforward: ethics as edge requires embodiment, not performance. Every ethical claim must be testable through behaviour.

Return to the motif: ethics compounds because it creates compounding pathways. A person who deals fairly today becomes the one others consult tomorrow. An organisation that publishes its failures becomes the one auditors favour. A community that rewards constructive critics becomes the one that attracts serious builders. Each instance strengthens the next. The compounding is slow at first but accelerates as the system matures.

The quiet power of this idea lies in its reciprocity. Ethical conduct does not merely influence how others treat you; it alters what kinds of opportunities seek you out. It tilts the environment. It shapes the flow of invitations, disclosures, and collaborations. And it establishes a durable edge precisely because it is difficult to fake over time.

The final tension, then, is this: how does one maintain ethical clarity when velocity rises, incentives shift, and visibility increases? What habits ensure proportion when pressures tempt distortion? And which behaviours—documented, visible, repeatable—will serve as the bedrock of trust when the next cycle tests every assumption we hold?

A simple pledge

In January 1962, in Omaha, Warren Buffett sent his partnership investors a short letter that began with what he called "ground rules". Before discussing performance, before arguing for any specific holding, he laid out how he would behave: he would invest alongside his partners, he would not market the partnership, he would accept responsibility for mistakes, and he would not guarantee results. The letter was not long. It read like a pledge. Yet those few paragraphs shaped decades of expectations between him and his investors. People who accepted the rules stayed. Those who disliked them redeemed. The outcome was concrete: fewer panicked withdrawals, less pressure to chase fads, and a culture in which decisions could compound quietly. A handful of sentences altered the trajectory of thousands of decisions. Digital asset markets lack an Omaha letter. There is no central figure whose pledge governs the whole field. Instead, every participant must draft a personal version—explicit, portable, small enough to remember when screens flash red. Five verbs serve as a workable spine: learn, verify, size small, review, stay kind. They fit on a card. They also cut across market cycles, protocols, and fashions. A simple sentence captures their spirit: *Principles must survive volatility intact.*

The first claim is that a written credo changes behaviour because it pre-commits the future self. Show this clearly. Imagine two researchers beginning to explore a new protocol launch. One has a one-page pledge stuck to their desk: *I will not allocate capital to anything I do not understand at a basic functional level.* The other relies on vague intuition that they will "be careful". When a charismatic founder presents a breathless thread, the difference in behaviour is immediate. The first researcher knows the pledge would be broken if they skipped the documentation. The second has nothing external to push against their impulse. Name this device: pre-commitment. Explain it: by expressing a standard in advance, one reduces the space for reinterpretation under emotional pressure. The implication is practical: a simple pledge is not about virtue signalling; it is a mechanism to constrain future panic.

"Learn" is the first verb for a reason. Learning here is not a lofty abstraction; it is visible in the trail one leaves. Meeting notes, bookmarked whitepapers, annotated block explorer queries, recorded conversations with more experienced peers—these are its metrics. A person who claims to care about understanding but leaves no trace of inquiry is signalling hope, not discipline. The pledge to learn means that before any significant commitment of time or capital, there is an observable period where the only output is understanding. That might be a weekend reading the protocol documentation, a notebook of basic questions, or a mock transaction carried out with trivial amounts. The implication is structural: portfolios anchored in learning tend to be smaller, slower, and less chaotic. Less noise leaks in.

Yet "learn" without "verify" collapses into credulity. The second verb insists on friction. Verification means checking claimed facts against independent sources: a protocol's TVL figures against on-chain data; a custodian's assertions against audit reports; an influencer's enthusiasm against longer-form research or code activity. Show this behaviour. In 2021, when a new yield platform claimed high "risk-free" returns, the users who verified looked up the smart contract on Etherscan, inspected the external calls, and realised that a single admin wallet held privileges to change core parameters. Those who skipped this step discovered the vulnerability only after funds were drained. Name the difference: verification gap. Explain it: both groups had access to the same information, but only one invested energy in cross-checking. The implication: the pledge to verify is a commitment to incur small, repeated costs now in order to reduce the risk of large, invisible costs later.

The motif of the pocket card appears again here. A personal credo printed on a small card can literally sit beside the keyboard. Every time a trader hovers over the "confirm" button, the verbs are there: learn, verify. This is not magic. It is a nudge. It brings the slow brain into a fast moment.

"Size small" addresses the most concrete dimension of risk: how much can be lost if everything goes wrong. It moves ethics from philosophy into arithmetic. A pledge to size small translates into behaviours such as limiting any single speculative idea to a modest percentage of liquid net worth, or capping the cumulative exposure to unaudited protocols.

It is visible in numbers. A researcher can look at a spreadsheet and see whether the pledge is kept. This matters because judgement fails intermittently; position sizes remain written down. A credible counter-example illustrates the cost of neglecting this verb. During the 2022 meltdown around algorithmic stablecoins, some participants had 70–80 per cent of their liquid capital in one design. They understood the mechanism. They had verified documentation. But they broke the "size small" principle. When the peg failed, knowledge did not shield them. Reconcile this with the earlier claims: learning and verification manage *quality* of decisions; sizing manages *consequence*. A simple pledge must address both.

"Review" keeps the credo from calcifying. A pledge that never meets its own audit becomes superstition. Review is the commitment to return to prior decisions and ask: did this thesis still make sense, given the data that arrived? Behaviourally, it might look like an annual "thesis day" where one reads back the original rationale for a position and compares it with actual events: protocol upgrades shipped or delayed, regulatory news, usage metrics, and governance outcomes. The metric here is not performance alone, but calibration. Did events surprise more than expected? Were certain risks underweighted? Did certain sources prove consistently unreliable? The implication is that the pledge itself may need to evolve. Principles stand; their specific thresholds (for example, how small "small" is) may change as experience deepens.

The card motif returns, now annotated. A person might literally rewrite their card once a year, adjusting the phrasing while keeping the verbs. Perhaps "size small" is sharpened into "size so that a total loss irritates, but does not destabilise, your life". Perhaps "review" gains a frequency: "quarterly, regardless of market noise". The pledge remains simple yet living.

The last verb—"stay kind"—may seem out of place beside hard-edged commitments to verification and sizing. It is not. Kindness, in this context, is not vague benevolence; it is a set of observable behaviours in an environment that rewards sharp elbows. It shows up in how one treats support staff when an exchange halts withdrawals, how one addresses developers when reporting bugs, how one disagrees with strangers in governance forums, how one speaks about people who have lost money. Metrics exist here too, even if informal. Screenshots of conversations, public comments on proposals, recorded calls—these form a record. The pledge to stay kind is a safeguard against becoming the sort of participant whose short-term gains come at the expense of a corrosive atmosphere.

Communities that honour kindness as a norm have measurable advantages. Open-source projects with codes of conduct and visible enforcement tend to retain contributors for longer. Online forums that actively reward well-reasoned disagreement and civility, as some early Ethereum research channels did in 2017–2018, often surface better ideas because more people are willing to risk looking foolish when asking questions. The implication is strictly practical: kindness is not softness; it is lubricant for collective intelligence. A simple pledge that ignores interpersonal conduct is incomplete.

A counter-example shows the cost of neglecting this dimension. During periods of speculative mania, social channels can devolve into harassment campaigns against sceptics, or mockery of those who publicly record losses. In such climates, honest feedback vanishes; people stop reporting vulnerabilities or questioning unsound designs because the social penalty is too high. The result is worse code, weaker governance, and more severe blow-ups. Reconciling this with the previous discussion clarifies the point: a pledge focused solely on personal outcomes, without regard for the health of the surrounding community, undermines the very information channels on which good decisions depend.

The quiet power of a simple pledge lies in its transmissibility. When someone shares their credo with a colleague, a friend, or a small group, the verbs become shared language. One might hear, "We have not really verified this yet," in a meeting, or "This position looks too large for our 'small' rule," in a review. The pledge graduates from private mantra to collective standard. Opportunity flows differently in such groups. They avoid certain traps automatically because the language to describe those traps is already present.

There is, however, a limitation. A pledge cannot substitute for competence. A group may faithfully recite "learn, verify, size small, review, stay kind" and still make unwise choices if their analytical methods are weak or their data is poor. The credo is a frame, not a guarantee. Reconciling this is straightforward: the pledge shapes *how* people behave as they try to improve; it does not make improvement effortless. Its edge comes from the way it disciplines attention.

The motif of the card returns one last time. A physical object—or its digital equivalent—anchors the pledge in daily life. Some investors maintain a short "investment constitution" at the top of their research notes. Some pin a message in their chat channels. Some write the verbs on a whiteboard behind their desk. Each method gives the credo a place in the environment, not just in memory. Under stress, people regress to habit; the pledge's purpose is to make those habits slightly better.

What remains is a decision that no writer can take for the reader: whether to make such a pledge explicit, to write it down, to share it with someone else who has permission to point to it when actions drift. The unresolved question is simple and demanding: if your future self could look back on the next decade of choices in digital markets, what five or six words would that person be grateful you kept, even when it was inconvenient?

About the Author

Anaya Korvelle writes at the intersection of money, technology, and human judgement. Her work helps readers slow down in fast markets, replacing hype with clear thinking and practical safeguards. She focuses on first principles, ethical decision-making, and the everyday habits that keep investors safe. Drawing on case studies from past booms and busts, she treats crypto as part of a longer story about innovation and speculation, from railway manias to today's digital currencies. Her mission is simple: equip beginners with calm methods for complex systems, so they can build confidence without confusing luck for skill. She believes good investing starts with curiosity, compassion for one's future self, and respect for risk.

www.ingramcontent.com/pod-product-compliance
Lightning Source LLC
Chambersburg PA
CBHW031336230926
51848CB00002B/263
* 9 7 8 9 3 7 4 5 9 1 0 9 3 *